Currents in

Twenty-First-Century

Christian Apologetics

Currents in Twenty-First-Century Christian Apologetics

Challenges Confronting the Faith

JOHN J. JOHNSON

WIPF & STOCK · Eugene, Oregon

CURRENTS IN TWENTY-FIRST-CENTURY CHRISTIAN APOLOGETICS
Challenges Confronting the Faith

Copyright © 2008 John J. Johnson. All rights reserved. Except for brief quotations in critical publications or reviews, no part of this book may be reproduced in any manner without prior written permission from the publisher. Write: Permissions, Wipf and Stock, 199 W. 8th Ave., Suite 3, Eugene, OR 97401.

ISBN 13: 978-1-55635-539-4

Manufactured in the U.S.A.

All scripture quotations, unless otherwise indicated, are taken from the HOLY BIBLE, NEW INTERNATIONAL VERSION®. NIV®. Copyright © 1973, 1978, 1984 by International Bible Society. Used by permission of Zondervan. All rights reserved.

Contents

Acknowledgments vii
Introduction ix

Part One
How Do We Adjudicate Religious Truth-Claims?

1 · Is Cornelius Van Til's Apologetic Method Christian, or Merely Theistic? 5

2 · How a Muslim Could Employ Van Til's Apologetic System: A Response to Frame and Hays 18

3 · Is John Hick's Concept of the "Real" an Adequate Criterion for Evaluating Religious Truth-Claims? 34

4 · A Case for "Reformed Evidentialism" 50

5 · The Implausible Foundations of Nietzsche's Attack Upon Biblical Religion 75

Part Two
What Can We Believe about the Resurrection of Jesus?

6 · Were the Resurrection Appearances Hallucinations? Some Psychiatric and Psychological Considerations 99

7 · Hans Frei as Unlikely Apologist for the Historicity of the Resurrection 111

Part Three
Christianity, Judaism, and the Holocaust

8 · A New Testament Understanding of the Jewish Rejection of Jesus: Four Theologians on the Salvation of Israel   131

9 · Should the Holocaust Force Us to Rethink Our View of God and Evil?   154

10 · Are We Asking the Wrong Questions about the *Shoah?* Eliezer Berkovits as Post-Holocaust Jewish Apologist   167

Bibliography   189

Acknowledgments

All articles are reprinted by permission of the publishers.

1. "Is Cornelius Van Til's Apologetic Method Christian, or Merely Theistic?" originally appeared in *Evangelical Quarterly* 75 (2003) 257–68.

2. "How a Muslim Could Employ Van Til's Apologetic System" originally appeared in *Global Journal of Classical Theology* 5 (2006). Online: http://www.trinitysem.edu/journal/5-3/TOCv5n3.htm.

3. "Is John Hick's Concept of the 'Real' an Adequate Criterion for Evaluating Religious Truth-Claims?" originally appeared in *Themelios* 27 (2002) 45–57.

4. "A Case for 'Reformed Evidentialism'" from *Churchman* 117 (2003) 7–32.

5. "The Implausible Foundations of Nietzsche's Attack upon Biblical Religion" originally appeared in *Evangelical Journal* 23 (2005) 82–94. Used by permission of Evangelical School of Theology.

6. "Were the Resurrection Appearances Hallucinations? Some Psychiatric and Psychological Considerations," from *Churchman* 115 (2001) 227–38.

7. "Hans Frei as Reluctant Apologist for the Resurrection" originally appeared in *Evangelical Quarterly* 76 (2004) 135–51.

Acknowledgments

8. "A New Testament Understanding of the Jewish Rejection of Jesus: Four Theologians on the Salvation of Israel," originally appeared in the *Journal of the Evangelical Theological Society* 43 (2000) 229–46.

9. "Should the Holocaust Force us to Rethink our View of God and Evil?" from *Tyndale Bulletin* 52 (2001) 117–28.

10. "Are We Asking the Wrong Questions About the Shoah? Eliezer Berkovits as Post-Holocaust Jewish Apologist" from *Conservative Judaism*, 57 (2004) 65–86. Reprinted with permission of the Rabbinical Assembly.

Introduction

WORKS OF apologetics are often viewed in today's intellectual climate as an oddity at best, or as an example of an intransigent fundamentalism at worst. The apologetic endeavor's tumble into disrepute began in the eighteenth century, when Immanuel Kant and David Hume raised serious objections to the theistic arguments from design and cosmology that had long been staples in the apologetic arsenal. Then, in the nineteenth century, Darwin's *Origin of the Species* and Lyell's *Principles of Geology* seemed to provide scientific support that made the case of skeptical Enlightenment philosophers even stronger. Also in that century, the corrosive influence of German biblical criticism began to take its toll, and many of the devout found themselves wondering just how much of the faith remained a viable option. In the twentieth century, thinkers like Karl Barth welcomed the abandonment of apologetics; Barth reveled in what some have called a fideistic brand of Christianity. In this same vein, late in the twentieth century, many Reformed thinkers, under the influence of Cornelius van Til, also rejected the traditional apologetic approach, opting instead for a "presuppositional" approach to the Christian faith, in which the tenets of Christianity are taken as a starting point, rather than something arrived at through evidential argumentation. Given all of this, it is easy to understand why many Christians began to think that apologetics' day had come and gone.

And yet, Christians are called by Scripture to present intellectually convincing reasons why the Christian faith should be taken seriously. First Peter 3:15 tells us we should "always be prepared to give an answer to everyone who asks you to give the reason for the hope that you have." That is, the New Testament writers conceived of the new religion as one of the head, as well as of the heart. Needless

Introduction

to say, St. Paul, with his rabbinical training, was hardly averse to rational argumentation in the service of advancing religious truth. His epistles bear this out to no end. A man like Barth, who was already a Christian, may have seen apologetics as futile, indeed, even idolatrous. But what about the average man or woman who is not a Christian? Surely some of them would be interested in Christianity, if only they thought it had some intellectual respectability to it. To those who claim that apologetics do not "work," I would point out the example of C.S. Lewis, who became a Christian largely because of what he took to be the good evidence for Christ's bodily resurrection. The same applies to Lutheran theologian John Warwick Montgomery and popular apologetic author Josh McDowell. There are other examples, too, but these three famous ones should suffice to give pause to those who think that apologetics is a futile endeavor. It would take a truly confident (arrogant, perhaps?) theologian to claim that God never uses evidential arguments in order to bring someone to faith. Indeed, if Christianity does not have at least some recourse to rational argumentation when confronted by its critics, it is hard to see why an increasingly secular, educated world should be bothered with it at all. To fall back upon a fideistic sort of faith may be acceptable for some, but it hardly does justice to the great intellectual tradition of the Church Fathers, the Catholic and Orthodox Churches, and the Protestant Reformers. A Christianity that is not apologetic is either complacent or frightened, and Christianity should be neither.

The essays in this book are not standard forays into apologetics. That is, I do not attempt to defend the cosmological, teleological, or moral arguments for God's existence. I have no interest in trying to square the book of Genesis with the findings of biology and geology. Nor am I concerned with attempting to prove that the Bible is "inerrant," whatever that phrase may mean to various audiences. Rather, each essay in this book is a response to a challenge raised about the validity of certain Christian doctrines. For instance, does an especially grievous example of suffering, the Holocaust, render the Jewish-Christian concept of a loving God null and void? Or, must the central Christian doctrine of the physical, bodily resurrection of Jesus be abandoned in light of the current revival of the "visions hypothesis" in certain more liberal theological circles? Or, given the pluralistic age in which we now live, does it still make sense to insist on the uniqueness and salvific nature of the Christian revelation, or must we now assume that all the world's great religions are equally valid paths to God?

These essays, then, are not a systematic attempt to defend each doctrine of Christian faith from creation to consummation. Instead, they seek to show how Christianity in the twenty-first century is still able to answer various intellectual challenges that confront it, all in keeping with the advice given by Peter two thousand years ago. I do not offer these essays as "proof" for the truth of Christianity. The idea that the faith can be proven true beyond all doubt is a position that advancements in science, philosophy, and biblical scholarship over the past two hundred years render untenable. My goal simply is to show that Christians have little to fear when their faith is challenged, for ours is a faith that does not originate in doubt and confusion, trembling "in a corner" (Acts 26:26). Today's Christian proclamation may be as bold as it was that first Easter morning, because it is from God, and God is not the author of falsehood.

PART ONE

How Do We Adjudicate
Religious Truth-Claims?

THE DEBATE over precisely how to conduct the Christian apologetic endeavor is a heated one. There are various camps, all claiming to have the most effective method for presenting Christian truth to the unbeliever. However, two methods, the presuppositionalist and the evidentialist, seem to have clashed with each other the most over the years. The presuppositionalist view (largely a product of Reformed theologians, particularly Cornelius Van Til, late professor of apologetics at Westminster Seminary in Philadelphia) insists that argument alone will never convince the skeptic that Christian truth-claims are valid. Rather, the presuppositionalist contends that the non-believer must submit his sin-impaired reason to the worldview presented in Scripture, and accept its presuppositions—theological, philosophical, or otherwise. Then, the argument goes, the non-believer will see that it is only the biblical understanding of reality, arrived at through prepositional means, that provides rational coherence for human life and thought. On this view of things, the unbeliever will see that the Christian gospel is necessarily true.

All well and good, the evidentialist maintains, but why should the skeptic accept the presuppositions of the Bible and its attendant Christian presuppositions? John Warwick Montgomery realized that this was precisely the question for which the presuppositionalists do not have a real answer, in a witty, yet theological astute piece entitled "Once Upon an A Priori." This essay was published in a volume entitled *Jerusalem and Athens*, a collection of papers grappling with the thought of Cornelius Van Til. I always found it interesting that in his rebuttal to Montgomery's challenge, Van Til mounted no serious counter attack to Montgomery's arguments. His reply was friendly and gracious, but it was in no way a rebuttal of anything Montgomery had written.

Chapter 1 follows in the Montgomery tradition, posing the question, what criterion do we use to assess religious truth-claims? The Christian will use her set of beliefs, the non-Christian believer will use his, and both will expect the rest of us to submit to the presuppositions of their respective systems. But without some kind of evidence to prompt us to choose one set of presuppositions over another, there simply is no basis for choosing, and the non-religious person is left in an agnostic limbo-land. I therefore present the idea in this chapter that a Muslim could use the Van Tillian presuppositional system just as well as a Christian.

This chapter was originally published in *Evangelical Quarterly* (Summer, 2003). In the following issue of the same journal, ardent Van Tillians John Frame and Steve Hayes presented a less than timid reply. And while I do not think that they have shaken the ideas I presented in my essay, their piece did convince me that I needed to be clearer as to precisely how a Muslim theologian could use the presuppositional system that, up until now, had been the domain of Christian Reformed thinkers. My attempt to do this is to be found in chapter 2, which was originally published in John Warwick Montgomery's online journal, *Global Journal of Classical Theology* 5 (October 2006) where I sought to show that Muslim presuppositions without evidence are no better, or no worse, than baseless Christian ones. To my knowledge, neither Frame nor Hayes has rebutted this essay in journal or book form.

Chapter 3 in this section is concerned with John Hick's religious pluralism. Hick, who began decades ago as an orthodox Christian thinker, has now moved to the other end of the theological spectrum and advocates a full-blown pluralistic view of the world's great religions. Now, there is much to commend his view, especially when one considers the havoc that has been wreaked upon the world when competing faith claims have clashed. Yet just because religions have often found themselves at each other's throat does not automatically justify the abandonment of the very idea of religion-specific truth-claims.

But what I find especially problematic for Hick is how does one determine which, if any, religion is "true"? By what objective standard can they be judged? Hick insists that any religion that causes moral improvement in the devotee makes that religion "true," and indicates that the adherent is therefore in touch with "The Real," Hick's phrase for what most of us would call God. But how would Hick handle, say, The Nation of Islam? Its reputation for improving the lives of young black men is well known, but so is its history of bigotry and racism. Are men who give up drug use and criminal activity at one with The Real, even if they believe and preach hatred? Or, when Muslims and Christians disagree over the events of Christ's life (Muslims deny Christ was crucified, putting them at odds with virtually all historians, regardless of religious persuasion), shouldn't we be guided by standard methods of historical investigation into these alleged facts, rather than simply glossing over them in an attempt to foster an artificial religious "understanding" between the two faiths? My article on Hick originally appeared in *Themelios* 27, (Spring, 2002.)

Chapter 4 naturally flows out of the preceding chapter. If Hick is reluctant to take a definitive stand regarding the evidence for any one religion as being stronger than the evidence for another, the so-called Reformed epistemologists, lead by Alvin Plantinga, fall into the opposite error. They claim that Christian faith requires no "evidence" in the normally understood meaning of that word, because Christian faith can be considered a fundamentally "basic" belief. But this is simply the polar opposite view taken by Hick. Either way, if there is no evidence that Christianity is true, it is hard to understand why it should be preferred over any other religion. My goal in this chapter is to suggest that Plantinga's position could be greatly strengthened with a dose of old-fashioned evidentialism.

Finally, I close this section with my take on F. Nietzsche's now infamous attack upon religion in general, and Christianity in particular. Nietzsche, of course, was not a believer like Van Til and Hick, yet I have grouped him with those thinkers because all of them are concerned with the issue of how and why religious faith becomes manifest in the believer's life.

Nietzsche has been largely influential in theological as well as philosophical circles for his insights into why people cling to Christian beliefs. These beliefs, he claims, are for the most part harmful, and prevented humanity from reaching its true potential. This, then, was of course picked up only a few years later in the writings of Sigmund Freud, and the Nazis and communists seized upon it as they sought to create a new humanity, free of the shackles of outdated, religio-superstition.

However, as much as Nietzsche has been attacked over the years by the faithful, I think many of the weaknesses in his position have often been overlooked. For example, he insisted that Christianity inculcated in people hatred and the desire for revenge, that it led to egotism and self-absorption, and that it was a religion based on weakness and fear. I try to show in this essay that Nietzsche has largely misunderstood the Bible and the Christian tradition, which in turn caused him to level charges against the Christian faith that were for the most part unfounded. This essay originally was published in *Evangelical Journal* 23 (Fall, 2005).

I

Is Cornelius Van Til's Apologetic Method Christian, or Merely Theistic?

IN THE field of Christian apologetics, the ongoing battle between the two dominant approaches, evidentialism and presuppositionalism, is well known, at least within conservative Christian circles. Evidentialism is, of course, the "traditional" approach to Christian apologetics, which relies upon arguments and "evidences" (e.g., Aquinas's famous Five Ways, or William Paley's "watchmaker" analogy) to convince the non-Christian that Christianity is true. The supreme example of evidentialist apologetics is found in the New Testament itself, where the various writers view the historic resurrection of Christ as proof not only of his divinity, but as a validation of the New Testament's entire salvific message. Presuppositionalism, on the other hand, completely rejects this approach to apologetics, arguing instead that until the non-Christian surrenders his sin-impaired autonomy and fully accepts the biblical worldview, along with all that worldview entails (e.g., the noetic effects of sin upon human reasoning, humanity's utter dependence on God, our natural inclination to rebel against our Creator and, *especially*, the *self-attesting truth* of the Bible), the non-Christian will never become a believer.

The late Cornelius Van Til, professor of apologetics at Westminster Seminary in Philadelphia, developed presuppositionalism in its most thorough and familiar form.[1] Van Til's system

---

1. Van Til was influenced by the nineteenth-century Dutch theologian Abraham Kuyper, who was a keen critic of evidentialist apologetics. See Knudsen, "Tendencies in Christian Apologetics," 275–76.

raises all sorts of complex questions, not only for apologetics, but for Christian epistemology as well; questions that would require far more attention than can be given here. But for the remainder of this chapter, I wish to concentrate on his system as it concerns one issue only. That is, how does a Christian use the Van Tillian system to convince a non-believer (be she atheist or agnostic, but especially if she is a committed adherent of *another faith*), that the Christian worldview is correct? I believe Van Til's system is simply inadequate for such a task. And I will use the writings of evidentialist apologete *par excellence* John Warwick Montgomery for assistance in this matter. Montgomery has been for several decades one of the most capable exponents of evidentialist apologetics, and has long been a critic of presuppositionalism. I will also examine the rebuttal to Montgomery's argument as supplied by two of Van Til's most ardent defenders, Greg Bahnsen and John Frame.[2] I hope to show that Van Til's system fails to be of apologetic benefit when confronting the non-Christian for the following reasons: one, it gives insufficient reason why the non-Christian should choose Christianity over another belief system, since any truth-claims that presuppositionalism makes in favor of Christianity could equally be made in favor of another religion, (especially a theistic one like Islam), and two, Van Til's system confuses the very different notions of *general* revelation and *special* revelation.

Van Til's "system" of apologetics, as he liked to call it, grew out of the fact that he believed evidentialism was an entirely backward approach.

> The traditional method had explicitly built into it the right and ability of the natural man, apart from the work of the Spirit of God, to be the judge of the claim of the authoritative Word of God. It is man who, by means of self-established intellectual tools, puts his stamp of approval on the Word of God and then, only after that grand act, does he listen to it. God's word must first pass

---

2. Bahnsen has written a great deal in Van Til's defense, while Frame is a former student of Van Til and has been called among the "most consistent and sophisticated presuppositionalists" (Sproul, *Classical Apologetics*, 299). And, if truth be told, both strike me as better expositors of Van Til's system than Van Til himself, whose prose was often difficult and sometimes vague.

man's test of good and evil, truth and falsity. But once you tell a non-Christian this, why should he be worried by anything else that you say. You have already told him he is quite all right just the way he is![3]

The outcome of Van Til's approach can be summed up with the following two main assumptions: "one, that human beings are obligated to presuppose [the biblical] God in all of their thinking, and two, that unbelievers resist this obligation in every aspect of thought and life."[4] Thus, it is easy to see how Van Til would have little use for, say, the arguments of an Aquinas or a Palely. For Van Til, the Christian must not meet the unbeliever "on his or her own ground" by admitting that God's existence is debatable and requires "proof" to be accepted. No, Van Til wants the unbeliever to understand that the God of the Bible necessarily exists from the *outset* of the discussion, and any attempt by the unbeliever to deny God's existence is the result of his or her own willful, sinful ignorance.

At first, it seems as if Van Til has a point. Those who are Christians know that the noetic effects of sin render human judgment less than reliable on all issues, especially spiritual ones. But is it not only because they are Christians that they know this? A person standing outside the Christian faith does not necessarily believe in judgment-impairing sin, so why should she not subject the Bible to her "sinful" judgment? Indeed, it is the only way she can possibly approach the Bible, or any other object in the world. (In fact, it is the only way Christians *themselves* can approach the reasoning process concerning any issue!) What Van Til wants does not seem possible, for man is a thinking, rational animal. All he can do, when presented with an argument, is examine the rationality from *his* point of view. It is simply the way we are "built."[5] I would go even farther and assert that part of what it means to be made in God's image is that we necessarily approach all things (including, and especially, the Bible!) in just the autonomous manner Van Til decries.

---

3. Van Til, "My Credo," 11.
4. Frame, "Van Til and the Ligonier Apologetic," 282.
5. For one of the most thorough arguments that Van Til's system is logically untenable, see Sproul et al., *Classical Apologetics*, 183–338.

Part One: How Do We Adjudicate Religious Truth-Claims?

In a whimsical, yet critical article of Van Til, the aptly named "Once Upon an A Priori,"[6] Montgomery rightly begins with a prefatory remark: "I do not wish to increase the height of what sometimes appears already to be a dangerously top-heavy pile of refutations and counter-refutations. At the same time, I am too concerned about the plight of the non-Christian in the contemporary world of growing secularity to by-pass the question apologetic method so ably raised by Van Til."[7] Quite true, and it reminds us of the true purpose of apologetics, which is often lost amongst the learned tomes written by those who either favor or reject the presuppositional position. The Christian worldview is under assault as never before, and the concept of religious pluralism is now almost a dogma of popular culture, rather than a rarified position held only by scholars and professors of religion. And, as I read Van Til and the writings of a defender like Bahnsen or Frame, I constantly find myself wondering: how can all of this be applied to the non-Christian, the person who doubts the validity of the Christian worldview, or perhaps has a strong devotion to a religion other than Christianity? Why would Van Til's system lead such a one to believe and embrace Christianity, and not some other faith as true? It is to this question that Montgomery addresses himself in his article, and to which I now turn.

Montgomery's essay actually contains three parables that raise important questions for those of the Van Tillian school in terms of how one can determine a "true" Christian view of reality as opposed to a "false" non-Christian view of reality. But it is the article's second "parable" that I will address in this paper. In it, Montgomery presents us with two extra-terrestrial races, the amusingly-named Shadoks and Gibis. He presents them as having mutually exclusive belief systems; each is certain that his religion is the true one, and each is certain that the facts support his case. However, each also realizes, in good Van Tillian fashion, that facts alone can never prove any one religion to be true (even though "brute" facts are all they presumably use to determine the veracity of virtually everything else in their lives! Why should the realm of religion be any different?). Thus, the Shadoks and Gibis debate each other on purely "presuppositional" grounds:

6. Montgomery, "Once Upon an A Priori," 380–403.
7. Ibid., 380.

Shadok: You will never discover the truth, for instead of subordinating yourself to revelational truth (Bible-Sh), you sinfully insist on maintaining the autonomy of your fallen intellect.

Gibi: Quite the contrary! [He repeats exactly the same assertion, substituting (Bible-G) for (Bible-Sh).] And *I* say what I have just said *not* on the basis of my sinful ego, but because I have been elected by God (Election-G) . . .

Shadok: Your religion is but the inevitable by-product of sin—a tragic effort at self-justification through idolatry. Let us see what God (God-Sh) *really* says in his Word (Bible-Sh).

Gibi: I will not listen to your alleged "facts." Unless you start with the truth, you have no business interpreting facts at all. Let me help you by interpreting the facts *revelationally* (Bible-G).[8]

This "conversation" between a Shadok and a Gibi, not surprisingly, sounds all too much like a debate between two presuppositionalists! And, of course, "[n]either viewpoint can prevail, since *by definition* all appeal to neutral evidence is eliminated."[9] The gist of their conversation comes down to the fact that each debater criticizes the other's position because he interprets the "facts" of reality and religion incorrectly, because he is blinded by self-delusion, and because he refuses to submit to the One, true God.

For our purposes, we may substitute a Christian and a Muslim for the warring Shadok and Gibi. Is it not easy to imagine a Christian (especially a presuppositional one!) insisting to the Muslim that the Muslim has everything wrong, primarily because his *willful* sinful nature makes embracing the truth an utter impossibility? But of course, the Muslim could *also* attribute the Christian's unbelief in Islam to his persistent, sinful refusal of Allah and His Koran: "[d]enying the truth of the message of God, that is, abandoning the right way or going astray, is associated in the Qur'an with following one's lust,

---

8. Ibid., 385.
9. Ibid.

the pursuance of excessive selfish desires."[10] Surely the Christian is "denying the truth" of Islam, otherwise, how could the Christian fail to see the beauty and perfection of the Koran? And, if the Christian happens to know Arabic, the Muslim may well be shocked that he is not already a follower of Islam. Can't this foolish Christian see the beauty and profundity of the Koran in its original Arabic? Surely this is a proof of its divine inspiration! The Van Tillian Christian will in turn reply that it is really the Bible, not the Koran that possesses an inherent, self-attesting truth.[11] This debate, of course, goes on *ad infinitum*, since each side has a different religious worldview, and hence a different criterion for deciding religious truth.

Montgomery's parable of the Shadoks and Gibis (and my battle between the Christian and the Muslim) really boils down to one essential issue, and it is this that the presuppositionalist must address: when examining which religious belief system is true, how is one to know? How does the *outsider*, who is an adherent of neither system, decide for herself which religion she should embrace?

The late Greg Bahnsen, an ardent defender of biblical Christianity and a devoted Van Tillian, addressed Montgomery's critique with a lengthy critique of his own.[12] In it, Bahnsen reveals why he (and by implication, Van Til) does not agree that when presuppositionalism and a different religious worldview collide, there is a dilemma such as Montgomery implies. I believe that Bahnsen's critique of Montgomery shows the fundamental problem with presuppositional apologetics. Namely, it is, when all is said and done,

---

10. Abu-Hamdiyyah, *The Qur'an—an Introduction*, 98.

11. The literary beauty of the Koran in the original Arabic has often been used by Moslem apologists as an indication of its divine origin. For further insight into Muslim apologetic technique, the interested reader should refer to Montgomery's "How Muslims do Apologetics," 81–89. In the article, the author explains how a leading apologist of the Islamic faith can approach his task with the same sort of presuppositionalist rigor as can a Van Tillian. For the well-known apologist in question, (Muhammad Ali), Islam is self-evidently true, just as Christianity is for the presuppositionalist Christian. It is so obviously true for Ali that he can confidently claim that, "Islam, more than any other religion, accords with the dynamic, evolutionary worldview of twentieth-century science and philosophy" (89).

12. Bahnsen, "Critique of the Evidentialist Apologetical Method."

Is Cornelius Van Til's Apologetic Method Christian, or Merely Theistic?

circular argumentation that proves nothing to the one who is not already a Christian.

Bahnsen begins his critique with the following statement: "the parable [of the Shadoks and the Gibis] either envisions a monotheistic or polytheistic framework. If the latter, there is no practical need to respond."[13] I assume Bahnsen is implying that, if either the Shadok or the Gibi is a polytheist, there is no reason for him to address the matter, since presuppositional apologetics is thoroughly monotheistic in orientation. But what if a Christian finds himself in a debate with a polytheist, be it a devout Hindu, or an adherent of one of the many new age cults that have gained such popularity in recent years? Is Bahnsen saying that Christians never find themselves faced with such an opponent? Or that such opponents are unworthy of a serious retort? Regardless, I think Bahnsen misses Montgomery's point here entirely. The religious framework of Montgomery's argument (whether polytheistic or monotheistic) is not important—what Montgomery is stressing is, *how* does one adjudicate between different religions' claims? The problem is the same whether the presuppositionalist Christian is debating a polytheistic Hindu or a strictly monotheistic Muslim.[14]

To further prove that Bahnsen does not seem to understand (much less adequately address) the simple point that Montgomery is making, I quote him at length:

> [if] the positions to be described in the story are and must be incompatible [and this, of course, is *always* the case when two religions lock horns in debate!] then . . . the type of argument put into the presuppositionalist's mouth . . . would not be that which appears at all. Instead the presuppositionalist would seek to find if the opponent has a theoretically justified epistemology (e.g. could answer the one and many dilemma, substantiate the assumptions of non-contradiction and uniformity,

---

13. Ibid., 4.
14. Oddly enough, Van Til himself, in a rebuttal to Montgomery's article, never seems to squarely address the simple point that Montgomery makes, i.e., how does one decide between a false religious truth-claim and a true one if all appeal to external evidence is ruled out? See Montgomery, "Once Upon an A Priori," 392–403.

etc.); he would attack at that fundamental level, bringing in the moral culpability of the unbeliever (i.e. law violations), and showing the strength and justification for his own world-view.[15]

So, basically, Bahnsen is appealing to "evidence" that would prove that Christianity is true (because it answers the one and the many dilemma, for instance). The source for this evidence? It must be Scripture itself, for where else do we learn about the Christian God? Bahnsen is assuming (or "presupposing") that Christianity does all of the things he thinks that it does. Let's start with the one and the many problem. I assume Bahnsen believes that the teachings of Scripture resolve this age-old philosophical problem. In other words, the triune God found in the New Testament, and the manner in which this God relates to the created universe, solves this knotty philosophical problem.[16] There is one problem, though. How do we know that such a triune God actually exists? If such a God truly exists, then that God may very well solve the one and the many problem. But what to do with a Muslim, who responds that the triune God of the New Testament does not really exist, that he is the product of first- and second-century minds that were more interested in creating a God who satisfied their Greek-inspired philosophical mindset rather than describing the Supreme Being as he actually exists?

Well, what could a good presuppositionalist do, other than appeal to a sort of fideism that demands blind acceptance of the New Testament portrayal of God? A much more sensible approach, though, would be to recommend to the unbelieving interlocutor a good book which refutes the idea that the Christian Trinity is the result of Greek philosophical speculation.[17] Or, what if our unbelieving non-Christian friend took another approach. What if he claimed the manner in which God in the New Testament is revealed (i.e., through the Man Jesus) is fallacious, since the New Testament documents were written two or three hundred years after the events

15. Bahnsen, "Critique of the Evidentialist Apologetical Method," 4.

16. For a valuable insight into Van Til's understanding of the Christian solution to the one and the many problem, see Rushdoony, "The One and the Many Problem," 339–48.

17. A comprehensive, evangelical book of this sort is Nash's *The Gospel and the Greeks*.

they purport to describe, and therefore are in no way historically trustworthy. What would anyone do when faced with the claim of an opponent they know to be false? They would supply the skeptic with *evidence* that his position is wrong.[18] There simply is no way to engage in a debate, much less win one, without some sort of appeal to evidence. This is true in every facet of human reasoning—why should it be different when we are discussing religion? Why does the presuppositionalist insist on changing the rules of logic and basic common sense when it comes to matters of religion, even though she would never think of abrogating those rules in any other area of human life?

But Bahnsen utterly rejects this line of reasoning. For Bahnsen, there is really no comparison between the Christian worldview based on the Bible, and the Muslim worldview based on the Koran, because the Bible is utterly unique, and teaches an entirely different sort of religion than does the Koran.[19] This may be true as far as it goes. In fact, as a Christian, I completely agree with Bahnsen (but of course, I am *already* a Christian!). But Bahnsen neglects the basic question: why should anyone trust what the Bible says? Maybe it was written by a bunch of clever, ancient presuppositionalists who wanted to invent a religion that would be impervious to attack, just like Bahnsen says Christianity is when it is defended from a presuppositional position. The simple fact of that mater is, evidentialist apologetics must be used when debating with a non-believer, and they must be used at the *very outset* of the debate. Otherwise, why should the non-believer accept this Bible that Bahnsen believes is so utterly unique and convincing? This, it seems to me, is part of the point Montgomery is making in his parabolic critique, a point that seems lost on Bahnsen, whose circular view of the veracity of Scripture leaves him with no room to convince others outside of the "circle" that his position is true.

Of course, this circularity of reasoning in the Van Tillian system has been noted before, even by one of Van Til's most ardent defend-

---

18. A fine place to start would be with Bruce's *The New Testament Documents*. See also Montgomery, *Where is History Going*, 44–52.

19. Bahnsen, "Critique of the Evidentialist Apologetical Method," 4.

ers, John M. Frame.[20] What Frame has to say regarding this is quite interesting, and so I quote him at length:

> But what is the alternative [to the circularity of the presuppositionalist method]? Again, the alternative seems to be that an unbeliever begins his quest, either with no criterion at all or with a "provisional" criterion of a non-Christian (or perhaps "neutral") sort; then by linear, noncircular reasoning, he learns hat he must adopt the Christian criterion. But, as we have noted earlier, this construction violates Rom 1:18ff and 1 Cor 10:31. According to Scripture there is no one in this position—no one without a knowledge of God's criteria. Those who seek to adopt non-Christian standards (and there are no "neutral" ones) are simply disobedient to the *Revelation* they have received [emphasis mine].[21]

This leads us into the second major difficulty with the presuppositionalist position that I want to address now. Frame, here, is of course criticizing the "traditional" approach to apologetics, as exemplified by someone like B.B. Warfield, which tries to begin the apologetic task on "neutral" ground with the unbeliever. Warfield, of course, started with "general" revelation (the innate awareness of God which all men have), and progressed to "special," Christian revelation.[22] For Warfield, the first step in the traditional method is to get the non-believer to consider the fact that there may exist a "God" who created the universe. This could be done, perhaps, through one or more of the classical "proofs" for God's existence. Once this was accomplished, the field must be narrowed down, through the use of evidentialist apologetics, to prove that the "God" who probably exists is the God of the Christian Bible.

20. Frame, "Van Til and the Ligonier Apologetic," 288.

21. Ibid., 288. Why Frame mentions 1 Cor 10:31 here is a bit mysterious, since it really has no bearing on the question of apologetic method. He mentions earlier in his article that, because the Corinthians passage mentions doing everything "to the glory of God," it is wrong to use an apologetic method that does not assume God's existence, since to do so would be to dishonor him, which is forbidden by the Corinthians passage (287). This seems to me to be a classic example of taking a text of Scripture out of context!

22. Sproul, et al., *Classical Apologetics*, 38.

Frame seems to be saying that in Rom 1:18–21, Paul is employing some sort of Van Tillian presuppositional technique which proves that unbelievers intentionally turn away from the Christian revelation. But Paul says nothing in these verses about Jesus, the Trinity, or the inspiration of the New Testament. In short, he mentions nothing specifically *Christian*. Paul is simply saying that all humans have an innate knowledge of God—he certainly is not saying that all men and women instinctively know that Jesus is God's Son, or that the gospel Paul is preaching about the resurrection of Christ is known by all to be true!

That this is the correct interpretation seems quite clear from Paul's own words in this passage, not to mention his actions in Acts 17. There, Paul gives the Athenians credit for being religious, for "knowing" God—but it is an *unknown* God they worship! He does not fault them because they do not know that the God in question is the God of Abraham, Isaac, and Jacob.[23] Rather, Paul builds on their basic theism (just as Warfield would have done), and explains that the God they believe in is actually the Christian God, the Father of Jesus. And, in verse 31, Paul says something that must surely warm the heart of any Christian evidentialist: "He has given *proof* of this to all men by raising him from the dead." In short, Paul here is showing that "in the New Testament the honest intellectual problems of unbelievers are respected and dealt with on their own ground."[24] The same apologetic technique is on display in Acts 26, when Paul appears before Festus and Agrippa. Here again, Paul is arguing the Christian case based on the evidence of the resurrection, which can

---

23. Van Til's comments on this passage prove interesting: "Paul does not place himself on their level in order with them to investigate the nature of being and knowledge in general, to discover *whether* the God of Abraham, Isaac, and Jacob might possibly exist. He tells them straight out that what they claim not to know, he knows. He tells them that their so-called ignorance is culpable, for God is as near to them as to their own selves" ("My Credo," 7). Van Til surely misses the point that Paul certainly *does* place himself on their level, for he obviously gives them credit for their theistic belief, misguided though it may be. However, once he places himself on their level, then he moves beyond to reveal the *specifics* of Christian faith, i.e., God's revelation in Christ.

24. Montgomery, "Apologetics," 36.

only mean, *contra* Van Til, that Paul thinks "these sin-blinded sinners can evidentially arrive at the facticity of the resurrection."[25]

Paul obviously did not think it was presumptuous, or a "violation" of 1 Cor 10:31, to reason with non-Christians, to try to "prove" the truth of Christianity based on the facts. If Paul, as well as the rest of the New Testament writers, did not think it was somehow inappropriate (even sinful!) to appeal to the fallen human intellect by arguing the truth of Christianity based on the evidence (i.e., the resurrection of Christ, the cornerstone of New Testament preaching), why should a Van Tillian? The Van Tillian would have us believe that the traditional apologetic method is flawed because it leaves the question of the truth of Christianity in the realm of the erring, fallen intellect of man. But, as Montgomery shrewdly points out, it is actually the Van Tillian who forces unbelievers to rely on their own intellect when faced with differing religious truth-claims from two opposing sources:

> Note that, under these conditions, an individual standing outside these two commitments has no way of "testing the spirits" to see which view, if either, is worthy of *his* commitment . . . In the absence of an apology that will make sense to the uncommitted, it is impossible, *even in principle,* to decide between these views. But if this is where the religious decision is left, then the non-Christian will make an *arbitrary* decision—which will be dependent on *himself alone* (not on evidence outside himself)—and his commitment (even if to the true position) will be man-centered.[26]

In short, the letters of Paul, and the rest of the New Testament writings, are replete with appeals to the evidence of Christ's resurrection. It is the resurrection that convinces the apostles that Jesus is who he claimed to be. It is the powerful preaching of Paul, and Peter, preaching based on Christ's resurrection and his fulfillment of Old Testament prophecy, that forms the basis of the New Testament witness to the truth of Christianity. Were one to stop at what Paul says about our innate knowledge of God in chapter one of Romans, why

25. Ibid., 78.
26. Ibid., 152.

shouldn't this knowledge lead to a belief in Allah, and his prophet Mohammed? Surely Muslims can use this very verse to prove that all men should embrace Islam, just as Frame seems to use it in favor of Christianity. After all, Muslims accept the Bible so long as it does not contradict the Koran. But Paul (and the other New Testament writers) did not stop at the first chapter of Romans, for the obvious reason that to do so would be to leave us unaware of God's plan of reconciliation with humanity through his Son.

To sum up, the point of Christian apologetics is to bring non-Christians to Christ. The question is, how best to do this? Shall we use the techniques of argumentation and debate that are used in every other realm of human intercourse whenever two sides disagree? Or, should we (in opposition to the evidentialist approach used by St Paul himself!) employ a method of apologetics which makes perfect sense to those already "in the loop," but which can only be utterly circular and non-convincing to the one outside of the privileged circle? Evidentialist apologetics certainly is not without flaw; since the time of David Hume, various attacks have been leveled against it with often damaging results. But if evidentialism is imperfect, presuppositionalism of the Van Tillian kind is even more so. For it fails to realize that any presuppositionalist claim that can be made for Christianity can be made for any religion. And, it confuses the general revelation that the New Testament says all men are privy to, with special revelation, which is a different matter entirely.

2

How a Muslim Could Employ Van Til's Apologetic System: A Response to Frame and Hays

THIS CHAPTER is a result of a piece published in *Evangelical Quarterly*[1] on the merits of Cornelius Van Til's presuppositional system of apologetics, in which I took the position that his approach may indeed prove the validity of theism in general, but not Christianity in particular. In fact, I suggested that a Muslim apologist could use Van Til's system with as much success as could a defender of Christianity. Dr. John Frame and Steve Hays published a rebuttal in a subsequent issue of *EQ*, in which they took me to task for failing to properly understand Van Til's thought, and, more importantly, not adequately demonstrating how an Islamic apologist could use Van Til's ideas to defend Islam. My rebuttal was published elsewhere as *EQ*'s editorial staff did not wish for the debate to continue in its pages.[2]

I would like to begin by thanking John Frame and Steve Hayes for their rejoinder. Their response was all the more gratifying when one considers that Dr. Frame is a giant in the field of Christian apologetics, and has devoted his life to powerfully presenting the gospel to a

1. Johnson, J., "Van Til's Apologetic Method," 257–68.
2. Johnson, J., "How A Muslim Could Employ Van Til's Apologetic System." As far as I know, neither Frame nor Hays has published a response. Hays did inform me, via email, that he might post a response on his Internet blog, but since this does not constitute a formal scholarly reply (i.e., in the form of a book or print journal article), I will not address it here.

skeptical modern world. Also, I agree with them that my paper would have been stronger had it included more interaction with books by, and about, Van Til. To that end, in this essay I will quote fairly extensively from Van Til, and also from Frame's writings, since he considers his own work on the subject to be a "major exposition" of Van Til's thought.[3] By delving deeply into the writings of these two men, I hope to show, more thoroughly than I did in my previous essay, that all of the major presuppositional assumptions that Van Til and Frame make for Christianity can just as easily be made for Islam. My point is not that Islamic apologists are using the Van Tillian system to promote Islam.[4] Rather, I wish to show that they easily could if they so desired. And, if this is the case, the Van Tillian method for doing apologetics must be seriously questioned as to its ability to prove the reality of the *Christian*, as opposed to the Islamic, God (or any similar theistic being).[5]

In their rejoinder, Frame and Hays take me to task because I stated in my critique of Van Til that a Muslim could agree with what

---

3. Frame and Hays, "Johnson on Van Til," 227–39. I will consider Frame to be an "orthodox" Van Tillian for the purposes of this response. I realize he does not agree with every one of Van Til's points, and he is not afraid to criticize the man whom he considers to be "the most important Christian thinker of the twentieth century." He says this in *Cornelius Van Til*, 3. In many places, Frame candidly admits that Van Til assumed that his method of apologetics accomplished a bit more than it actually does. In contrast to Van Til, Frame writes that, "I have suggested that we distinguish between the certainty of the *evidence* for Christian theism, which is absolute, and our human *arguments* for Christian theism, which are fallible and often uncertain" (301). Frame seems to think that Van Til was a bit too sure that his presuppositional method of apologetics could prove Christianity to be true. Still, it is fair to say that Frame agrees with Van Til in the main regarding Van Til's approach to apologetics. Thus I will consider Frame to be an enthusiastic spokesman for Van Tillian apologetics.

4. Some Muslim apologists may have done so. However, I am not conversant enough with Muslim scholarship to know if this is the case.

5. The Van Tillian approach works best when it is used against the position of atheism or agnosticism. Van Til was at his strongest when pointing out how Christianity is a far more satisfying worldview than any non-theistic outlook. Francis Schaeffer did much the same thing when he showed that atheists simply could not live consistently with the God-less world they envisioned. See, for instance, his most important writings, available in the one-volume *Trilogy*. But, Van Til's system seems far less effective when he pits the God of Christianity against other theistic worldviews, as I hope to show in this chapter.

PART ONE: HOW DO WE ADJUDICATE RELIGIOUS TRUTH-CLAIMS?

Paul says in chapter one of Romans. They write that a Muslim could not accept what Paul says there, because, for one thing, Muslims do not accept the New Testament as divinely inspired Scripture. Also, Paul is basing his argument on the twin concepts of natural revelation and original sin, and Muslims do not have a doctrine of original sin.[6] Frame and Hays have a point; I should have clarified what I meant. I will do so now.

First, I agree that Muslims do not consider Paul's words as infallible Scripture. But, on the other two matters, sin and natural revelation, any Muslim could agree, in principle, with what Paul says in chapter one of Romans. I will address the issue of sin first, since it is of enormous importance for the Van Tillian method of apologetics. The Fall of man, as recounted in Genesis, is essential to understanding Van Til's apologetic method. In many places in his writings, he insists that only a literal, historical understanding of the Fall can account for the perversity of the human condition.[7] The Fall, and its resultant noetic effects upon humanity, cause the unregenerate man to rebel against his Creator even though he knows, deep down, that God is real, and deserves man's worship and love. Frame writes that "Van Til often refers to the process described in Romans 1: fallen man suppresses what he knows to be true about God, exchanging it for a lie."[8] Thus, man is a rebel against God; he refuses to accept his authority, even his existence, all the while knowing that God must exist, as Paul claims in the first chapter of Romans.

The upshot of all of this for Van Til is that the so-called "point of contact," that is, the intellectual common ground where a Christian can address a non-believer, is narrow at best, and always tenuous. The unregenerate man cannot understand the things of God, because his reasoning process is so severely damaged. His presuppositions are therefore false, and they need to be replaced with biblical ones. This is why Van Til is so insistent upon establishing sound biblical presuppositions in an unbeliever's mind; there simply is no other way the unbeliever can begin to understand the gospel without such foundations. Traditional evidentialist apologetics do not work because

6. Frame and Hays, "Johnson on Van Til," 229 (footnote 13).
7. See, for example, his *The Defense of the Faith*, 14, where Van Til says that the "Fall of man needs emphasis as much as his creation."
8. Frame, *Cornelius Van Til*, 188–89.

they assume that unregenerate man's reason is working properly, and therefore trust he is able to understand and respond favorably to "proofs" that Christianity is true. Van Til writes that if the presuppositional apologist addresses unregenerate man as if he actually had the pre-fall ability to understand God's truth, the apologetic is doomed to failure, because "if we allow the legitimacy of the natural man's assumption of himself as the ultimate reference point in interpretation in any dimension we cannot deny his right to interpret Christianity itself in naturalistic terms."[9] In Van Til's understanding, the natural man will never understand Christianity until he realizes that his entire atheistic worldview is false. Thus, Frame can write that, "we may ask the unbeliever to think on Christian presuppositions, because in one sense he already does. Our plea is that he drop the unbelieving presuppositions that dominate his thought and give heed to those principles that he knows but suppresses."[10]

Now, listen to one Muslim commentator talking about the apostasy of Adam's descendants. Note that his words here sound not only a lot like Van Til, but also are very reminiscent of what Paul says in Rom 1:

> ... in the succeeding centuries, by and by, people swerved from the straight way of life (Islam) and adopted different crooked ways. They not only lost the Guidance owing to their negligence but also tampered with it because of their wickedness. They attributed to others the qualities and powers of Allah and associated others to rank with Him as gods and ascribed His rights to others. They invented different kinds of religions (ways of life) by mixing up all sorts of superstitions, wrong theories and false philosophy with the Guidance that was given by Allah. They discarded the right, just and moral principles taught by Allah and corrupted them and made such laws of life as

---

9. Van Til, *The Defense of the Faith*, 93.

10. Frame, "Presuppositional Apologetics," 218. When Frame says that the unbeliever "already does" think along Christian presuppositional lines, he is referring to the Van Tillian idea that the human thinking process itself is only possible because the God of Christian theism has created a world in which human logic is possible. I will address the problems with this view later in the paper.

suited their prejudices and lusts, and filled Allah's Earth with chaos.[11]

Or consider the following from an Islamic scholar, whose description of humanity's sinful rejection of God could (except for the reference to the Koran!) have been penned by Van Til himself: "The perversity of rejection *(kufr)* can only be understood in terms of men's refusal to have faith in or believe in what they secretly know. The Old Testament, Gospels and the Koran concur that men willfully reject their Creator. But this implies that men can disbelieve in what they know; knowledge does not entail faith although faith may entail, indeed encompass, knowledge."[12]

Islam (along with Van Til, Frame, and Hays) teaches that man is sinful, and willfully rejects the God he knows to exist. So, right away, the apologetic endeavor is in trouble. Both sides are using the same argument, but to argue for *different* Gods, namely, Jesus and Allah. But perhaps the Van Tillian has an objection at this point. Perhaps he will point out that the presuppositional approach (along with Christianity as a whole) teaches the doctrine of original sin, whereas Islam teaches no such doctrine. Islam admits the reality of sin, yes, but it does not teach that humanity is in any way "fallen."[13] Well, this is true, but does it really matter? Whether a man is an original sinner (Christianity) or merely a "non-original" sinner in the Koranic sense, the result is the same—the One, true God is rejected, even though his existence is stamped permanently upon the hearts of all men.

The Van Tillian may claim, though, that the doctrine of original sin does not entail only a rejection of belief in God's existence, but also leads fallen man to confuse true morality with false, and even to reject the moral and ethical demands that God makes upon his life. In other words, the Fall does more than merely turn one away from God; it also thoroughly confuses man's moral compass.

11. Mawdudi, *An Introduction to the Koran*, 5.
12. Akhtar, *A Faith for All Seasons*, 30.
13. Ibid., 91–92. However, even in the Koran, there seem to be hints of a fall-like contagion that plagues humanity. "Several *surahs* make cryptic references to an actual disease (*marad*), presumably spiritual, which flourishes in the sinful hearts of hypocrites and rejecters alike (K:8:49; 33:12) and which is increased by Allah as a recompense for the hard-hearted perversity of man (K:2:10)."

But Islam, even without the distinctly Reformed doctrine of utter depravity,[14] teaches much the same thing. Rejection of Allah seems to go hand in hand with the attempt to deny the moral obligations Allah has placed upon wayward humanity. Thus, those who reject Allah's existence also attempt "to seek release from duties they secretly acknowledge as binding."[15] And although it is often said that Islam sees sin more as a forgetting of the righteous path to God, rather than deliberate rebellion against him, "the Quran itself depicts fallen human beings as more than merely forgetful." Humans are described in the Muslim Scriptures as sinful (K:14:4), ungrateful (K:14:34), boastful (K:11:9–10), and rebellious (K:96:6).[16] True enough, sin in Islam is not the result of the contagion of original sin, but it is still a *willful* rejection of God's laws. Sin "is acquired not inborn, emergent not built-in, avoidable not inevitable. It is a deliberate conscious violation of the univocal law of God."[17] With or without original sin, in Islam man sinfully violates what he knows to be God's truth, just as in the Van Tillian understanding of sin.

Perhaps the Van Tillian will claim that the willful rejection of God entails more than just fallen man's desire to escape moral and ethical duties. Original sin has actually impaired our very reasoning process; we can no longer "think straight" as a result of the noetic effects of sin. Indeed, Van Til says of fallen human reason that "we cannot grant that it has *any right to judge* in matters of theology, or, for that matter, in anything else. The Scriptures nowhere appeal to the unregenerated reason as to a qualified judge."[18] Again, Islam can take this position, too; such theology is not dependant upon the Calvinistic stress on man's depravity. True enough; Islam does not say that man's reason has been badly damaged by a fall from primordial purity. Because man has never fallen, he is largely the way Allah intended him to be. Thus it is only natural that Muslim think-

---

14. Van Til and Frame are committed to Reformed theology. They consider the presuppositional approach to apologetics to be the one that is most faithful to a Christianity that stresses the teachings of Calvin and the Westminster Confession.

15. Akhtar, *A Faith for all Seasons*, 27.

16. George, *Is the Father of Jesus the God of Muhammad?* 115.

17. Abdalati, *Islam in Focus*, 33.

18. Van Til, *The Defense of the Faith*, 212.

ers have more faith in human reason than a committed Calvinist would. Nevertheless, Islam teaches that man's rational ability (what Van Til so often describes as man's alleged "autonomous reason") is defective, and certainly cannot presume to make definitive judgments upon Scripture. Muslim scholar Shabbir Akhtar explains the role of human reason *vis-à-vis* faith as follows: "[w]hat, then, is the role of independent reason in the interpretation of scriptural claims? What is the true office of reason in theology? . . . in the final analysis, faith has decisive priority over reason . . . An intellect unenlightened by God's grace cannot judge faith while an intellect enlightened by God's grace can only judge faith favorably . . . faith is indeed, in religious domains, the arbiter of reason and its pretensions."[19]

For all the stress that Christian presuppositionalists place upon the Fall of man, and the necessity to approach the apologetic task presuppositionally, it seems that Islamic thinkers, though less radical in their understanding of human sin, are pretty much in agreement with Van Til and Frame regarding man's sinful rejection of God, his willful suppression of the duties God has placed upon him, and the second-place status of human intellect vis-à-vis divine teachings.

Another area of agreement between Paul and Muslims is the theater of God's glory, the created world. The world-as-evidence-for-God argument is quite a powerful one, and it is only to be expected that Muslims, who attribute to Allah absolute sovereignty over the universe, would see in the creation proof of his handiwork. Paul insists every human being is without excuse for unbelief because the awe-inspiring universe testifies to the God who created it. Frame, commenting upon Paul's argument in Romans, states that "the facts of God's creation bear clear witness of him even to the minds of sinners."[20] Similarly, when disobedient men "see Allah's portents in Nature and elsewhere, they turn a blind eye."[21]

---

19. Akhtar, *A Faith for all Seasons*, 34. Akhtar goes on to explain that the "predominant view among Muslim theologians today as in the past is the view called 'fideism' in Christian thought" (34). How ironic that Van Til has often been accused of fideism himself! And while I do not think that this charge is accurate, it is easy to see why many, especially those unfamiliar with the complexities of his thought, would consider Van Til guilty of this charge.

20. Frame, "Presuppositional Apologetics," 210.

21. Akhtar, *A Faith for All Seasons*, 83.

How a Muslim Could Employ Van Til's Apologetic System

Van Til and Frame both believe that their presuppositional approach is largely successful because it posits that a certain type of God (the biblical, triune, Christian God) and only this type of God, can account for the world as we know it. Frame realizes, of course, that there are other versions of God among the religions of the world, but he tends to dismiss them, one reason being because he sees most of them as derivative of the biblical God. Thus, these gods are not serious candidates because, after all, they are only poor copies of the triune God of the Bible. Listen to what he says on this matter: "Christian heresies are religions influenced by the Bible, but which deny the central biblical gospel. Among the Christian heresies are not only those designated as such in history (Arianism, Gnosticism, Sabellianism, Docetism, Eutychianism, etc.), but also the historic rivals of Christianity, namely, Judaism and Islam."[22] When I first read this, I was not sure but that I had encountered a typographical error. Judaism, a religion that preceded Christianity by centuries, and eventually gave birth to it, is a *Christian* heresy? I will leave it to the reader to puzzle out what Frame could possibly mean by this. But perhaps he says this because he knows that his apologetic system would work as well for a Jew as for a Christian. After all, the God of the Old Testament is the God of the New Testament!

As for Islam as a Christian heresy, this is much more likely. Still, the matter is not as clear-cut as Frame would have us believe. Yes, the Koran obviously borrows many key themes from Christianity, like monotheism, the Day of Judgment, the idea of hell as an eternal abode of the wicked, etc. And the Koran plagiarizes many characters and stories from the pages of the Old Testament. But, Islam hardly fits into the same mold as obvious Christian heresies, like Mormonism or Jehovah's Witnesses. Many Christians would classify these groups as heretical based on two criteria: alteration and addition. That is, these groups take specifically Christian doctrines and alter them in an unorthodox manner. For instance, the Jehovah's Witnesses accept the divinity of Jesus (which is anathema to Muslims) but they consider his divinity inferior to that of the Father. They are, in effect, modern-day Arians. The Mormons admit that the New Testament is God's word (which Muslims do not), but they add to this the Book of Mormon, which for them is a superior source of divine revelation.

22. Frame, *Apologetics to the Glory of God*, 38, (footnote 7).

PART ONE: HOW DO WE ADJUDICATE RELIGIOUS TRUTH-CLAIMS?

The Koran certainly is full of ideas taken directly from the Bible. But, Islam does not share with genuine Christian heresies important doctrines like the divinity of Jesus, the sacrificial nature of his death, etc.[23] Walter Martin, in his encyclopedic work on cults and non-Christian religions, avers that Islam is "a major world religion distinctly different from Christianity."[24] Additionally, I think many others, both Christian and non-Christian, would have trouble with Frame's assessment of Islam as a Christian heresy. By assigning Islam (and Judaism!) to the disreputable realm of Christian heresy, Frame artificially strengthens his case that only the Christian God can account for the world as we know it. Frame and Van Til believe that the God of Christianity, because he is absolute, is able to account for the created order. And, because he is personal, he is able to serve as a reference point for things like morals and ethics. Both Van Til and Frame see the personal God of Christianity, as manifested in the Trinity, as the only God who can truly explain all aspects of our universe, from the physical to the moral. Thus Frame writes: "Islam's doctrine of predestination often has the ring of an impersonal determinism rather than the wise and good planning of the biblical Lord. And Islam's Allah can make arbitrary changes in his very nature, in contrast with the abiding, dependably personal character of the God of Scripture."[25] Frame, like his mentor Van Til, assumes that the God of Christianity is the One who not only explains the world, but makes possible the intelligibility of the world: "God must be nothing less than the Trinitarian, sovereign, transcendent, and immanent absolute personality of the Scriptures."[26]

Now, Van Til and Frame here are certainly correct when they point out that the Christian God is much more of a "person" than the God of Islam. The triune God possesses personality in that the divine logos became incarnate in a human being, walked among us,

---

23. In fact, the Koran does not even teach that Jesus was crucified. Rather, it teaches that another man was crucified in his stead, thus apparently deceiving all the onlookers. Sura 4 of the Koran states that "[t]hey did not kill him, nor did they crucify him, but they thought they did." This passage is quoted from *The Koran*, 382.

24. Martin, W., *The Kingdom of the Cults*, 364.

25. Frame, *Apologetics to the Glory of God*, 48.

26. Ibid., 89.

and told and showed us what God is like. The Holy Spirit, often described with personal pronouns in Scripture, is no impersonal force, but a personal manifestation of God's three-in-oneness. By contrast, the God of Islam often seems remote, impersonal, almost more like the God of deism than the loving, personal God of the New Testament. But this impression of Allah is true only up to a point. For instance, Christian philosopher and apologist Norman Geisler, certainly no defender of Islam, points out that contrary to much Christian misconception, Allah is viewed by Muslims as a God of absolute love: "Allah is a God of love. Indeed, some of God's names depict this very characteristic."[27] Love, of course, is no abstract quality; it can only be predicated upon personhood. And, even the much-vaunted plurality within the Christian Godhead (which Van Til and Frame insist is necessary in order for God to truly be a God of love) is not without precedent in the Islamic understanding of Allah. Geisler, in discussing Islamic theologians' understanding of Allah's revelation of the Koran to Muhammad, notes that Muslims understand Allah's speech to be an "eternal attribute of God that is not identical to God but is somehow distinguishable from him." If this were so, Geisler reasons, "it would seem that the Islamic view of God's absolute unity is, by their own distinction, not incompatible with Christian trinitarianism."[28] As to the charge that Van Til and Frame seem to level against Allah, namely, that he is too far removed and distant (i.e., not immanent enough) to truly be the source of all logic, order, and morality, Muslims have no difficulty in maintaining that Allah is indeed the force that binds the universe together in a coherent, rational manner. Muslims believe that the world was "created by the will of a Designer and sustained by Him for meaningful purposes. Historical currents take place in accordance with His will and follow established laws."[29]

Do I personally think that Allah makes as good a candidate for the creator of the world as does the biblical God? No. I think Van Til and Frame are correct to point out that the personal, trinitarian character of the Christian God is a *better* candidate for the ultimate source of our universe. But two things must be said in this regard.

27. Geisler, "Islam," 370.
28. Ibid., 371.
29. Abdalati, *Islam in Focus*, 51.

First, just because Allah does not seem as "qualified" does not a priori rule him out. He could still be the One, true Creator of all; Frame is certainly aware that a Muslim could easily make this claim.[30] A Muslim could do so because Allah, as portrayed in the Koran, seems to be described in much the same way as God is in the Bible, that is, as the absolute master of the universe. In fact, when "Christians read the Quran, they are often struck with how similar the Quran's depiction of God sounds to that of the Bible."[31]

Now, If Van Til, Frame, and Hays simply said, with appropriate humility, that the God of the Bible seems to be a more *likely* candidate than Allah for the role of Supreme Creator, then I would be in full agreement. And to his credit, Frame does hint at this position when he says that "Islam, Judaism, and various sects like the Jehovah's Witnesses also approximate biblical personalism, though I think inconsistently. But their personalism, such as it is, is due to the influence of Scripture."[32] But, even if Muhammad fashioned Allah after the God of the Bible (and this seems obvious to me) it is not obvious to Muslims, who take the Koranic descriptions of Allah to be infallible revelation, and thus a sure basis for apologetics. Therefore, a Muslim apologetic based upon the personhood of Allah, even though it is not the fully orbed personhood of the biblical God, is certainly a live option.

Despite the somewhat tentative nature of Frame's statement above, Van Til (and to a lesser extent, Frame) ultimately thinks that the supremely personal God of the Bible is the only explanation for the universe. Van Til, writing about the natural world and human ability to understand it correctly, said that:

> the existence of the God of Christian theism and the conception of his counsel as controlling all things in the universe is the only presupposition which can account for the uniformity of nature which the scientist needs.

30. Frame, *Cornelius Van Til*, 316.
31. George, *Is the Father of Jesus the God of Muhammad?* 71.
32. Frame, "Presuppositional Apologetics," 224 (footnote 27). Elsewhere Frame also suggests that the God of the Bible is a better candidate than any other God, seemingly eschewing the dogmatic insistence he displays elsewhere that only the Christian God could have created our world (228). But, this certainly was not Van Til's position, and Frame himself does not usually speak this way.

> But the best and only possible proof for the existence of such a God is that his existence is required for the uniformity of nature and for the coherence of all things in the world . . . Thus there is *absolutely certain proof* for the existence of God and the truth of Christian theism [italics mine].[33]

As a Christian, my faith tells me that such a God exists, too. But can I have "absolutely certain" proof of it? Muslims also believe that Allah gives order, structure, and purpose to the world: "the human mind was devoid of fertility till the bright rays of learning and science of the Quran awakened the human race, and spread in the four corners of the world."[34] Or again, concerning the natural world, Muslims think that if there "were not a Regulator of the whole of this system behind the scenes, the system would fall into chaos."[35] A Muslim can make the same kinds of statements as can a Reformed Christian presuppositionalist; the Muslim God may not seem as strong a candidate, but that certainly does not rule him out. Frame, though not quite as confident as Van Til in this area, is still able to write that "Van Til is also right, I believe, to emphasize that Christian theism is the only basis for intelligible predication . . . As we have seen, the alternative to Christian theism is ultimate impersonalism, which offers no intelligible explanation for the order and value of the world."[36]

As a Christian, I find the Christian God far more attractive, and more intellectually satisfying as well as morally satisfying, than the God of Islam. But I still fail to see how Allah could not be the creator of the world. Frame might reply that only a *fully* transcendent and *fully* immanent God could be responsible for the world as we know it. But how does he know that? Because it seems logical? Well, perhaps, but Muslims, and the ever-growing numbers who convert to Islam each year, do not see Christianity as logically superior in this regard. They think that Allah, even though he is not fully immanent and fully transcendent in the way that Christians conceive of God,

---

33. Van Til, *The Defense of the Faith*, 103.
34. Ahmad, M.G., *Islam Universal Religion*, 38.
35. Ahmad, Z., *Philosophy of the Teachings of Islam*, 47.
36. Frame, *Cornelius Van Til*, 276.

is responsible for the world as we know it. Metaphysical speculation about which God, Christian or Muslim, would make a better creator does not do much for the Van Tillian position. Geisler, writing about Van Til's insistence that only the triune God of Christianity can explain the world, says that "Certainly, as Van Til argues, it is necessary to posit a God to make sense out of the world. However, he has not shown that it is necessary to posit a triune God. This is true whether or not one accepts his argument that only the Trinity solves the problem of the one and the many."[37]

Van Til, contrary to much popular belief, is not opposed to using evidences to help prove the truth of Christianity. In fact, he welcomes the use of evidence, provided it is presented as part of the overall Christian presuppositional worldview. What Van Til will not allow is for man, with his so-called autonomous reason, to examine the traditional apologetic evidences on their own merit, apart from the Christian presuppositions that Van Til says these evidences depend upon. Van Til is radically opposed to allowing men, with their sin-beclouded minds, to judge whether or not the God of the Bible exists based only on so-called "neutral" evidence (e.g., the traditional evidentialist appeal to the resurrection as proof that Christianity is true). He writes that "if man is not autonomous, if he is rather what Scripture says he is, namely, a creature of God and a sinner before his face, then man should subordinate his reason to the Scriptures and seek in the light of it [sic] to interpret his experience."[38] Van Til is always insistent that the unbeliever must accept the Christian Scriptures, because they are infallible testimony to the God of Christianity and, as shown above, only the Christian God can, in Van Til's system, satisfactorily explain the universe. The Bible, then, for Van Til, is *the* presupposition behind of all of his other presuppositions, for the Bible reveals the presuppositions upon which Van Til builds his entire system of apologetics (e.g., the Fall of man, the noetic effects of sin, the triune personal God). He writes that "I take

---

37. Geisler, "Islam," 758. Van Til's insistence that only the doctrine of the Trinity solves the ages-old dilemma of the one and the many problem is one of the reasons he believes that only Christian theism can explain the world. For a good analysis of Van Til's position on the Trinity, see Frame, *Cornelius Van Til*, 63–78.

38. Van Til, *The Defense of the Faith*, 108.

what the Bible says about God and his relation to the universe as unquestionably true on its own authority."[39]

Now, what does the Muslim apologist claim? He claims, not surprisingly, that *his* Scriptures are the only true revelation of God. In fact, the Muslim in this instance actually goes Van Til one better, for the Muslim claims that his Koranic presuppositions involve accepting the belief that the Bible contains errors and is not trustworthy! Just as Van Til insists that sinful, unregenerate man cannot be trusted to sit in judgment upon Scripture, so the Muslim insists that the Bible is inferior to the Koran. Christians have no right to judge the Koran based upon the Bible, because the Bible contains willful misrepresentations of divine truth. The "revelations to Muhammad were a renewal of God's earlier revelations to Adam, Abraham, Moses, Jesus, and many other prophets, revelations that Muhammad said had been corrupted."[40] This willful corruption of the Bible sounds a great deal like the sinful, deliberate rejection of God that Van Til claims all unbelievers are guilty of.

The Christian can easily counter the Muslim claim that the Bible has been corrupted; the manuscript evidence, for the New Testament especially, is so great as to virtually guarantee that the New Testament text we read today is essentially the same as what was contained in the autographs.[41] But of course, this does not matter at all to the Muslim apologist; his Koran says the Bible is corrupt, and that is all there is to it. Well, he must say this; there are too many contradictions between the Bible and the Koran. The Muslim apologist will not let textual scholars, with their Van Tillian "autonomous reason," sit in judgment upon the Koran in this matter, any more than Van Til will let a non-believer sit in judgment upon the Bible. We thus seem to have reached a stalemate. Both Van Til and his Muslim counterpart argue that their particular Scripture must be trusted, and all others rejected.[42] All of this will strike the unbeliever as fideism.

39. Ibid., 195.
40. Armour, *Islam, Christianity, and the West*, 18.
41. See, for instance, Bruce, *The New Testament Documents*.
42. For the absurdity that results when two combating apologists both claim to be in possession of their own inerrant set of *self-authenticating* Scriptures, see Montgomery, "Once Upon an A Priori," 380–92.

It is at this point that an apologist in the evidentialist school might attempt to use the traditional arguments for Christianity to break the theological impasse. As previously noted, Van Til is not opposed to the use of evidence, so long as it is used within what he considers to be a proper Christian presuppositional framework. But the problem with Van Til's approach to Christian evidences is that, once a non-Christian accepts the presuppositions that Van Til insists upon, he is *already* a Christian! What is the point of arguing, say, for the historicity of the resurrection if the person with whom the apologist is debating already accepts all of Van Til's preconditions about the nature of the debate?

For instance, if someone accepts the idea of a literal, historical fall, (and this is a major Van Tillian presupposition, without which his apologetic endeavor simply is not possible) and the resultant curse upon man's intellect, at that point he is already a Christian. Who but a Christian believes that there was a "fall" from original righteousness? Who but a Christian believes that we are tainted with original sin as a result of this fall? I could also add, who but a strict Calvinist believes that the Fall has done as much damage to men and women as Van Til claims that it has?[43] Or, once one accepts that God is three-in-one (another basic Van Tillian presupposition), why does the apologist need to go further? Only orthodox Christians accept this view of God. It seems that if a non-believer accepts *any one* of Van Til's presuppositions, he is by default already a Christian.

The same could be said for the Muslim presupposition that the Koran is the theological corrective to a textually corrupt Bible. Once someone accepts this basic presupposition, he is *already* a Muslim—no one but a Muslim believes that the Koran contains the very words of God, words that pre-existed in heaven before being revealed to Muhammad. If appeals to outside evidence are rendered

---

43. Van Til, in good Calvinist fashion, stresses the idea that the Fall not only adversely influenced mankind, but also deeply harmed every aspect of the human condition, especially our reasoning process. The fact that Roman Catholicism, Eastern Orthodoxy, and many forms of Protestantism do not see the Fall as damaging human reason to this extreme extent puts Van Til's system somewhat at odds with the majority Christian position, and will probably prove to be a stumbling block to anyone not in agreement with his strict Calvinistic interpretation of the "utter depravity" that resulted from Adam and Eve's disobedience.

unnecessary by both the Van Tillian as well as the Muslim approach, how can a non-theist ever decide which of these great world religions is true? A Van Tillian would say that Christianity is obviously true, because it teaches what all men instinctively know, namely, that there is a God, and that unbelievers knowingly reject him despite the fact that they know better. But Islam teaches this very doctrine, too. The Van Tillian might then claim that the Bible alone presents a God who is able to account for the universe. But as we have seen above, a Muslim can make the same claim almost as strongly as can the Van Tillian. The Van Tillian could claim that Christianity is true because the Bible teaches that it is true. But the Koran teaches the same thing about Islam. What about an appeal to evidential arguments like the resurrection? Van Til rules this out unless one views it with the spectacles of Christian presuppositions. And it is precisely those presuppositions that are the problem, for they are no more convincing than the presuppositions that an Islamic apologist could use in the defense of his faith.

I do not wish to claim that there is no value in the Van Tillian system, far from it. As I stated above, Van Til (and Frame) does a masterful job of showing how the non-theist has no rational basis for his perceptions of the world, since he will not allow for a proper theistic foundation for those perceptions. But, as I have shown in this rebuttal, Van Til's system does not fair nearly so well against a theistic, in this case a Muslim, position. Thus, I find myself returning to the premise of my original article, namely, that the Van Tillian system is more theistic than specifically Christian. I believe I have shown how a Muslim apologist could use this approach to apologetics to validate the Islamic faith in much the same way that a Christian could use it to authenticate the truth-claims of Christianity. So, are Christians lost amidst the seas of religious doubt and despair when debating Muslims? Certainly not. But the Christian must use evidence that is unique to biblical religion, and not an apologetic system that lends itself to more than one version of theistic truth. Thus I insist on the resurrection of Jesus as strong, objective evidence for Christianity, evidence that is not dependent upon presuppositions that are not uniquely Christian.

3

Is John Hick's Concept of the "Real" an Adequate Criterion for Evaluating Religious Truth-Claims?

As is well known, John Hick has done much to advance the popularity of the concept of religious pluralism over the past several years. As a Christian, Hick has worked assiduously to revamp the faith so that Christians will finally start to acknowledge the salvific nature of the other great world religions. Hick's goals are, to a certain extent, understandable. For too long, Christians have often been arrogant in their assurance of the truth of their position, when in fact humble thanksgiving is the proper attitude for the Christian to assume in light of God's gift of redemption through his Son. However, in his zeal to create a version of Christianity which does not suffer from "theological imperialism," or "the scandal of particularity," Hick reduces the truth or falsity of all religious experience to what he terms the "Real." In other words, any religion that establishes a genuine relationship between the devotee and the Real (i.e., God) must be considered a valid form of faith. Proof that one is in contact with the Real is evidenced in a changed life, in a turning away from selfishness towards selflessness. In short, there is ongoing moral improvement in the person's life. However, two serious, insurmountable problems arise from this view of religion: one, it allows for religions which are based on seemingly false premises to be labeled "true," and two, it precludes, *a priori*, an honest *evidential* comparison and contrast between the conflicting truth-claims of the various religions.

Is John Hick's Concept of the "Real" an Adequate Criterion?

To begin with, let us look briefly at Hick's criterion for determining a religion's truth: the concept of the Real. Once a person begins to renounce his or her self-centeredness in favor of *Reality-centeredness*, what is the result? It is what Hick terms "salvation/liberation," although the traditional Christian understanding of salvation is not foremost in Hick's mind here: "salvation is not a juridical transaction inscribed in heaven, nor is it a future hope beyond this life (although it is this too), but it is a spiritual, moral, and political change that can begin now and whose present possibility is grounded in the structure of reality."[1] Hick is not denying an "afterlife" in the Christian sense, but his definition of salvation/liberation is primarily a "here and now" one. The result of this is an awakening to the "peace and joy and compassionate kindness toward all life."[2] Basically, Hick is defining religion as a turning away from selfishness, and a turning towards God, or the Real. This change of heart makes it possible for members of the religions to become, to put it simply, better human beings. And, since every culture, regardless of its religion, contains many examples of devout men and women whose lives seem to be getting "better," this is for Hick proof that all religions are equally salvific: "Their [the religions] soterical power can only be humanly judged by their human fruits, and . . . these fruits seem to me to be found more or less equally within each of the great traditions."[3]

Hick's insistence that all religions are equally valid, and therefore equally salvific, has mainly been confined to the major world faiths (Christianity, Judaism, Islam, Hinduism, and Buddhism). However, if a genuine encounter with the Real is the test for spiritual veracity, why should not this criterion apply to other, lesser-known religious groups, or religions with fewer adherents than the great world faiths? Surely Hick, who has so tenaciously fought for the concept of religious pluralism, would not want to deny the validity of one's spiritual life simply because that person does not belong to one of the five "major" religions? It is here that Hick's notion of the Real encounters its first serious hurdle. I have in mind religious "cults," or unorthodox religious groups that make claims that most other thoughtful religious people will find hard to accept.

1. Hick, "A Pluralistic View," 43.
2. Ibid., 50–51.
3. Ibid., 44.

PART ONE: HOW DO WE ADJUDICATE RELIGIOUS TRUTH-CLAIMS?

For example, what is one to make of the Nation of Islam, the radical "black" version of Islam, currently led by Louis Farrakhan? This group has attracted thousands of members of the African-American community in the United States. However, it is well known that many orthodox Muslims (both in the US and abroad) reject the group as heretical (because, for one thing, its theology is based not only upon the Koran, but also many extra-Koranic teachings). It is also a fact that the group's spokesmen have made numerous anti-white, but especially anti-Jewish, remarks in the press. So frequent have been these attacks that "Farrakhan and his aides are now characteristically known as 'bigots' who have labeled Jews 'bloodsuckers,' Judaism a 'gutter religion,' Israel 'an outlaw state,' and Hitler 'a very great man' (albeit 'wickedly great')."[4]

It is, therefore, little surprise that when Farrakhan spoke at New York's Madison Square Garden in 1985, the Jewish Defense League organized a "Death to Farrakhan" march.[5] If all of this were not enough to ignite the ire of Jews, a publication put out by *The Nation*, entitled "The Secret Relationship Between Blacks and Jews," accuses Jews of playing a disproportionately large (almost demonic) role in the African slave trade.[6]

The racist rhetoric of the Nation of Islam is unavoidable, really, given the nature of the sect's cosmological beliefs. The Nation's beliefs about the origin of the world and the creation of man are, to be blunt, somewhat cartoon-like, and it is hard to imagine anyone who is not within the Nation taking them seriously.[7] To put it briefly, Allah created humanity, but all the first men were of the so-called Asiatic black race (Asia being the original name for earth). These first blacks were created in a pristine state, and were "not the true source of moral evil in the world, for the production of such misery is against their nature."[8] (It is only when blacks reject the truth of Allah and Islam that they can be said to cause evil.) Whites, however, are a different story entirely. They were not "created" by Allah, but

4. Lieb, *Children of Ezekiel*, 185.
5. Ibid., 184.
6. Ibid., 185.
7. For a good summary of the Nation's outlandish beliefs about human origins, see Pinn, *African-American Religious Experience*, 128–34.
8. Ibid., 151.

rather "made" by an evil one named Yakub. This Yakub groomed his creations ("white devils," if you will) to the point where they became the masters of the globe and held blacks in thrall.[9] It is this evil domination of blacks by whites which continues to this day, and which the Nation of Islam has so forcefully railed against. Ironically, this all sounds very similar to what various *white* supremacist groups believe when they describe people of color as "mud people," inferior beings who are to be distinguished from the superior white race, whose members are the true descendants of Adam.

Surely, such a religion that teaches the inherent evil of Jews, black superiority, and white inferiority, cannot be a true expression of Hick's "Real"? Surely no one in touch with the loving being Hick insists on equating with the Real could be responsible for the theology of the Nation of Islam? But wait a moment. The Nation of Islam *does* seem to do, in many cases, what Hick claims true religion should do: change one's orientation from selfishness to the "Other." The Nation of Islam can boast several moral success stories. For example, the Nation has "gained national recognition and respect" for liberating inner city black neighborhoods that were formerly controlled by drug dealers and addicts.[10] The Nation of Islam can also boast great success in converting and rehabilitating many black men who are incarcerated in the nation's prisons: "NOI [Nation of Islam] officials have received numerous awards for their rehabilitation programs."[11] Farrakhan himself has "become a respected presence in mediation and counsel" concerning the black-on-black gang violence which has wreaked such misery in the black community.[12]

Even if Hick were to claim that the overt racism of the group indicates they are not truly in touch with the Real, I would respond, why not? Their racism is a sin, but all truly religious persons manifest sin in their lives. Sin in one area (racial prejudice) does not cancel out all of the obvious turnings toward the Real which Nation members make in other areas, any more than a sincere Christian's trouble with, say, pornography or a bad temper, does not nullify all the truly Christian traits he or she evidences in other areas. All Hick's

9. Ibid., 132–33.
10. Lincoln, *The Black Muslims in America*, 271.
11. Gardell, *Elijah Muhammad*, 306.
12. Lincoln, *The Black Muslims in America*, 271.

criterion of the Real requires is that religious persons are making moral progress, that they have turned away from self and toward the divine; moral perfection is never attainable. When one sees the well-groomed, smartly dressed members of the Nation of Islam passing out literature on the streets of major US cities (some of whom no doubt terrorized those same streets before their conversion), it is hard to think that they are not morally progressing, albeit imperfectly, towards Hick's Real.

In fact, the culmination of the Nation's positive influence can clearly be seen in Farrakhan's crowning achievement, his famous Million Man March. This was not a gathering of a few fanatics to spread racial hatred, as is so often the case with "skinhead" and KKK rallies. This was the largest civil rights march in the history of the United States, and it drew anywhere from 650,000 to 1.1 million persons.[13] That this was a "respectable" civil rights march can be judged by the black civil rights luminaries and scholars who supported and or attended it: Rosa Parks, Jesse Jackson, the Southern Christian Leadership Conference, Maya Angelou, and Cornel West.[14] West's words seem to sum up best the positive nature of the event: "the Million Man March was an historic event—called by Minister Louis Farrakhan, claimed by black people of every sort and remembered by people around the globe as an expression of black men's humanity and decency. Never before has such black love flowed so freely and abundantly for so many in the eyes of the world."[15]

Here Hick would seem to be caught on the horns of a dilemma of his own making. The Nation of Islam teaches racial superiority along with racial hatred; this racism has its roots in Allah himself, and his racist preference for blacks over whites. Surely this cannot be a religion that is truly in touch with the divine, with what Hick terms the Real. Yet many of its members have changed their orientation in a way that Hick insists is a mark of true religion. And, in Hick's system, it is not the *content* of the religion, but only its *results* in the lives of the faithful that determine its validity. Using Hick's criterion, those whose lives have been changed by the Nation of Islam seem to

---

13. Lieb, *Children of Ezekiel*, 190.
14. Ibid., 190.
15. Ibid.

indicate that the transforming power of this religion is quite powerful, and quite real.

The Church of Jesus Christ of Latter Day Saints—the Mormons—pose a similar problem for Hick. Most Christian scholars would define them as a cult, not because they wish to denigrate Mormons, but because they are associated with the things characterized by cults. They take an established religion (Christianity) and add their own unique interpretation to it (the Book of Mormon); they have their own "inspired" religious leaders (the leader of the Church, or the Prophet, the first of which was Mormon founder Joseph Smith); and they demand unswerving allegiance from their followers, and freely practice excommunication if their behavior is unsatisfactory.

However, be they a cult or not, the Mormons have a widespread reputation for morally upright living.[16] I personally know several Mormons, and they are obviously devout, sincere people. Their devotion to God and family, and their eschewal of vices like drinking, smoking, and pre-marital sex, are well known. Many readers of this essay could probably confirm this through personal encounters with Mormons in their everyday lives. Yet there is a problem with Mormonism: it is, in my estimation of the evidence, demonstrably *false*. Or, at the very least, it rests upon foundations that seem to have very little going for them in terms of verifiability. Many religions do not offer much in the way of negative *or* positive evidence for their truth-claims, so it is difficult to assess the veridicality of such faiths (for instance, can anyone prove one way or another that the Nirvana of Buddhism does or does not exist?). But unlike some religions that are not capable of being decisively proven to be true or false,

---

16. Martin, W., *The Kingdom of the Cults*, 167, 169. This book is considered by many to be the standard reference work on religious cults written from an explicitly evangelical viewpoint. However, some of the entries in the book, like Islam, are clearly world religions, not cults. Also, Martin has sometimes been criticized for his polemical tone in this work. However, the attacks he levels against the alleged historicity of the *Book of Mormon* have never been refuted (as far as I know), and this is the reason I cite him here. And although Martin is quite critical of the Mormons, even he admits their reputation for "clean living," "sound moral traits," and devotion to church and family. Thus, they seem to be in tune with Hick's concept of the Real.

PART ONE: HOW DO WE ADJUDICATE RELIGIOUS TRUTH-CLAIMS?

Mormonism *can* be shown to contain so many errors that its likelihood as a true path to Hick's Real must be seriously questioned.

The first problem arises from the Book of Mormon itself. It was supposedly discovered by Mormon founder Joseph Smith, who translated it from the original "Reformed Egyptian" via the use of a type of magical spectacles. The only problem here is that Reformed Egyptian does not exist, nor has it ever existed, according to "every leading Egyptologist and philologist ever consulted on the problem."[17] But the content of the Book of Mormon proves even more troubling. The Book claims to be a history of two ancient civilizations, one that left the Tower of Babel region and relocated to the east coast of what is now Central America around 2250 BC (according to Mormon reckoning). The second group left Jerusalem just before the Babylonian captivity, and settled on the west coast of South America.[18] Of course, outside of the Book of Mormon, there is absolutely no evidence that such civilizations ever left the Middle East for the New World. In addition to this, the Book claims that there were thirty-eight great cities that were established in the Americas after the arrival of these transplanted Middle Eastern races. However, the "Mormons have yet to explain the fact that leading archaeological researchers not only have repudiated the claims of the Book of Mormon as to the existence of these civilizations, but have adduced considerable evidence to show the impossibility of the accounts given in the Mormon Bible."[19] Much like the cosmology of the Nation of Islam, the alleged history of the Book of Mormon must seem utterly fantastic to anyone who is not a dedicated Mormon.[20]

17. Martin, W., *The Kingdom of the Cults*, 172.
18. Ibid., 178.
19. Ibid., 183. It must be realized that these are not mere archaeological discrepancies, as are often found when the Christian Bible is examined. There are parts of the Old Testament, for example, which cannot be verified by archaeology, and some parts that seem to be undermined by it, but on the whole, there is obviously a historical basis to the Old Testament writings. And it has long been recognized that the New Testament is firmly anchored in historical reality. See, for instance, Bruce, *The New Testament Documents*, 80–99. This is not so with the Book of Mormon, where all the historical foundations of the book seem to be fabricated.
20. For a thorough refutation of the "historicity" of the Book of Mormon, see W. Martin, *The Kingdom of the Cults*, 178–87.

Finally, there are the "prophetic" utterances of Mormonism's founder, Joseph Smith. If he was a prophet, as Mormons to this day believe, his prophetic skills (or lack thereof) could have gotten him stoned to death in ancient Israel, where false prophets were not suffered to live! His prophecy concerning the American Civil War predicated that England would become involved, and that the conflict would escalate into a world war. He also predicated that he would occupy his home in Nauvoo, IL "for ever and ever." The truth is that neither he nor his descendants remained in the house. In fact, the house was destroyed by fire, and the Mormons eventually sojourned into Utah.[21]

What are we to make of Mormonism then, in light of John Hick's criteria for determining a religion's truth? Without a doubt Mormon people seem to be living moral, "holy" lives, which Hick insists is proof of a genuine encounter with the Real. However, what would a critical scholar like Hick do with the obviously false historical framework of the Book of Mormon? He certainly is not reluctant to discount portions of the Bible that he does not believe are historically accurate,[22] and the Bible is undoubtedly more firmly rooted in history than the Book of Mormon! What would he make of the false prophecies by the religion's "inspired" author? As with the Nation of Islam, Hick would have to ignore these glaring problems, since, according to his theory, Mormons are genuinely engaged with the Real, based on the lives they lead.[23]

---

21. Ibid., 190–91. As with the seriousness of the historical inaccuracies mentioned above, so with these false prophecies. Joseph Smith is not a minor figure in the history of Mormonism, who can be allowed a bit of prophetic "leeway." He is the founder of the religion itself, and his false predictions do not bode well for the faith he claims to have discovered.

22. Hick, "A Pluralistic View," 31–36.

23. The same approach I have taken with the Nation of Islam and the Mormons could probably be taken with atheists, as well. They, of course, deny belief in any type of religion whatsoever, yet it is common knowledge that there are many "good" atheists among us. How would Hick explain the existence of atheists who lead charitable, loving lives? Surely they are not in touch with the divine? Or, if they are, it is a "secret" relationship, similar perhaps to Rahner's concept of "anonymous Christianity." Surely Hick, given his Christian commitment, would condemn atheism as a false worldview. Yet how to explain the reality of "good" atheists?

How might Hick respond to such criticisms as those listed above? First, he rightly concludes that not all religions are valid paths to the Real. The twisted religious ideas of, for example, the Nazis, Jim Jones, or David Koresh, certainly are not salvific, for obvious reasons. Plus, many religions/cults are too new, and a fair assessment of their validity cannot yet be made.[24] With this I fully agree. However, the Nation of Islam and the Mormons cannot be so easily dismissed, for, as previously explained, both religions meet Hick's criterion for religious validity. Also consider Hick's comments, taken from a passage where he is discussing the way to determine the validity of cults, and those faiths that are not among the major world religions: "[a]ny judgement about them has to be based on a close examination of each particular movement, and all that one can say in general is that the same criterion must apply as in the case of the great world faiths: are they effective contexts of the salvific transformation of human beings from self-centredness to a new orientation centred in the Real as authentically known in a particular human way?"[25]

Both the Nation of Islam and the Mormons provide a way for their adherents to make this transformation. And although Hick believes that a religion may be a genuine path to the Real, while at the same time containing elements "that have little or no religious value, or indeed that work directly against the salvific transformation,"[26] I do not think this approach will work in the case of the Nation of Islam and the Mormons. For the problems I have pointed out with these religions (i.e., racism, and dubious scriptural records) are not peripheral matters. Rather, they lie at the very core of each religion. The inherent evil of the white race, and the inherent superiority of the black race, are essential to Nation of Islam theology. And the Mormon religion itself would not be possible without the Book of Mormon.

The above-mentioned discrepancies encountered with the Nation of Islam and the Mormons are a serious problem for Hick, who sets up a self-created, arbitrary criterion to define true religion: self-improvement through contact with the Real. I suggest that one should examine the evidence (or lack thereof) for each religion and

---

24. Hick, *A Christian Theology of Religions*, 44.
25. Ibid., 110–11.
26. Ibid., 44.

evaluate it, the same way one would evaluate the evidence for any other sort of truth-claim, secular or otherwise. Someone who does not share Hick's definition of religion could simply examine the religions described above (and all others as well), look at the pros and cons of each, and decide if the religion being scrutinized is true. For someone who believes God (or the Real) is a God of love, that person would have to reject the Nation of Islam's cosmology and theology, which portrays God as caring more for dark-skinned than for light-skinned persons. Someone who takes seriously the question of scriptural records (and this includes the closely-related matters of archaeology and history) upon which a "historical" religion like Mormonism is based, would necessarily have to reject that religion, for the history espoused in the Book of Mormon seems to be entirely fanciful.

But such an honest look at the evidence for the world religions is something that Hick simply will not consider.[27] Why? For one thing, he does not think it is possible to acquire *enough* empirical knowledge about any of the religions in order to be certain that that particular religion is "true." Hick states that, because we cannot empirically prove, beyond a doubt, the truth of any religion: "[religious truth-claims] are not matters concerning which absolute dogmas are appropriate. Still less is it appropriate to maintain that salvation depends upon accepting any one particular opinion or dogma concerning them." [28]

The kind of absolute evidence Hick desires is quite unrealistic, considering we almost never have this type of evidence regarding the

---

27. One reason for Hick's reluctance here is the fact that he believes his interpretation of religion will allow the world religions to live in a more harmonious atmosphere, once such exclusionary religions like Christianity stop insisting the Christian faith is the only true faith: "a religion that accepts the other great traditions as equally authentic can join with them to promote international peace and to solve the problems of planetary ecology and two-thirds world poverty, malnutrition and disease, and the vast periodic disasters of war and famine," in Hick, *The Metaphor of God Incarnate,* 134. These wonderful things may indeed come about if religious claims to exclusivity cease, but the issue at hand is, how does one know if a religion is true or false? As laudable as the goals mentioned by Hick are, they really do not have anything to do with the determination of which, if any, religion is in tune with the Real.

28. Hick, *The Metaphor of God Incarnate,* 145.

PART ONE: HOW DO WE ADJUDICATE RELIGIOUS TRUTH-CLAIMS?

most important decisions we make every day. I, for instance, may drive a certain route to work. I may consider it to be a very safe route (light traffic, no hairpin turns, etc.). I consider the road in question so safe that I drive it every day, almost certain that nothing untoward will happen to me on it. Of course, I could be wrong—tomorrow, on that very road I could be involved in a fatal car crash. Yet I consider this event so unlikely that I am willing to continue driving that road. In short, I am "dogmatic" about the safety of this road! Or, take for example, a man who has been married for twenty-five years. His wife is devoted to him, and has never shown him anything but love and affection. Now, it is possible that when she says she is going to the local mall, she is really going to meet a man with whom she is having an extra-marital affair. The husband would never consider this because, based on the evidence of twenty-five years of faithful marriage, the idea is preposterous. He, too, is "dogmatic" about his wife's fidelity. Not because he can empirically prove beyond a doubt that she is faithful, but because the *evidence* (not ironclad proof) indicates that she is so. If such deeply important things like life and death driving decisions, and life-long marriage relationships do not require one hundred percent empirical verification, why should a religious decision? The simple fact is: there is no area of life where we have absolute certainty, yet we continue to go on making very important decisions based on what evidence we *do* have.[29]

Hick's lack of confidence concerning religious evidence results in an inability to see that the issue of truth-claims must be addressed, or else one is forced to accept outright contradiction among the religions (that the major world religions do indeed teach mutually exclusive concepts of man, sin, God, salvation, revelation, etc., has been pointed out more than enough times, so there is no need to belabor the point here). But it is not just contradiction of the theological kind, which Hick, of course, explains away by teaching that various, equally valid paths to God are available. The contradictions are *historical* in nature. This is especially apparent when addressing the issue of Christ's death on the cross. In the New Testament we are told

---

29. I am indebted to the work of Christian apologist John Warwick Montgomery here, who often employed this sort of thinking when arguing for the strength of the evidential approach to Christianity. See, for instance, his *Human Rights and Human Dignity*, 152–54.

that Christ dies on the cross, and that he was resurrected. However, the Koran denies that Christ died on the cross.[30] Here Hick makes the following statement: "All that one can say in general about such disagreements, whether between two traditions or between any one of them and the secular historians, is that they could only properly be settled by the weight of historical evidence. However, the events in question are usually so remote in time, and the evidence so slight and uncertain, that the question cannot be definitively settled."[31] I find this statement to be quite surprising. First, he does not seem to take seriously the fact that the very truth, indeed, the very existence, of both Christianity and Islam rest on the issue of what happened to Christ on the cross. If Jesus did not die, as the Koran asserts, then Christianity is based upon a lie, and Christians are, as Paul once said, the most miserable of all men. If, however, Christ did die upon the cross, and later rose, then it is Islam that is based upon a false premise (i.e., that Jesus was only a prophet, rather than the One whose resurrection verified the early Christians' claim that he was indeed the divine Messiah).

What I find truly astounding is that Hick thinks that the evidence for the death of Christ upon the cross to be "so slight and uncertain." Has Hick's desire for religious pluralism, based on his concept of the Real, blinded him to the great amount of evidence that has been put forth by Christian apologists in support of the New Testament's description of Christ's death and resurrection? This evidence has been set forth and vigorously defended by numerous scholars.[32] Simply put, when one considers the major pieces of evi-

---

30. To Hick's credit, he does offer the New Testament version as a "historical report," while he labels the Koranic version a "theological inference—that God would not allow so great a prophet to be killed" (*The Metaphor of God Incarnate*, 146). It must also be admitted that Hick is not here presenting an in-depth study of what happened to Christ on the cross. He is using the cross experience to show how historical records can vary from one religion to another. Still, I think the criticisms that follow are entirely warranted, based on Hick's overall approach to obvious contradictions among the world's religions, and his apparent disinterest in analyzing religious truth-claims from an evidentialist viewpoint.

31. Ibid,, 146.

32. The literature in the area is enormous, but some of the best works are as follows: *Did Jesus Rise from the Dead?* This work contains a debate between Christian apologist Gary Habermas and renowned atheistic philosopher Antony

PART ONE: HOW DO WE ADJUDICATE RELIGIOUS TRUTH-CLAIMS?

dence, it is far easier to accept the authenticity of the resurrection narrative found in the New Testament, rather than to posit alternate explanations (such as the now thoroughly discredited "swoon theory," where Christ allegedly fainted on the cross, then was later revived).

There are several major pieces of evidence. One, the tomb of Christ was empty. Had he not risen, hostile Roman and Jewish authorities could have easily produced the body, thus squelching any talk of a risen Messiah. Such talk would have been blasphemy to the Jewish religious leaders, and potentially seditious as far as the Romans were concerned. The idea that the disciples stole and hid the body, then later claimed that Christ was resurrected, is ludicrous. The disciples suffered greatly for the gospel that they preached. They certainly gained no worldly benefits from preaching their message. Ultimately, tradition tells us, most of them died as martyrs. It is highly unlikely that twelve men would suffer and die for a religion they knew to be based on a lie.

Two, the resurrection must have actually occurred, for it is these appearances that obviously turned a rag-tag group of Jewish peasants into the mighty evangelists who began to preach the resurrection and divinity of Christ. How else would we explain the fact that these simple men, who were so dejected when their Master was executed, suddenly became witnesses unto death for that same Master? That these resurrection appearances were only visions, or hallucinations, is entirely untenable, for no twelve men (not to mention the 500 that Paul mentions!) can be expected to have the same hallucinations!

Three, the story of the resurrection was preached in the presence of "hostile witnesses," that is, Jewish authorities who would have gladly discredited the story had they been able to do so. Suffice to say that the death and resurrection of Christ is easily the best-attested event in the New Testament, if not the entire Bible. Can we know with one hundred percent proof that this happened? No, but as I pointed out earlier, such proof is never required when it comes to

---

Flew. The debate is rather one-sided, however, as Flew is unable to refute any of Habermas's arguments supporting the New Testament account of the resurrection. In a similar vein, see the debate between William Lane Craig and John Dominic Crossan in *Real Jesus Please Stand Up?* Also of interest are Davis, *Risen Indeed*, and Montgomery, *Where is History Going?* 37–74.

making important decisions (like, for instance, a religious decision to believe in Jesus because of the New Testament evidence that he rose from the dead, thus verifying his divinity). Even Hick himself, in the passage quoted above, says that the "weight of historical evidence," not proof beyond all doubt, is required to resolve such issues. The weight of the historical evidence clearly favors the New Testament account of what happened to Jesus on (and after) the cross. The importance of this kind of evidence for the Christian faith cannot be overestimated, for such evidence simply does not exist for any of the other world religions. Consider Islam, for example: John Warwick Montgomery writes, concerning the evidence for the resurrection juxtaposed with the evidence for the Islamic faith, that "[n]o such attesting evidence for Muslim revelational claims can be marshaled, for it simply does not exist."[33]

Hick also seems unwilling to admit just how central the death and resurrection of Christ is to the Christian faith. In one of his works, where he is discussing the "historical" beliefs that separate different religions from each other, he lumps the resurrection of Christ in with such beliefs as the Buddhist belief that Buddha literally flew from India to Sri Lanka, the Muslim belief that Muhammad flew between Mecca and Jerusalem, and the Jewish belief that, at Joshua's command, the sun remained immobile in the sky for twenty-four hours.[34] Now, the problem here is that the resurrection of Jesus is a central (indeed, *the* central) belief for the Christian. A Muslim could dispense with Mohammad's airborne travel, as could a Buddhist with the story of Buddha's flight, and nothing of essential theological significance would be lost to either religion. These miraculous stories are really not important to either religion in terms of their respective theologies and belief systems. As for Joshua's commanding the sun to stop, this is hardly an essential part of Jewish theology. Besides, Joshua is not even the founder of Judaism! But Christianity stands or falls based upon the historicity of the resurrection. Ironically, it is Christianity that can offer solid empirical evidence that the miraculous event upon which it is based actually happened.

33. Montgomery, *Human Rights and Human Dignity*, 119. For Montgomery's critique of Muslim attempts at apologetics, see his "How Muslims do Apologetics," 81–99.
34. Hick, *An Interpretation of Religion*, 363–64.

PART ONE: HOW DO WE ADJUDICATE RELIGIOUS TRUTH-CLAIMS?

A final word must be said regarding Hick's incorporation of Kantian thought into his pluralistic theology. When confronted with criticism of his views, Hick has often sought refuge in Kant's theory that there is a difference between reality as such, and the *perception* of reality which we as human beings experience. Hick believes that, as each human has a different perception of the outside world, so human experience and interpretation of God can vary. This, combined with different historical and cultural settings, goes far in explaining the variety of religions in the world: "It is the variations of the human cultural situation that concretize the notion of deity as specific images of God. And it is these images that inform man's actual religious experience, so that it is an experience specifically of the God of Israel, or of Allah, or of the Father of our Lord Jesus Christ, or of Vishnu or Shiva."[35] This view, however, faces serious problems, especially in regard to the criticisms I have raised. First, it does not resolve the historical contradictions among the world's religions. If the Christian perception of reality is that Christ died on the cross, while the Muslim perception is that he did not, *one* of these perceptions must be erroneous. Kant can be invoked to explain these different interpretations, perhaps, but one must still decide which perception is historically, objectively, true. Similarly, Kant might be used to explain, but certainly not defend, the racist teachings of the Nation of Islam, since racism clearly violates Hick's own definition of what it means to be in touch with the Real. And, I definitely do not see how he could use the Kantian theory to defend the glaring historical fabrications that are the basis of the Book of Mormon. The events the Book purports to describe either happened, or did not happen. It is a question of historical fact, not human perception.[36]

35. Hick, *God Has Many Names*, 105–06.
36. Hick offers the following example of how human perception can view the same object differently. He uses an intentionally ambiguous drawing which, depending upon how one looks at it, either looks like a rabbit or a duck. Hick explains that the drawing will look like a rabbit to one who is acquainted only with rabbits. However, if one is familiar only with ducks, he can see in the drawing nothing but a duck (*A Christian Theology of Religions*, 24–25). This is true as far as it goes, since the object in question is only a drawing. However, if it were an actual object, it would be either a rabbit, or a duck. It would have an objective reality, and this reality is in no way dependent on the viewer's perception. If the object is actually a duck, and the onlooker perceives it to be

Is John Hick's Concept of the "Real" an Adequate Criterion?

Clearly, Hick's criterion of the Real is not an adequate basis for assessing religious truth-claims. We must not look only at the moral improvements in the lives of religious believers (admirable as these changes may be), but rather at the religions *themselves*. A man or woman may evidence moral and spiritual improvement, yet still adhere to a faith that espouses racism. Can such a faith truly be a path to the Real? Equally, one may lead an exemplary moral life, yet be a member of a religion that rests on allegedly historical Scriptures, which in fact have no basis in reality. Is the path to the Real based upon myths masquerading as fact? Christianity, on the other hand, can boast of moral growth in the lives of its followers but, unlike other faiths, it can *also* offer convincing evidence that it is a religion based on empirical fact.

---

a rabbit, he is simply wrong. Surely, such errors occur in the realm of religious perception, too, which at least partially explains the glaring contradictions among the world's religions.

4

A Case for "Reformed Evidentialism"

THE TASK of apologetics has long been of concern to evangelical theologians. The dominant approach to apologetics among evangelicals has been the evidentialist one. Evidentialist apologetics has always been rational regarding the defense and promulgation of the Christian faith; it has sought to anchor the validity of biblical Christianity on the tri-foundation of logic, common sense, and objective evidence. The evidentialist school of thought has strong roots in the Enlightenment and the idea that human reasoning can determine the validity of any intellectual position, religious or otherwise. However, the postmodern period, with its rejection of Enlightenment ideals, has rendered suspect the idea that anything can be "proven," especially something as nebulous as religious belief. To counter this position, the so-called Reformed epistemologists emerged in the 1980s and attempted to justify Christian belief independent of any type of evidentialist, rationalist proof. This chapter will examine the strengths of the Reformed epistemological position concerning apologetics, comparing and contrasting it with traditional evidentialist apologetics, and ultimately arguing that the Reformed epistemological approach cannot succeed as a tool of Christian apologetics without a healthy infusion of evidentialism.

The traditional evidentialist approach to apologetics, sometimes called the classical approach,[1] has a long and illustrious history. In

---

1. The terms "evidentialist" and "classical" are often used interchangeably, but according to one thinker there is a major difference. Classical Christian apologists believe that God's existence must be proved before any specific

fact, the New Testament writers themselves were evidentialists in the purest sense of the word. For them, the resurrection of Christ was an objective event in time-space history that verified the claims of the new faith the disciples were preaching. In Acts 17:31, Paul, who is debating with the Athenians, explicitly states that there is objective evidence for his religion, since God "has given *proof* [italics mine] of this to all men by raising [Jesus] from the dead." The same apologetic technique is on display in Acts 26, when Paul appears before Festus and Agrippa. Here again, Paul is arguing the Christian case based on the evidence provided by the resurrection. Indeed, so central is the resurrection for Paul that he plainly says the Christian faith stands or falls based on the veracity of this event (1 Cor 15:12–19). The writer of 1 John, in his attempt to defend the gospel against Gnostic corruptions, stresses the objective fact of the gospel. The apostles have "seen," "touched," and "felt" the One they now worship as Lord. Thus, it can be said that the New Testament is strongly evidentialist in its approach to the faith. Yes, it teaches that the Christian life is one based on faith, but it is a faith based upon historically verifiable events. This type of evidentialist approach to the defense of Christian theism was surely the most popular approach to Christian apologetics in the twentieth century.[2] A representative example is B.B. Warfield of Princeton Seminary. Warfield, who is best characterized as a classical/evidentialist apologist, began the apologetic task on "neutral" ground

---

arguments for Christianity can be considered, while evidentialists believe that the specific arguments themselves not only provide proof for the existence of God, but also suggest that this God is most likely the God of the Christian Scriptures. However, the line is often blurred between these two approaches. For more on this, see Habermas, "Evidential Apologetics," 92.

2. Another popular strain of apologetics in the twentieth century was presuppositional apologetics. Cornelius Van Til, the late professor of apologetics at Westminster Seminary in Philadelphia developed this system of defending the faith. Presuppositionalists reject the very idea of Christian evidences, arguing, as did Karl Barth, that there is no point of contact, or common ground, between Christians and non-Christians. What is needed, Van Til maintained, is to make the non-believer realize that all thinking, religious or otherwise, is predicated upon the existence of the God of the Bible. Thus, the unbeliever must not be permitted to evaluate arguments for Christianity and "decide" if Christianity is true. He or she must humbly submit to the authority of the God of the Bible. For a devastating critique of this position from a classical/evidentialist position, see Sproul et al., *Classical Apologetics*, 183–338.

PART ONE: HOW DO WE ADJUDICATE RELIGIOUS TRUTH-CLAIMS?

with the unbeliever. Warfield started with "general" revelation (the innate awareness of God that all people have, according to Paul in chapter one of Romans), and progressed to "special," Christian revelation. For Warfield, the first step in the traditional method was to get the non-believer to consider the fact that there may exist a "God" who created the universe. This could be done, perhaps, through one or more of the classical proofs for God's existence. Once this was accomplished, the field must be narrowed down, through the use of evidentialist apologetics, to prove that this God who probably exists is the God of the Christian Bible.

One common approach that Christian evidentialists will employ is to appeal to the general reliability of the New Testament documents. The point is often made that the writings of the Christian Bible are the best-attested documents of the ancient world. They were composed within only a few decades after the events they describe. In addition, the large number of extant New Testament manuscripts (literally in the thousands), ensures that the Christian Scriptures we have today are substantially the same in content as the original autographs.[3]

An even more common approach, though, is to focus on the person of Christ, specifically his death, burial, and resurrection. The historicity of the resurrection has taken somewhat of a beating in the last several decades; many scholars have been so reluctant to declare the resurrection a historical fact that they have sought refuge in the realm of a "history beyond history." That is, they maintain that the resurrection indeed happened, but not in the realm of observable, verifiable history. Of course, this is merely theological double-talk; there is no such realm, at least not that we know of. Past events either

---

3. For a good summary of the reliability of the New Testament, see Bruce, *The New Testament Documents*, 80–99. Also of interest is Montgomery, *Where is History Going?* 44–52. Of course, the integrity of the New Testament documents does not in any way guarantee that their contents are "true." But, the fact that our current New Testament has come down to us more or less in the form in which it was originally written is a powerful argument against those who might be inclined to suspect that the texts have undergone significant editorial redaction. Also, by arguing that the New Testament has a firm historical basis, it can be distinguished from a work like the Book of Mormon, for which there is no supporting historical evidence. For the lack of historicity regarding the Mormon Scriptures, see W. Martin, *The Kingdom of the Cults*, 178–87.

happened, or they did not. Indeed, the phrase "historical event" cannot even be understood apart from the idea that something actually occurred in space-time history. But, even if such a meta-historical realm does indeed exist, why would it be any easier for God to perform miracles there than in our own historical realm? If God cannot work miracles, then he cannot work miracles, regardless of the "world" in which he operates! Rudolf Bultmann was one of the most famous advocates of this supra-historical view of the resurrection. For Bultmann, "God is beyond space-time history. His acts are transcendent; they are above observable human history . . . Miracles are not of this world. They are acts in the spiritual world. In brief, Bultmann has defined them out of existence."[4] But appeal to a make-believe realm of supra-history does nothing to settle the matter one way or another. Indeed, from an apologetic viewpoint, this retreat into the non-historical realm seems to be a tacit admission that the resurrection need not be taken too seriously, since it seems to be like so many other religious stories—purely mythical, regardless of the effect it may have had on the disciples.[5] Evangelical distaste for such a view is captured in the following words from Gregory Boyd and Paul Eddy: "A good deal of liberal theology is premised on the mistaken notion that people can embrace the symbolic meaning of an event while denying the event ever literally took place . . . Evangelicals have always regarded this line of thinking implausible, if not incoherent."[6]

Another common approach has been to assume that the resurrection appearances were visions. This approach is interesting because it takes seriously the experiences of those who saw the risen Christ. Proponents of this view seem to sense that it will not do to deny the experiences of the disciples; there is no way to account for the existence of Christianity otherwise. Why would men steeped in Jewish monotheism proclaim a human being was divine? Why would

---

4. Geisler, *The Battle for the Resurrection*, 90. For a good, succinct summary of Bultmann's views on the historical (or non-historical) character of the New Testament, see Michalson, "Rudolf Bultmann," 102–13.

5. Although Bultmann insisted that the resurrection was not a physical, objective event in history, the "event" of the resurrection nonetheless sparked the rise of the kerygma in the apostles. For his skepticism regarding the historicity of the gospel accounts, see his *The History of the Synoptic Tradition*.

6. Boyd and Eddy, *Across the Spectrum*, 71.

they endure hardship, persecution, and eventually death unless they had had an experience that convinced them Christ was indeed alive after his crucifixion? Even orthodox Jewish scholar Pinchas Lapide is compelled to assert: "No vision of hallucination is sufficient to explain such a revolutionary transformation [in the disciples]. For a sect or school or an order, perhaps a single vision would have been sufficient—but not for a world religion which was able to conquer the Occident thanks to the Easter faith."[7] There are other problems with the hallucination hypothesis. As I have shown elsewhere, the psychological nature of hallucination, as well as mass-delusion, simply does not lend itself as a plausible explanation of the origins of the Easter faith.[8]

Fortunately, there have been several major works within the past two decades in which the historicity of the resurrection has been ably defended. A host of evangelical scholars have produced rigorous defenses of the historical reliability of Christ's resurrection. Even the esteemed atheist Antony Flew faired quite poorly when he tried to counter the arguments in favor of the resurrection in a debate with evidentialist Gary Habermas.[9] Flew's intellectual ability was not the problem; he simply had no effective response to the numerous pieces of evidence Habermas advanced in favor of the New Testament account of Christ's rising from the dead.

Reformed epistemology (hereafter RE) was born in the wake of postmodernism and the concomitant collapse of Enlightenment foundationalism. Foundationalism is a term used to describe the idea that "though many beliefs are based on other beliefs, some beliefs must be held in a basic or foundational manner in order to avoid an infinite regress of beliefs." These basic beliefs were viewed as "self-evident or experientially certain."[10] Thus defined, foundationalism

---

7. Lapide, *The Resurrection of Jesus*, 49. As an Orthodox Jew, Lapide does not view Christ as the Jewish Messiah. However, he does believe that his resurrection proves that he is God's Messiah to the *Gentile* world.

8. Johnson, J., "Resurrection Appearances Hallucinations?" 227–38.

9. The debate can be found in Habermas and Flew, *Jesus Rise from the Dead?* For a similar debate, see the exchange between William Lane Craig and John Dominic Crossan, in *Real Jesus Please Stand Up?* Also of interest is Stephen Davis's *Risen Indeed*.

10. Evans, *Pocket Dictionary of Apologetics*, 46.

is almost a synonym for common sense. For instance, if I know it is raining, I will take an umbrella when I leave the house. This is based on the "foundational" knowledge (acquired through objective observation as well as experience) that without the umbrella, I will get wet. However, foundationalism refers to more than this type of indisputable logic. Under the influence of Descartes and the Enlightenment, foundationalism became the idea that all of our philosophical and theological thinking could be grounded upon some irrefutable premise.[11] It is against this definition of foundationalism that postmodernism has rebelled, so much so that, for Christian thinkers at least, only two options remained: "blind acceptance of classical Christian doctrine by appeal to the Bible (or the church) or the skeptical rationalism that seemed to be the final product of the enlightened mind."[12]

With the demise of foundationalism, enter the Reformed epistemologists. Those at the vanguard of this movement were interested in establishing Christian faith as a viable option in the modern world, despite the fact that Christians could no longer appeal to the surety of foundationalism. They therefore embarked upon a theological undertaking that they thought would safeguard Christian belief from the ravages of postmodern, anti-foundationalism. In the pages that follow, I will point out what I consider to be the strengths of the RE position. Then, I will attempt to reveal some of the weaknesses that are inherent in this apologetic system.

Simply put, the RE position can be summed up as follows: "belief in God, like belief in other persons, does not require the support of evidence or argument in order for it to be rational."[13] These are the words of Kelly James Clark, one of RE's foremost advocates. He points out that RE can claim the support of no less than John Calvin, who had little use for evidential arguments, rather arguing that all humans have an innate sense of the divine which is not de-

---

11. Grenz, "Articulating the Christian Belief-Mosaic, 110–12.

12. Ibid., 111–12.

13. Clark, K.J., "Reformed Epistemology Apologetics," 267. The reference here to "other minds" goes back to Alvin Plantinga's argument that we believe that other minds besides our own exist, even though this is impossible to prove. So it is with faith in God.

pendent on any type of alleged evidence.[14] Clark makes the salient point that, if there is a God, it seems strange that he would expect us to master the intricacies of arguments and counter-arguments about his existence which fill learned articles and books. "Why put that sort of barrier between us and God?" he asks.[15] Certainly, the Bible never assumes its readers are required to master complex arguments in order to come to faith. An RE epistemologist is happy to take his stand with St. Paul, who in the first chapter of Romans proclaims that the existence of God is clearly revealed to everyone; only human sin makes anyone deny this fact. In fact, RE thinkers do not believe they have any choice but to take this position. There is no universal standard of human reason, contra the evidentialists, who can establish the validity of any religious truth-claim. But then, how then is religious truth, especially Christian truth, decided?

Concerning the question of whether or not belief in God is warranted without evidence, the premier RE thinker, Alvin Plantinga, has done much to reinforce the traditional Calvinist view that no such evidence is required. For Plantinga, belief in God is "properly basic" so long as certain conditions are met. Those conditions arise within the Christian community itself. That is, the Christian community largely determines the faith of its individual members. For those inside the Christian community, Christian faith is properly basic, and therefore as valid a belief as any other belief.[16] For Plantinga, the Christian community shares certain beliefs about God. These beliefs gave shape to that community, and provide the basis of its worldview. These beliefs are shaped by Scripture, but also by the experiences that Christians within the community share, such as "guilt, gratitude, danger, a sense of God's presence, [and] a sense that he speaks."[17] The Christian may not be able to convince everyone that his beliefs are true, but this does not render his faith invalid, according to Plantinga. One scholar sums up Plantinga's position as follows: "For example, I might *know* that I am hungry, even if I can't convince you through an argument. In the same way, the believer might know that God exists in some immediate or non-inferential way, but not be

14. Ibid., 267.
15. Ibid., 272.
16. Grenz, "Articulating the Christian Belief-Mosiac," 131–33.
17. Plantinga, "Reason and Belief in God," 81.

able to convince others of her knowledge."[18] Again, note the reliance here upon Paul's argument in Romans, as well as Calvin's teaching that we possess an innate sense of the divine. Plantinga's point is that, for a Christian, the Christian worldview "makes sense" and seems to be a valid approach to life, even if one cannot "prove" that her faith is true beyond a doubt. Still, for the Christian, her belief can be termed properly basic, because it does not rest upon any "foundational" belief. For Plantinga, belief in God is its own foundation, if you will.[19]

There is much to recommend this view of Christian faith, at least from an evangelical viewpoint. First, and perhaps most obvious, it takes the internal witness of the Holy Spirit seriously. Jesus assured his disciples that the Spirit would "guide them into all truth" (John 16:5–16). Evangelicals (especially those of charismatic and Pentecostal persuasion), take seriously the reality of the Holy Spirit in the believer's life. Thus, RE, with its emphasis upon the Spirit-inspired, inner-assurance of the believer, surely will find favor with many evangelicals. On this point, RE has two thousand years of Christian orthodoxy on its side.

But there is much more to RE that the evangelical will find appealing. For too long, Christians have been on the defensive, as the largely secular intellectual world expected Christians to prove beyond a doubt that their faith was true, or at least logically sound. The logical positivists of the last century, adopting a secular, atheistic framework, tried to force Christians into a logical quandary. Their attempt was to render Christianity logically unverifiable. However, the logical positivists were vulnerable to the very same objections they leveled against Christianity, namely, inconsistency: "positivists held that for a proposition to be meaningful it must either be analytic or at least in principle empirically verifiable. The critics of positivism simply asked: Is the positivist criterion itself either analytic or

---

18. Hatcher, "Plantinga and Reformed Epistemology," 88.

19. Here, Plantinga reminds me very much of the presuppositionalist approach to apologetics developed by Cornelius Van Til. For Van Til, too, Christian belief could not be deduced from any sort of argument. It simply is a God-given fact, and it provides the Christian with the correct way of viewing and interpreting the world.

empirically verifiable? Obviously, it is neither, so it should be rejected on its own grounds."[20]

For Plantinga, the word-games of the positivists, as well as the complexities of evidentialist arguments and rebuttals, are not necessary. Why is it Christians who must always defend their view of the world, Plantinga asks? Why do non-theists automatically assume that their position is any more sound than the Christian one? Plantinga writes: "The Christian will of course suppose that belief in God is entirely proper and rational; if he does not accept this belief on the basis of other propositions, he will conclude that it is basic for him and quite properly so. Followers of Bertrand Russell and Madelyn Murray O'Hare may disagree; but how is that relevant? Must my criteria, or those of the Christian community, conform to their examples? Surely not. The Christian community is responsible to *its* set of examples, not to theirs."[21] Plantinga's point is well-taken. Why do atheists so often assume that their position is preferable? Can they produce evidence that Christianity is untrue? If, as it is so often maintained, the burden of proof is upon the accuser, let those who deny theism, or Christianity in particular, offer definitive arguments against Christianity, and in favor of atheism. Since the atheist has never done such a thing (at least not to the satisfaction of the millions of believers in the world!), Plantinga's point is a sound one: Christian belief can be just as properly basic as can the tenets of atheism.[22] Both seem properly basic to their adherents, and both seem to make sense of the world for their respective followers.

Another realm in which Plantinga's approach will be appreciated is that of biblical studies. Evangelicals have often been suspi-

20. Hatcher, "Plantinga and Reformed Epistemology," 87.
21. Plantinga, "Reason and Belief in God," 77.
22. Of course, the problem of evil is a serious obstacle that all Christians must face. Many atheists consider this to be their trump card. For them, the reality of evil seems to rule out the possibility of the all-powerful, all-benevolent God of Christian belief. However, the problem of evil, difficult as it is for Christian thinkers, is not insurmountable. One of the best attempts to tackle the issue from an evangelical viewpoint comes from Gregory A. Boyd, who is currently at work on a trilogy that grapples with the problem of evil from an evangelical, biblical perspective. The first two books in the series are: *God at War* and *Satan and the Problem of Evil*. Also of interest here is Hick's classic theodicy, *Evil and the God of Love*.

cious of the historical-critical method, but not because they think this approach has no merit. Indeed, the spectrum of those calling themselves evangelical is so broad as to include ultra-conservatives who have serious doubts about biblical criticism,[23] to far more moderate evangelicals who embrace much of the findings of modern biblical scholarship. However, one thing that most evangelicals definitely disdain about this approach to Scripture is that it tends to reduce Scripture to a merely manmade document. The historical-critical approach has often been marked by a deep skepticism toward the miraculous elements in Scripture. Many biblical scholars conduct their work as if the miraculous element is assumed, *a priori*, to be fictitious, a pious addition to the otherwise mundane texts they analyze. Edward John Carnell summed up the matter well when he wrote, "[i]t does not occur to the higher critic that he has started off with his philosophy of life in a way that makes the consistency of redemptively conceived Christianity impossible."[24]

The Jesus Seminar, often castigated by both conservatives and liberals for their extreme views concerning the historical reliability of the Gospels, represents an example of the anti-supernatural bias in scholarship taken to the extreme. Because the members of the Seminar are so deeply influenced by a modernist, anti-miraculous worldview, their scholarship cannot but be seen as biased. For them, "any record of supernatural events in the gospels must be rejected as inauthentic. Recorded supernatural events are either mythic fictions created by the early church, or else they can now be accounted for by naturalistic explanations."[25] Admittedly, the members of the Jesus Seminar are not part of the mainstream of New Testament scholarship, but the biases that they bring to the table are inherent in many non-evangelical scholars. Indeed, even so illustrious a New Testament scholar as Rudolf Bultmann was guilty of the same sort of *a priori* anti-supernatural bias as is the Jesus Seminar.[26] Evangelicals, on the other hand, tend to give Scripture the "benefit of the doubt": "If we have sufficient reasons for believing in God (e.g., from scientific or philosophical evidence and argument), then we must bring to our

23. See, for instance, Kaiser, *The Old Testament Documents*.
24. Carnell, *An Introduction to Christian Apologetics*, 194.
25. Wilkins and Moreland, *Jesus Under Fire*, 4 (introduction).
26. Habermas, "Did Jesus Perform Miracles?" 128.

study of [biblical] history a prior rationally justified acceptance of theism. In other words, we cannot exclude the possibility of miracles before we even investigate historical evidence; rather, the evidence itself must ultimately win the day."[27]

It is often those who deny the miraculous element in Scripture who portray themselves as "objective" scholars, while viewing the evangelical position as somehow less than intellectually honest.[28] Plantinga, in keeping with his insistence that the Christian worldview (and the miraculous happenings it champions) is intellectually warranted and properly basic, rejects the idea that the premises of critical scholars are the *only* acceptable ones. (He does not, of course, reject all of the findings of biblical criticism). In fact, he views higher critical methods of Bible study as so biased by an anti-supernatural worldview that he sees little reason to take the "findings" of the critics too seriously. When higher criticism first began to gain prominence, we were often told that it produced "assured results." This simply is not the case, Plantinga maintains. For one thing, the critics are often at odds with each other regarding the findings of their own science. Plantinga remarks that "[w]e don't have anything like assured results (or even reasonably well-attested results) that conflict with traditional Christian belief in such a way that belief of that sort can continue to be accepted only at considerable cost; nothing at all like this has happened."[29]

Plantinga is not denying that modern criticism has been helpful in determining matters like the authorship and dates of the various books. Rather, he is claiming that higher criticism has not given evangelical Christians any compelling proof that the central tenets of the faith, like the existence of God, or the resurrection of Jesus,

27. Wilkins and Moreland, *Jesus Under Fire*, 5 (introduction).

28. On this point, Carnell maintains that it is actually conservatives who are the more honest, for they take Scripture as what it claims to be on virtually every page: a miraculous, God-inspired work: "let us not soon forget that the Christian, not the higher critic, has actually faced and conquered the facts as they stand. If one assumes that the Bible is a human product, it becomes meaningless; but if one assumes the existence of the God who has revealed Himself in Scripture, he can explain, not deny, the basic facts of the text of the Bible." (*An Introduction to Christian Apologetics*, 205–06.)

29. Plantinga, *Warranted Christian Belief*, 421. Plantinga's full treatment of this subject spans pages 374–421.

are mythical. A telling example of the over confidence of biblical critics is that of Rudolf Bultmann. Bultmann, of course, is famous for his attempt to demythologize the Bible. This was necessary, he believed, because modern people simply cannot believe the miraculous worldview that the Bible presents. Of course, he gives no reasons why we who live in the modern era cannot believe in both technological progress *and* the miraculous as found in the pages of the New Testament. He simply assumes that the two worldviews are incompatible, and then proceeds to build his entire theological outlook on that unproven assumption.[30] That Bultmann's position lacked the certitude he thought it did is proven by the fact that most of his students eventually went in the opposite direction and asserted the New Testament is far more historically reliable than their teacher thought it was.

Although there is much for the evangelical to appreciate in Plantinga's system, there are several serious problems with it in terms of its apologetic usefulness. All of these problems contribute to his system's inability to answer the question: how does one adjudicate between the truth-claims of different religions? Evangelicals are characterized by their insistence on the uniqueness of the Christian faith, and their adherence to the teaching that salvation is possible only through Christ. Therefore, the defense of the Christian faith as the only path to God has always been of great importance to evangelicals. This is not to say that evangelicals see no value in other religions. Many evangelicals are willing to grant that God has revealed at least some truth in all of the great religions.[31] However, the fullness of God's truth, his saving truth, is to be found in Christianity alone. Therefore, any apologetic system that cannot adequately distinguish the plenary truth of Christianity from the partial truth of other world religions raises great difficulties for the evangelical. The purpose of any Christian apologetic system should be to defend the veracity of the Christian faith, and give reasons why it, and not some other faith, is the truest worldview. It is here that Plantinga's system encounters serious difficulties.

30. See his "New Testament and Mythology," 1–44.
31. See, for example, McDermott, *Evangelicals Learn from World Religions?* See also Pinnock, *A Wideness in God's Mercy.*

Part One: How Do We Adjudicate Religious Truth-Claims?

The first problem with Plantinga's system is the manner in which he tries to prove God's existence. He compares the existence of God to things that simply are not at all analogous to God. For example, Plantinga uses the following hypothetical example. Police take him in for suspicion of a crime. However, at the time the alleged crime took place, he was far away, hiking in the hills. But, no one saw him on the hiking trail, so he states, "I hold a belief for which I can't give an argument and which I know is disputed by others. Am I therefore guilty of epistemological egoism? Surely not. Why not? Because I *remember* where I was, and *that* puts me within my rights in believing that I was off hiking, even if others disagree with me."[32] Plantinga's point here is that he is justified in maintaining his innocence because he knows, based on his memory, where he was when the crime happened. He has epistemological certitude about this, just as Christians have about the existence of God. But the analogy does not work because, assuming his memory is functioning properly, he really *was* hiking in the hills. Had anyone else been there, they would have seen him. Had a camera been rolling at the time, it would have filmed him strolling along. If he goes back to the trail he hiked, his boot-prints will be there. If he was careless, perhaps he lost a few personal items (like a wallet with his identification in it) on the trail. A hermit who lives in the hills may come down to the police station to verify Plantinga's story. The point is, there are many ways Plantinga's story could be confirmed, based on *evidence* (eyewitnesses, boot-prints, etc.). But what evidence does RE offer for the similar belief that the Christian has in God? There is no evidence, only the believer's inner-confidence that this God exists.

RE thinker Kelly James Clark, following Plantinga, also rejects the idea that all of our beliefs must be based on evidence. As examples, he cites the following: that he believes there is a country called Paraguay, even though he has never been there; that he believes e=MC2, even though he cannot understand or prove it; and that he believes he ate breakfast this morning, although all he can offer as proof is his memory of the event.[33] As with the example cited by Plantinga, none of these examples is analogous to faith in God, because they all can be *proven*. Clark may never have visited Paraguay,

---

32. Plantinga, *Warranted Christian Belief*, 450–51.
33. Clark, K.J., "Reformed Epistemology Apologetics," 269–70.

A Case for "Reformed Evidentialism"

but he can talk to those who have. He can view photographs of the country. And, he can book a flight to Paraguay any time he wishes. As for e=MC2, he may not be able to understand it or prove it himself, but there are plenty of persons in the world who do understand it, can prove it, and can offer evidence as to how the equation functions in the natural world. As for Clark's breakfast, the experience does not rest solely on his memory. Someone could have seen him eating his breakfast. Or, he could root through his trash to find evidence (a banana peel, for instance) verifying what he ate. All of these things can be confirmed by an appeal to objective *evidence*. These things are objectively true in and of themselves. But how is belief in God anything like these examples? What outside evidence can be marshaled in defense of the belief? Within RE, precisely none, because the RE theologian does not think any is valid, required, or even exists!

This failure to understand the importance of external, objective evidence to the enterprise of Christian apologetic thinking constitutes the great flaw in RE thinking. RE apologists want to ground belief in the Christian faith on purely subjective grounds, without any appeal to evidence outside the believer's own consciousness. However, once this approach is adopted, how is it possible to adjudicate between the truth-claims of Christianity and, say, Islam, or Buddhism? The RE apologist may say that Christian faith does not need evidence, based on what St. Paul says in Romans. But he or she would only be partially correct. Paul does indeed teach in Romans that the creation itself proves God's existence; no further argument is needed. But any Jew or Muslim would agree with what Paul says in the first chapter of Romans. However, Paul never says that the creation proves anything specifically *Christian*. Neither Paul nor any other New Testament writer ever says that the doctrines of Christianity (like the triune nature of the Christian God, or humanity's innate depravity) are apparent to everyone. That is why, when it comes to most important Christian doctrine of all, the resurrection of Christ, Paul argues for its validity in an evidential manner, as discussed early in this chapter.

Paul's argument may prove that there is a "God" who created the universe. And the more we learn about the breathtaking complexity of the universe, the more sound his argument seems. But why is this God necessarily the Christian God? Could it not be the God of Islam? And as for Plantinga's claim that the witness of the Christian community confirms the veracity of Christianity, the same can be said for virtually any other religious community. Why is Plantinga willing to allow that the Christian community's belief is warranted and properly basic, but not allow the same to be said for the Muslim faith community, the Hindu faith community, etc? Once the appeal to objective evidence in favor of a religious truth-claim is dismissed, then all religious truth-claims are pretty much equal.[34] They are all subjective, all based on personal beliefs or inner-experiences, and all subject to rightful skepticism on the part of the unbeliever.

Plantinga has tried to deal with this objection to his system, but I do not believe that he has done so successfully. At one point, he responds to what a detractor of his RE might call the Great Pumpkin objection. That is, if RE requires no external evidence, does this not mean that *any* religion, no mater how bizarre it seems, can be held with complete conviction? Recall the mighty faith that Linus from the Charlie Brown comic strip had in the Great Pumpkin. The critic asks Plantinga, is not Linus justified in his belief, silly as it may be? No, says Plantinga. But why? Because it is an irrational belief, and therefore does not qualify as properly basic. After reading Plantinga several times on this point, I think he is saying that belief in Great Pumpkinism is not warranted because it does not have the support of a large, historically entrenched community, as does Christianity. In other words, "the Reformed epistemologist holds . . . that there are widely realized circumstances in which belief in God is properly basic; but why should that be thought to commit him to the idea that just about *any* belief is properly basic in any circumstances, or even to the vastly weaker claim that for any belief there are circumstances in which it is properly basic?"[35]

Granted, there does seem to be a much stronger case that the tenets of RE work better when there is a large, well-established religious community, like Christianity, than when there is a quirky religion like Pumpkinisn that has only one adherent (Linus!). But, Plantinga still has not proven that Great Pumpkinism is false,[36] so I don't think it can be ruled out completely, silly though it may seem. But what if

---

34. This point is well made by Hatcher in "Plantinga and Reformed Epistemology," 90–91.
35. Plantinga, "Reason and Belief in God," 74.
36. Hatcher, "Plantinga and Reformed Epistemology," 90–91.

the critique of RE is applied to another unorthodox religion, namely, voodoo? Voodoo has far more adherents than Great Pumpkinism; it has been practiced for hundreds of years, and those who believe in it would certainly tell you that voodoo gives structure and meaning to their lives. The world makes perfect sense to them when filtered through the faith of voodooism. Hence, for voodoo practitioners, this faith is properly basic.[37] Plantinga rejects the charge that voodoo should be construed as a properly basic belief, but the reasons why he rejects it are not quite clear, at least not to me. From what I can gather, Plantinga is saying that voodoo practitioners may *think* their belief system has warrant, but they could be mistaken, perhaps because their religion is based on a misunderstanding of nature, or because they learned voodoo from their parents, and their parents were simply mistaken about the truth of voodoo. Hence, Plantinga can write:

> It could certainly happen, therefore, that the views of the Reformed epistemologist are legitimate in the sense of being warranted, and those of the voodoo epistemologist, who arrives at his views in structurally the same way as the Reformed epistemologist, are not. That could be if, for example, the central claims of the Christian faith are true and voodoo belief is false. It is therefore not the case that if the claim that belief in God and in the great things of the gospel is properly basic with respect to warrant is itself warranted, then by the same token the claim that voodoo belief is properly basic with respect to warrant is itself warranted.[38]

The above statement is true as far as it goes. Christianity may be ontologically true, hence warranted, while voodoo may be ontologically false, therefore not warranted. But how is one to *know*? Plantinga's system allows for no evidence, pro or con, regarding either faith. How does one know that the beliefs of the voodoo adherents should be rejected, while the beliefs of Christians should be accepted? Without some type of appeal to evidence, there simply is no way to prove which religion is warranted and which one is

---

37. Martin, M., *Atheism: A Philosophical Justification*, 272.
38. Plantinga, *Warranted Christian Belief*, 349.

not. To the non-Christian, the central tenets of Christianity seem just as bizarre as do the beliefs of the voodoo priest to Plantinga. Thus, when Plantinga talks about the need to reject a community that espouses "clearly crazy" beliefs,[39] he does not seem to realize that his Christian beliefs seem just as crazy to many a non-Christian. Consider the words of Jewish scholar Samuel Sandmel, describing the reaction that many Jews have upon reading the gospel for the first time: for "a Jew, reading as sympathetically as he is able, the gospels create a bewilderment, not an appreciation. I can report that many a Jew, prior to reading the gospels, has an estimate of them which the actual reading reduces."[40] Suffice to say, the beliefs of Christians can look just as odd to Jews as the practice of voodoo practitioners do to Christians.

Plantinga spends a fair amount of time refuting a probably false faith (Pumpkinism), and a non-mainstream religion (voodoo). Both of these religions are so unlikely to be veridical that the RE apologist (and some evidentialists) will probably tend to give Plantinga's argument against them a bit more weight than it deserves (even though he has not offered one shred of evidence as to why Pumpkinism or voodoo are not true). But, what does the RE theologian do with a major world religion, like Islam or Hinduism? Here are two faiths that have hundreds of millions of followers. They have both existed for centuries; they have both significantly shaped the cultures in which they have been practiced. And, if you were to ask a Muslim why she believes the way she does, her answer would probably sound pretty much the same as the RE believer's reasons for accepting Christianity. If one lives in, say, Saudi Arabia, believing in Islam, and belonging to a Muslim community, it is as natural and as evidently "true" to the Muslim as the faith of an RE Christian raised in a devout Christian environment. And, what of Judaism? Here is a faith that not only is older than Christianity, but which actually gave birth to Christianity. If I were a Jew, why would I even consider the truth of Christianity, especially when I have strong reasons, based on historical evidence, to believe that Judaism is "the truth"?[41] If RE

---

39. Ibid., 349.
40. Sandmel, *We Jews and Jesus,* 126–27.
41. Even Christian theologian Karl Barth, often criticized for his ambivalent attitudes toward the Jews, was fond of quoting a conversation between Frederick

offers no reason for someone to convert to Christianity, it can hardly be called an effective Christian apologetic.

Clearly, RE fails as an apologetic system, since it offers no reasons why a non-Christian should ever consider embracing Christianity. It is precisely at this point that evidentialist apologetics is at its strongest. The world is a welter of competing religious claims, and evidentialism seeks to show that Christianity is demonstrably true. This approach has its critics, of course. Both Kierkegaard and Karl Barth had little use for attempts to "prove" the Christian faith: "Barth agrees with Kierkegaard that reason cannot defend the Christian faith. Either Jesus was or was not what he claimed to be—the unique Son of God . . . The man who would prove it implies, implicitly or explicitly, that he has some criterion higher than revelation, he does not need revelation."[42]

This was basically the same line taken by Cornelius Van Til, who thought it was wrong to submit divine revelation to the "higher" criterion of human reason. A common thread that runs through the thought of men who oppose the evidentialist approach is the belief that one cannot be reasoned into Christianity; conversion is purely the work of God acting upon the unbeliever. Of course, no evidentialist would argue that God himself is not the primary agent in the conversion process. Yet the fact remains that evidentialist arguments *do* aid greatly in that process. This is obvious from looking at Scripture, where Thomas believes in Christ as Lord only after he examines the crucifixion wounds. Paul was converted on the road to Damascus by an actual encounter with the risen Jesus; there was nothing fideistic about Paul's faith.

In a similar vein, if evidence cannot help produce conversion in the human heart, then why bother preaching the gospel at all? Gospel preaching is, after all, a type of apologetic. Why not assume a sort of hyper-Calvinist position and abandon preaching, evangelism, and missions altogether, secure in the knowledge that the Holy Spirit

---

the Great and his personal physician, Zimmerman: " 'Zimmerman, can you name me a single proof of the existence of God?' And Zimmerman replied, 'Your majesty, the Jews!' " (*Dogmatics in Outline*, 75). For a treatment of the veracity of Judaism from the point of view of a Jewish apologist, see Berkovits, *Faith After the Holocaust*.

42. Horndern, *Layman's Guide to Protestant Theology*, 134.

Part One: How Do We Adjudicate Religious Truth-Claims?

will convict and convert those whom he has chosen? As far as I know, RE does not advocate this position. Why? For one reason, preaching the gospel, like offering evidences for its validity, is commanded by St. Paul himself: "how can they believe in the one of whom they have not heard? And how can they hear without someone preaching to them?" (Rom 10:14). Paul makes this statement because preaching is efficacious for conversion—but so is apologetics. For proof, we can point to the example of many of the great twentieth-century apologists themselves. C.S. Lewis was brought to faith, albeit "kicking and screaming," because he found the evidence for Christianity so compelling.[43] The same type of event occurred in the life of popular apologist Josh McDowell.[44] These are only two examples, but then again, they are famous examples. Surely large numbers of everyday men and women have come to faith in Christ in precisely the same way.

I do not have space in this chapter to go into all the various ways evidentialists have used to advance the Christian faith. However, one of the most common techniques is to employ a "defensive" evidentialist approach regarding the death and resurrection of Jesus. Such a defense would basically proceed as follows. One, the tomb of Christ was empty. Had he not risen, hostile Roman and Jewish authorities could have easily produced the body, thus squelching any talk of a risen Messiah. Such talk would have been blasphemy to the Jewish religious leaders, and potentially seditious as far as the Romans were concerned. The idea that the disciples stole and hid the body, then later claimed that Christ was resurrected, is ludicrous. The disciples suffered greatly for the gospel that they preached. They certainly gained no worldly benefits from preaching their message. Ultimately, tradition tells us, most of them died as martyrs. It is highly unlikely that twelve men would suffer and die for a religion they know to be based on a lie. Two, the resurrection must have actually occurred, for it is these appearances which obviously turned a rag-tag group of Jewish peasants into the mighty evangelists who began to preach the resurrection and divinity of Christ. How else to explain the fact that these simple men, who were so dejected when their Master was executed, suddenly became witnesses unto death for that same Master?

43. Lewis, C.S., *Surprised by Joy*, 223–24.
44. McDowell, *Evidence that Demands a Verdict*, 363–67.

That these resurrection appearances were only visions or hallucinations is entirely untenable, for no 12 men (not to mention the 500 that Paul mentions!) can be expected to have the same hallucinations! Three, the story of the resurrection was preached in the presence of "hostile witnesses," that is, Jewish authorities who would have gladly discredited the story had they been able to do so.[45]

The evidentialist approach differs from that of RE in that it offers particular reasons not only for accepting Christianity, but also for *not* accepting the truth-claims of other religions. Here the Christian evidentialist employs "offensive" apologetics. For instance, how should a Christian adjudicate between the truth-claims of Christianity, and those of Islam? In RE, both religions can only be seen as equal. That is, both religions have millions of followers, have existed for centuries, and are logically coherent to their respective devotees. Well, the evidentialist would do two things. First, he or she might point out some of the historical problems with Islam. One of the most damning criticisms has to do with the Koranic belief that Christ did not really die on the cross. According to Sura 4.156 of the Koran, "they did not slay him, neither crucified him, only a likeness of that was shown them."[46] Now, this belief raises serious problems for the Muslim, for I know of no New Testament scholar, conservative, moderate, or liberal, who denies that Christ did indeed die on the cross (whether or not he subsequently rose from the dead is of course another matter!).[47] The notoriously skeptical Bultmann considered this to be one of the few incidents in the Gospels that could be considered a historical fact. Confirmation of Christ's death comes even from non-theological quarters in the form of papers published in *The Journal of the American Medical Association*, as well as other

---

45. For a fine treatment of this type of approach, see Montgomery, *Where is History Going?* 53–74.

46. Quoted from Hick, *The Metaphor of God Incarnate*, 146.

47. In fact, even John Dominic Crossan, one of the primary members of the Jesus Seminar, does not deny that Christ actually died on the cross. This is significant, when one considers his radical reinterpretation of the rest of the Gospels. For instance, his version of what happened to Jesus after death is unique. He believes Jesus was buried in a shallow grave, and that wild dogs eventually consumed his corpse. For more on this, see Habermas and Flew, *Jesus Rise from the Dead?* 142.

PART ONE: HOW DO WE ADJUDICATE RELIGIOUS TRUTH-CLAIMS?

medical journals.[48] So, when Muslims deny that Christ truly died, they are obviously speaking from their own faith perspective, rather than from one of objective, historical investigation.

The Christian evidentialist might also ask, how does the Muslim know that the Koran is God's inspired word? How does he or she know that Muhammad was indeed inspired by God? As noted above, there is good historical evidence for believing that Christ rose from the dead, thus verifying his claims (and/or those of his followers) regarding his right to serve as God's divine representative on earth. What can Islam offer in the way of this type of evidence for the founder of their faith? John Warwick Montgomery writes that "[n]o such attesting evidence for Muslim revelational claims can be marshaled, for it simply does not exist."[49]

Or, consider the Mormon religion. An evidentialist might challenge the claims that are made in the Book of Mormon. Joseph Smith, founder of the Mormon faith, claims to have translated the Mormon Scriptures from a language he called "Reformed Egyptian." Now, the only problem is that scholars know of no such language; it never existed, based on the opinion of "every leading Egyptologist and philologist ever consulted on the problem."[50] But what is recounted in the Book of Mormon is equally troubling. The Book tells the story of two ancient civilizations that left the Middle East centuries before the time of Christ. One group is said to have settled on the west coast of South America, while the other group settled the east coast of what is now Central America. The Book goes on to describe how these two groups of persons established thirty-eight great cities in the New

---

48. See, for instance, Edwards et al., "Physical Death of Jesus Christ," 1455–63, and Ball, "Crucifixion and Death," 77–83.

49. Montgomery, *Human Rights and Human Dignity*, 119. Muslims often point to the beauty of the Koran's language in its original Arabic as proof of the Koran's divine origin. However, literary beauty is not proof of divine inspiration. No one claims that Shakespeare wrote under divine inspiration, even though the beauty and profundity of his work has never been equaled in English. Muslims will also sometimes point to the internal consistency of the Koran, as opposed to the multiple authorship and apparent thematic contradictions of the Bible. But the Koran could easily be wrong in what it teaches, yet still be completely coherent and consistent in its error. For more on Islamic apologetic techniques, see Montgomery, "How Muslims do Apologetics," 81–99.

50. Martin, W., The *Kingdom of the Cults*, 172 (footnote 11).

World. Obviously, the problem is that no one outside of Mormonism believes that any ancient immigrants ever left the Middle East and established great cities in Central and South America. Why? Because there is absolutely no proof that this occurred: "Mormons have yet to explain the fact that leading archaeological researchers not only have repudiated the claims of the Book of Mormon as to the existence of these civilizations, but have adduced considerable evidence to show the impossibility of the accounts given in the Mormon Bible."[51] So, an evidentialist apologist need not spend his or her time wondering about whether or not Mormonism meets the claims of "properly basic" belief. Such speculation is rendered moot by the fact that there seems to be no historical basis for this faith. Evidence (or, in this case, the lack thereof), should give a potential convert serious pause before embracing this faith. Even if the would-be convert were impressed with the properly basic faith he saw among members of the Mormon community,[52] how important would that be to him, if he knew that that faith seemed to have no grounding in verifiable history?

Finally, the evidentialist approach is realistic. It does not claim that Christianity can be proven beyond all doubt. An apologetic system that delivered irrefutable proof would make a mockery of the claim; found throughout the New Testament, that faith is the key to the Christian life. Yet, as was pointed out above, the New Testament writers do not advocate a fideistic faith, but rather one built upon solid evidences. The evidence for Christ's death and resurrection is strong, but it is not so strong as to make the resurrection an undeniable fact of history (but of course, how could one prove that any event that happened two thousand years ago is irrefutably true?) John Warwick Montgomery, one of the ablest evangelical defenders of the resurrection in the twentieth century, constantly stressed this point in his writings. Although he believes that the evidence for the

---

51. Ibid., 183. For a thorough refutation of the alleged historical basis of the Book of Mormon, see pages 178–87.

52. I have known several Mormons personally, and I have always been impressed with their deep faith and the manner in which that faith issues in godly living. Mormons are therefore fully justified in claiming the RE understanding of religion for themselves. If their lives are as holy, or more so, than many Christians, how would an RE theologian account for this, given the fact that Mormonism and Christianity are two very different religions? They cannot both be right, even though they both seem to produce the same fruits.

resurrection is strong, he knows it is not irrefutable. But what of that? As Montgomery wisely points out, we live our lives based on probabilities.[53] For example, I may drive home from work every day on a certain road. This serpentine road is known for its many fatal accidents. Despite the fact that I know there have been several bad car wrecks on this road, I still continue to drive on it. Why? Because I know the chances are quite slim that I will ever be involved in one of those crashes. Thus, I am willing to risk my life based on the probable (not certain) knowledge that I will not become a fatality on this road. Montgomery has often made the point that all of life is based upon such decisions; we never have absolute certainty regarding important life-decisions, so why should our religious decisions be any different? As I have pointed out elsewhere, it simply is not possible to possess certitude about the decisions one makes in life, be those decisions secular or religious.[54] Edward John Carnell agrees with this position: "Christian faith . . . cannot rise above rational probability. Probability is that state of coherence in which more evidences can be corralled for a given hypothesis than can be amassed against it . . . . Since Christianity is a way of life, and not an unabridged edition of the Pythagorean theorem, it cannot enjoy the demonstrative certainty of the latter."[55]

Dr. Plantinga has rendered the Christian community a great service with his RE defense of the Christian faith. However, its deficiencies are such that the only cure seems to be a healthy injection of evidentialism. Such merging of the two systems would not only buttress the weaknesses in RE, it would also strengthen some of the weak points in the evidentialist system. For instance, evidentialism can sometimes devolve into a series of cold, calculating proofs whereby the apologist defends the faith with great intellectual acumen, but at the expense of genuine Christian warmth or godly example. Presuppositionalist John Frames writes that, "Apologists, therefore, must resist temptations to contentiousness or arrogance. They must avoid the feeling that they are entering into a contest to prove themselves to be righter or smarter than the inquirers with whom the

---

53. Montgomery, *Human Rights and Human Dignity*, 152–54.
54. Johnson, J., "John Hick's Concept of the 'Real,' " 52–55.
55. Carnell, *An Introduction to Christian Apologetics*, 113.

deal."[56] Frame goes on to point out that often an apologist can be more persuasive by the life she leads, and the example she sets, than she can with any amount of argumentation.[57] The RE Christian, secure in her faith and unconcerned with "proving" Christianity, may be more inclined than the evidentialist to demonstrate the truth of her faith by example.

Evidentialists can also sometimes forget that, ultimately, the Holy Spirit, not arguments, however strong they may be, is the cause of conversion in a man or woman's life.[58] All good evidentialists believe this, but it is easy to overlook it when carried along by the intellectual tide of argumentation. Alister McGrath wisely remarks that apologetics "is an excellent servant of the church; it can, however, too easily be allowed to become its master." A good evidentialist will realize the limits of apologetics, and allow room for the faith-creating work of God.[59] The RE Christian, however, with his Calvinistic inclination to see faith as a gift from God, is far less likely to fall into this trap.

Conversely, evidentialism can strengthen RE apologetics at its weakest point, namely, how does one adjudicate between different religions? The RE approach may make perfect sense for someone who is *already* a Christian, but its effectiveness with non-Christians will necessarily be severely limited, for reasons given above. If the primary purpose of Christian apologetics is to encourage non-Christians to embrace the faith, it is hard to see how the RE approach could possibly do this. Evidentialism also takes seriously the fact that, as RE thinkers themselves admit, there is not much in the world that we can know with absolute certainty (after all, this was the reason RE thinkers rebelled against foundationalism and created the RE move-

56. Frame, "Presuppositional Apologetics," 220.

57. Ibid., 220.

58. For the role of the Holy Spirit in apologetics, pertaining to both Christians and non-Christians, see Feinberg, "Cumulative Case Apologetics," 158–66.

59. McGrath, *Bridge-Building*, 81. Also helpful is the section on the limits of apologetics, 82-86. Evidentialist John Warwick Montgomery has often been accused of relying too much upon human reason, and too little upon God, for his apologetic method. And while it is true that he does stress the importance of human reasoning, he is fully aware that only God can bring about conversion. See his *The Shape of the Past*, 140.

ment!). If this lack of certainty is true in secular realms of living, there is no reason it should not obtain in the religious realm as well. Evidentialism is realistic in its assessment of the human predicament; it realizes and accepts that, aside from the realm of mathematics, human belief rest on probabilities, not certainties. But it can show that the probability of Christianity being true is quite high, while leaving actual conversion to God.

If the two approaches to apologetics, RE and evidentialism were blended, I believe a powerful apologetic system would emerge. It would be a matrix that could account for the biblical teaching that God's existence is knowable to all via the world he has created. But, this system would also take into account the fact that the New Testament clearly teaches that specific Christian truths are not revealed through nature, but through evidences, such as the resurrection of Jesus. This system would take seriously the beliefs of Christians who "know" that their faith is true, even though they might not be able to "prove" it through complicated theological argumentation. It would account for the reality of the Holy Spirit in a believer's life, and the work the Spirit does to confirm that the Bible, and the believer's faith, are genuine. Such a method would also provide a defense against the atheist, who seems to think that his position is somehow more rational than that of the Christian, even though he cannot prove this. The combination of RE and classic evidentialism would offer the Christian solid reasons for the faith that he or she holds. It would also allow the Christian to examine other faiths with a critical eye, and realize that they lack the evidential foundation that distinguishes Christianity from other religions, be they Pumpkinism or Islam. Finally, it would ground the Christian faith in objective truths, like the resurrection, that may not possess mathematical certitude, but do provide a more than adequate basis for deciding in favor of Christianity.

5

The Implausible Foundations of Nietzsche's Attack Upon Biblical Religion

GERMAN PHILOSOPHER Friedrich Nietzsche's vitriolic attack upon the Bible and Christianity is well known. Religion in general, and Christianity in particular, was a favorite target throughout his career, and the attack culminated in one of his final works, the aptly-named *Anti-Christ*. Nietzsche maintained that Christianity was a curse upon the Western world, that it was a religion that discouraged what was best and noblest in humanity, while promoting the base qualities of cowardice, fear, resentment, hatred, and revenge. However, Nietzsche's attack upon Christianity is based upon several assumptions, most of which are, upon close examination, either misinterpretations or outright fabrications.[1] I realize the problems of his critique of Christianity have been pointed out before, but not often, as far as I can determine, from an evangelical, *historical* perspective. Those critiques I did find did not address the issues I intend to take up in this writing. Therefore, I will look at evidence from the Bible,

---

1. Despite the critical tone I assume in this paper, I do not think that Nietzsche has nothing of value to say to Christians—far from it. For some instructive examples of how Christians can benefit from the writings of Nietzsche, see Westphal, *Suspicion and Faith*. Also helpful is his "Nietzsche as a Theological Resource," 213–26. That Nietzsche himself thought intelligent Christians could learn from him is revealed in his comment: "[w]hen I wage war against Christianity I am entitled to do this because I have never experienced misfortunes and frustrations from that quarter—the most serious Christians have always been well disposed toward me" (Nietzsche, *Ecce Homo*, 233).

as well as from Christian history, in an attempt to refute the following charges that Nietzsche levels against Christianity: that it is a religion based upon the debasement of normal human values; that it is fed by resentment, and the desire for vengeance; that it is a selfish, egotistical religion; and that it has historically attracted only those whose lives are characterized by fear and weakness.

Much of Nietzsche's work is filled with vehemence passages against Christianity. For him, Christianity was the opposite of everything it claimed to be. It was a religion of hate, not of love. It was a religion of low, base morals and instincts, devoid of anything that could truly be called noble. It was the religion with which the weakest tricked and defeated the strongest:

> Nietzsche regards Christianity as the typical slave morality. He believes that Christianity is an "artful device" consciously and unconsciously evolved for the self-preservation of the inferior classes. It is the revolt of the slaves against their masters, finding its supreme expression in the Crucifixion of Christ, which Nietzsche looks upon as a Jewish revenge whereby Israel subtly repudiated before the whole world her own instrument of revenge . . . The slaves wanted power and so they flung on to the landscape of Calvary the living epitome of those virtues which had to characterize their lives as inferiors, placarding them before the world on a cross of shame. The submissive spirit which Christianity extols is the outcome of a slave-coward's soul, and is aimed at destroying the strong . . . Christianity, in other words, is a system of revenge, a complete contradiction of the so-called Gospel of Love and Forgiveness which it preaches.[2]

Nietzsche saw, rightly, that Christianity had its origins in Judaism. He sometimes pointed out the irony of Christian anti-Semites who are not aware that they, as Christians, are merely the theological outgrowth of what began with Abraham four thousand years ago. In fact, the heart of Nietzsche's problems with Christianity are to be found, he claimed, in the pages of the Old Testament, where he thought that a "revaluation" of values had occurred that would eventually make its way into Christian theology. It is in the pages

2. Thompson, *Nietzsche and Christian Ethics*, 23–24.

of the Old Testament, Nietzsche maintained, that we find the writers of Scripture turning morality on its head. That is, what humans naturally admire, the Hebrew writers label as sinful, and what man naturally despises, the Jewish authors claim to be noble. Nietzsche says that "the Jews have brought off that miraculous feat of an inversion of values . . . their prophets have fused 'rich,' 'godless,' 'evil,' 'violent,' and 'sensual' into one and were the first to use the word 'world' as an opprobrium. This inversion of values (which includes using the word 'poor' as synonymous with 'holy' and 'friend') constitutes the significance of the Jewish people: they mark the beginning of the slave rebellion in morals."[3] Nietzsche's point here was not to stoke the embers of anti-Semitism. In fact, he had great admiration for the Jews, and at one point called them "the strongest, toughest, and purest race now living in Europe," a people who could easily have "mastery of Europe" if they so desired. He even thought that it might be a good idea to "expel anti-Semitic screamers from the country."[4] But what Nietzsche despises about Jews is the religion of the weak that they created, the ethos of which would eventually lay the foundation for Christianity.

The inversion of values that Nietzsche saw in Judaism happened, according to him, after the Babylonian Exile. Once the Jews had been conquered, and banished from their homeland, they began to "re-image" God. The God of the patriarchs had been a strong God, a God of war and conquest; a deity who summed up the best and bravest desires of his chosen people. The post-exilic God, according to Nietzsche, was a very different God that mirrored the pathetic situation in which the Jews now found themselves. The former God had been one of glory and power, much like the deities in Greco-Roman mythology. He was beyond good and evil, and capable of awesome displays of power that could not be understood in terms of cause (sin) and effect (God's wrath).

After defeat at the hands of Assyria and Babylon, the God who blessed the military exploits of the Hebrews in Canaan is no more. God is now a much more petty being; he punishes his people if they do not give him the worship he is due. "The God of affirmation and spontaneity, committed to the well-being of the nation

---

3. Nietzsche, *Beyond Good and Evil*, 108.
4. Ibid., 187–88.

through the warrior-king, becomes a God who rewards and punishes the nation because of sin. The defeat of the nation is interpreted as a punishment."[5] This new version of Yahweh rewards only those among his chosen people who debase themselves before him. He is now a God who values "humility and meekness over manly pride. The [Jewish] priests who interpreted that deity's will naturally were preferred to the now defeated warriors."[6]

The first area of difficulty for Nietzsche's hypothesis is that it simply does not match the evidence provided by the biblical record. Nietzsche would have us believe that God in the pre-prophetic parts of the Bible does not punish his people for "petty" moral infractions. Rather, God's displays of power are more "noble" than that. Yet consider this episode in 1 Chr: "Uzzah reached out his hand to steady the ark, because the oxen stumbled. The LORD's anger burned against Uzzah, and he struck him down because he put his hand on the ark" (13:9–10). Here is Yahweh killing a man for what would seem to be a very minor infraction. There were, however, rules that had been laid down previously that only Levite priests could move the ark, and then only with the aid of poles. After the exile, however,

> the once noble religion of a God beyond good and evil [was transformed] into its opposite by a people now dominated by a priestly caste who nourished an intense resentment and hatred of the natural expressions of power in noble men. The form of their revenge against their conquers (and, indeed, against all noble types) was supremely spiritual: with their most seductive and effective form of sublimated aggression, with their weapon of *psychological* warfare, they originated a moral-religious inversion of the values of their masters, even of those ultimate values enshrined in the faith of their fathers.[7]

Nietzsche would have us believe that the God of the early portions of the Old Testament is more "noble," because he is less demanding of submission from his people. But the absolute loyalty that is demanded of the people after the exile is surely demanded

5. Kee, *Nietzsche Against the Crucified*, 168.
6. Neumann, "The Case Against Apolitical Morality," 32.
7. Lewis, C., "Nietzsche's Concept of Biblical Religion," 70–71.

The Implausible Foundations of Nietzsche's Attack Upon Biblical Religion

of Abraham, too. Does not God force the patriarch to offer up his only son as proof of his devotion? Did God not explain that the purpose behind his horrifying testing of the patriarch was to test Abraham's loyalty: "now I know that you fear God" (Gen 22:12). Did not Nietzsche see in this act an example of the "slave morality" that he alleges only began to develop after the exile? Or, what of God denying Moses entry into the Promised Land for the apparently insignificant act of striking the water-producing rock with his staff, rather than speaking to it, as God had commanded (Num 20: 6–13). And consider all of the episodes in the Pentateuch that did not go in Israel's favor because the people disobeyed Yahweh in some way or another. Trouble most often resulted because the Jews did not heed God's solemn commands in Deut 4:1: "Hear now, O Israel, the decrees and laws I am about to teach you. Follow them so that you may live and may go in and take possession of the land that the LORD, the God of your fathers, is giving to you."

Nietzsche would have been far more consistent had he said that he disliked the idea of God presented in the entire Old Testament, for the same qualities that he exhibits after the exile are surely present long before the exile. These qualities are not the result of an oppressed and resentful people who have been conquered and now wish to turn morality on its head by inventing a new God. Rather, these seem to be qualities that are inherent to God as he is presented throughout the Old Testament. And while Nietzsche the atheist would not accept the idea that this is simply a reflection of the way God "is," he still should have come to terms with this question: why did the Jews in their warrior stage which Nietzsche so admired, portray God in the same way as did the Jews centuries later, after they had been humiliated by their conquerors? The mighty David, the great warrior king who exhibited many of the qualities that Nietzsche liked (ambition, military prowess, and ruthlessness in certain situations, a will to power if you will) could still exclaim, "I have sinned greatly in what I have done. Now, O Lord, I beg you, take away the guilt of your servant" (2 Sam 24:10).[8]

---

8. David's sin apparently lies in his decision to conduct a census to count his warriors. The footnote to this passage in the 1985 NIV of the Bible remarks that this "represented an unwarranted glorying in and dependence on human power rather than the Lord" (461). This is yet another example of the pre-prophetic

Nietzsche surely was familiar enough with the Bible to be well aware of the scriptural evidence I have just pointed out. He was the son of a pastor, and he "was exceptionally familiar with scripture."[9] Perhaps one explanation for his apparent disregard of Scripture is the fact that he had come under the spell of nineteenth-century German biblical criticism. Nietzsche, like so many others during this period who were possessed of a skeptical nature to begin with, embraced the new criticism as a form of liberation from the chains of biblical orthodoxy.[10] I personally think that the new "low" view of Scripture that was then flourishing encouraged in him a disdain for *all* of Judaism and Christianity that probably was not justified by the evidence. Nietzsche "was quite outspoken in the conviction that nobody familiar with scholarly methods could any longer base his weal and woe on so weak a foundation as that offered by religion."[11]

Just as Nietzsche's claim that the God of the later Hebrew Scriptures is a different sort of God from that which is found in the patriarchal narratives, he also misunderstands the moral stance taken by the prophets. In keeping with his theory that prophetic Judaism always sided with the weak and ignoble, while condemning the strong and the noble, he had this to say about the theology espoused by the great prophets of late biblical Judaism:

> "It was the Jews who, with awe-inspiring consistency, dared to invert the aristocratic value-equation (good=noble=powerful=beautiful=happy=beloved of God) . . . saying, 'the wretched alone are the good; the poor impotent, lowly alone are the good; the suffering, deprived, sick, ugly alone are pious, alone are blessed by God, blessedness is for them alone—and you, the powerful and noble, are on the contrary the evil, the cruel, the lustful . . . and you shall be in all eternity the unblessed, accursed, and damned!' "[12]

Yahweh acting in a manner that seems inconsistent with Nietzsche's thesis.

9. Salaquarda, "Nietzsche and the Judaeo-Christian Tradition," 94.
10. Ibid., 99–101.
11. Ibid., 99.
12. Nietzsche, *On the Genealogy of Morals*, 34.

The Implausible Foundations of Nietzsche's Attack Upon Biblical Religion

Now, there are two problems with Nietzsche's position. One, it simply is not true that the prophets can be portrayed in the manner that Nietzsche desired. As is often the case in Nietzsche's writings about religion, he took an idea that most people would agree with (in this case that the prophets often took the side of the poor) and turned it into an ironclad rule to support his religion-is-based-upon resentment theory. "Although the prophets and the priesthood did defend the cause of the poor, they were by no means antipathetic toward the strong and the noble per se, and they hardly viewed all of the poor as being virtuous and blessed."[13] The prophets certainly railed against the abuses of power, wealth, and privilege, but they just as strongly condemned covenant infidelity to Yahweh. Such infidelity, of course, was just as common among the poor as it was among the rich. A person is not blessed in the mind of an Isaiah or a Jeremiah simply by virtue of being poor and powerless. One is blessed because he or she proves to be a true child of Israel by living a life worthy of the calling of the Lord that the prophets extol above all else. The prophet Isaiah shows no favoritism when he attacks the leaders of Israel, *or* the fatherless and widows, "for everyone is ungodly and wicked" (Isa 9:13–17).

Additionally, just as strict, "slave-like" obedience is demanded by God in the pre-prophetic sections of Scripture (as pointed out in the above example of Abraham's near sacrifice of Isaac), so too is care for the poor found in the earliest history of the Jewish people: "the fact that a concern for the poor is exhibited in the pre-prophetic parts of the Old Testament shows that the prophets and priests, in defending the poor and lowly, did not, *contra* Nietzsche, introduce a radically new 'inversion' or 'revaluation' of traditional values— rather they insisted on conformity to certain of the old traditions and laws."[14] For instance, Jeremiah does not rail against the rich and powerful, but against *all* Jews because "My people have exchanged their Glory for worthless idols" (2:11). Walter Brueggemann has pointed out that alleged moral revaluation that Nietzsche thought only began with the Major Prophets was in fact already present in the work of Moses. Brueggemann states that when Moses rebelled against the Egyptian empire, he inaugurated a "break from both the religion of

13. Duffy and Mittelman, "Nietzsche's Attitudes Toward the Jews," 313.
14. Ibid., 313.

static triumphalism and the politics of oppression and exploitation . . . Moses dismantles the politics of oppression and exploitation by countering it with a *politics of justice and* compassion."[15] Based on such examples (and there are many more that could be cited), "it is difficult to see how one could justify the claim that the defense of the poor represents an inversion of the 'noble' values espoused . . . by the pre-prophetic Hebrews."[16]

Nietzsche so abhorred what he saw as the defense of weakness and lowliness in the Bible because he felt that it encouraged humanity to turn away from its rightful traits of dominance, power, and self-expression. In short, biblical religion deprives us of the will to power, which is the very essence of what it means to be human. Often in his writings, Nietzsche talked a sort of golden age of humanity, a time long before man was corrupted by the life-denying slave morality of biblical religion. Nietzsche imagined that, sometime in the distant past, the strong ruled the weak, and they *instinctively, naturally* thought themselves good and just. They felt no guilt because they ruled and oppressed their inferiors. In fact, they considered the poor and the weak to be necessarily base and evil. Their belief in the corruption of their inferiors was not based on any external teachings (such as a divinely-revealed Scripture), but rather upon their own sovereign judgment. Nietzsche's noble man "conceives the basic concept 'good' in advance and spontaneously out of himself and only then creates for himself an idea of 'bad!' "[17] This ancient, noble breed of men, "*felt* themselves to be 'happy'; they did not have to establish their happiness artificially by examining their enemies, or to persuade themselves, *deceive* themselves, that they were happy (as all men of *ressentiment* are in the habit of doing)."[18]

Not only were such noble souls happy because they were not plagued by religion-induced resentment, they had qualities of character that were truly admirable. For one thing they, like the earliest version of Yahweh, were capable of great deeds, as well as evil ones. Their life force issued in acts of heroism or cruelty, as was appropriate to their circumstances. But evil deeds were not dwelt upon,

15. Brueggemann, *The Prophetic Imagination*, 16.
16. Duffy, "Nietzsche's Attitudes Toward the Jews," 313–14.
17. Nietzsche, *On the Genealogy of Morals*, 39–40.
18. Ibid., 38.

says Nietzsche, as is often the case with Christianity, the religion of weakness and self-hatred. The "Greeks of the strongest, bravest age conceded [foolishness or ignorance] as the reason for much that was bad and calamitous—foolishness, *not* sin! Do you grasp that?"[19] Not only were the noble ancients free of the life-destroying concept of sin, they also exhibited a strength of character that was truly remarkable. Such a noble man was "incapable of taking one's enemies, one's accidents, even one's misdeeds seriously for very long . . . Such a man shakes off with a *single* shrug many vermin that eat deep into others; here alone genuine 'love of one's enemies' is possible—supposing it to be possible at all on earth. How much reverence has a noble man for his enemies!"[20] Thus, the noble type has no time for festering hatred or prolonged vendettas. He in fact respects his enemies, even as he fights manfully to defeat them. This nobility is to be contrasted with the slave morality of the one who has been unmanned by biblical religion, who sees himself as morally upright while viewing his enemy as entirely evil, an agent of the devil himself.[21]

Now, had there indeed been an epoch in human history during which such men and women walked the earth, Nietzsche certainly would have been at least somewhat justified in lamenting the fact that the Bible and its revalued morality has succeeded in eliminating such worthies. But when, and where, did such people live? Nietzsche is somewhat vague on this point. "Whether he first conceived the features of the true culture and then read them into early Greek culture, or whether he obtained his notion of true culture from a study of Antiquity, is a problem in itself."[22]

But, one can assume, based on his admiration for the ancient Romans and Greeks that they manifested these qualities to which he refers. At one point he lambastes Christianity for destroying the achievements of Rome, whose inhabitants possessed "manly-noble natures."[23] But, when one looks at them, what does one find? Yes,

19. Ibid., 94.
20. Ibid., 39.
21. Ibid.
22. Copleston, *Friedrich Nietzsche*, 51. Copleston concludes that the pre-Socratic period was probably the highlight for Nietzsche (55).
23. Nietzsche, *The Anti-Christ*, 193. Nietzsche goes on to offer his opinion that the ancient Greco-Roman world had already achieved everything that

there is heroism, and bravery, and often a healthy respect for competent enemies. But one also finds precisely the same kind of burning hatred that Nietzsche imagines is the result of biblical religion. Consider the case of Achilles in the *Iliad*. Achilles certainly embodies many of the manly virtues Nietzsche so admires, but there is another side to the man: "when Hector kills his [Achilles'] dearest companion Patroklos . . . the anger of Achilles is transformed into a form of rage that one can only describe as demonic and implacable. Achilles' rage is the theme of the *Iliad*. From the poem's beginning we ask ourselves: will his rage ever end, or will the spiral of destructive anger and vengeance continue in an unending cycle like some terrifying nuclear reaction?"[24] Such is the gruesome desire for vengeance on Achilles part that "even the gods are put off" by his desire to mutilate the body of Priam's son Hector.[25] Achilles' behavior must have been bloodthirsty indeed, if even the notoriously capricious Greek gods are sickened!

Or, consider the case of Oedipus. Does Oedipus look upon his actions (the murder of his father and the illicit marriage to his mother) as mere "foolishness," or as a simple mistake? Quite the contrary. Oedipus agonizes over his actions with as much self-loathing as any Christian who has committed some unpardonable sin. And while it is true that Sophocles portrays Oedipus largely as a victim of fate, Oedipus knows that his own guilt cannot be denied. Indeed, his guilt for what he has done is central to Sophocles' intentions. The "very heart of the play's symbolic action is Oedipus' insistence upon punishing himself."[26] This is a far cry from the Nietzschean ideal, where a great man does not mull over his sins, and certainly does not let them destroy him.[27]

---

was essential to successful human culture. Not only was Christianity not an improvement over the culture of the ancient world, it was a destruction of all the mighty achievements of pagan antiquity (194–95). However, Copleston rightly points out that "the Roman Empire, tending of itself to dissolution, would have passed away—Christianity or no Christianity" (69).

24. Hamilton, "Vengeance, Rage and Reconciliation," 2.
25. Ibid., 3.
26. Quoted in Vellacott, *Sophocles and Oedipus*, 240.
27. Nietzsche, the classical philologist, surely knew both of the examples I have cited from Greek literature. That he does not address them is not surprising,

The Implausible Foundations of Nietzsche's Attack Upon Biblical Religion

Of course, the examples of Achilles and Oedipus are fictional. Still, they represent two of the greatest characters in all of Greek literature. It is unlikely that Greek culture would have produced such literary characters as these if that culture did not identify with the vengeful wrath of an Achilles, or the soul-searching guilt of an Oedipus. That such characters still continue to be popular today proves exactly the opposite of Nietzsche's thesis. There never was a golden age when humanity was free of the weak values Nietzsche despises. Humans have always been vengeful to the point of obsession, and they have always been plagued by guilt when their actions disgusted themselves and the moral standards of their communities. The sin of vengeance, and anguish over ones' sin, did not begin with Christianity. Christianity offered a remedy to such maladies, but it certainly did not create them. Paul, in the first chapter of Romans, suggests that all persons have an innate understanding of right and wrong, regardless of whether or not they are Christians:

> In the Ancient World [*sic*], then, there was morality and there was religion, and where these were respected—according to the lights men had—there was a flowering of culture. But when men sinned against the light, degradation was the result. Those who strove to go beyond good and evil went—not *up*—but *down*... The Romans who neglected the light of conscience were given up to shameful vices: the Nazis who reject the moral law and the Kingdom of Christ are a fearful example of human degradation and anti-culture.[28]

Nietzsche believed that Christianity took up the hatred the conquered Jews had for their oppressors. Christianity, he felt, became the ultimate expression of hatred and vengefulness. It became the religion par excellence of *ressentiment*, the French word Nietzsche uses because "it retains its original intensity... *Ressentiment* is a mixture of frustration and fear, it is indignation but always with an element of jealousy."[29] Christianity began, of course, among the poor and the downtrodden, and for the first three hundred years of its existence

---

since they would only detract from his thesis.
28. Copleston, *Friedrich Nietzsche*, 202–03.
29. Kee, *Nietzsche Against the Crucified*, 64.

it was often a despised and persecuted faith. These oppressive beginnings, Nietzsche held, helped to form the foundation of the Christian faith. The hatred and desire for vengeance that the early Christians felt became one of the primary (subconscious) characteristics of the Christian man and woman. "The ancient Hebrews and then the early Christians, Nietzsche argues, simmered with resentment and concocted a fabulous philosophical strategy against their ancient masters. Instead of seeing themselves as failures in the competition for wealth and power, they turned the tables ('re-valued') their values and turned their resentment into self-righteousness."[30]

Nietzsche's writings are suffused with the idea that Christianity is the ultimate example of subconscious ressentiment, but the only documented proof he offers to support his thesis (at least as far as I know) is to be found in *On the Genealogy of Morals*, where he cites three specific examples. In chronological order, the first is the book of Revelation, about which Nietzsche says it is "the most wanton of all literary outbursts that vengefulness has on its conscious." Next, the Church Father Tertullian is damned by the philosopher, because Tertullian envisages the judgment that will fall upon the enemies of Christianity, and the joy that Christians will have in beholding the spectacle of the damned in the flames of hell. Finally, he quotes from Thomas Aquinas, where the angelic doctor says, regarding the damned in hell, "the blessed in the kingdom of heaven will see the punishments of the damned, in order that their bliss be more delightful for them."[31]

The first thing to be said about the examples that Nietzsche lists is their utter rarity. He offers no evidence from either the teachings of Christ, nor from the Apostle Paul, who, in keeping with much German biblical scholarship of the nineteenth century, Nietzsche considered to be the true founder of Christianity. He offers nothing from Augustine, or Luther, or Pascal, Christian thinkers whose work he knew quite well.[32] He finds no lustful desire in any of these think-

---

30. Solomon, "Nietzsche *ad hominem*, 208–09.

31. The three citations in question are to be found in Nietzsche, *On the Genealogy of Morals*, 49–53.

32. Father James Lehrberger of the University of Dallas pointed this out during his lecture at Baylor University in March 2003. His lecture dealt with Nietzsches's use of Aquinas.

ers that would indicate they relished the idea of the damned suffering forever in the depths of perdition. If Christianity truly is based upon the desire for vengeance, it is odd that Nietzsche finds only three examples in the course of a two-thousand-year history.

Now for a closer look at the three examples that Nietzsche offers. It is true that the author of the book of Revelation seems to take a certain satisfaction in the eventual destruction of the wicked and the vindication of God's elect. But can Revelation be said to be normative for the early Christian community's thinking about the fate of God's enemies? Many in the early Christian community did not accept this particular book as canonical. For example, Eusebius, the fourth-century bishop of Caesarea and author of the great *Ecclesiastical History*, did not approve of Revelation's placement in the New Testament canon, because "he could not reconcile himself to its millenarian teaching."[33] There were some Eastern churches that continued to doubt the authority of the book long after Eusebius' time.[34] Even during the Reformation, Martin Luther did not accord the same reverence to Revelation as he did to most of the other canonical books; he "mistrusted Revelation because of its obscurity."[35]

One could also cite numerous examples in the other New Testament books that express exactly the opposite view, namely, that the destruction of the wicked is a horrible thing indeed, and not something to be anticipated with glee by either God or man. Second Peter 3:9 tells us that "He is patient with you, not wanting anyone to perish, but everyone to come to repentance."

The example of Tertullian, it must be admitted, does seem at first blush to lend credence to Nietzsche's hypothesis, but again, this is the voice of only one theologian. Just as Revelation does not represent the entire New Testament attitude toward the fate of the wicked, I do not believe that Tertullian's opinion represents anything like a consensus among patristic writers. For one thing, the very nature of hell was disputed among the theologians of Tertullian's era. "The Apostles' Creed affirms that Jesus will return to judge the living and the dead at the end of history, though it does not spell out the exact nature of that judgment. One can find the idea of everlasting

---

33. Bruce, *The Canon of Scripture*, 199.
34. Ibid., 199.
35. Ibid., 244.

torment (in Tertullian), annihilation (in the *Didache*), and universalism (in Origen)."[36] By the time of the Reformation, both Luther and Calvin, though they believed in the reality of hell, tended to downplay the idea of a hell that contained literal flames and opted for a more metaphorical interpretation of the fiery passages that had so roused Tertullian's imagination. The great Princeton theologian Charles Hodge took a view similar to that of Luther and Calvin.[37]

As for the passage that Nietzsche quotes from Aquinas, it is the First Article of Question 94 in the Supplement of his *Summa Theologica*. However, in the Third Article Thomas makes clear what he means by speaking of the saints' "rejoicing" at the suffering of the dammed. He writes, in response to those who ask if the saved will enjoy the destruction of the lost:

> I answer that a thing may be a matter of rejoicing in two ways. First directly, when one rejoices in a thing as such: and thus the saints will not rejoice in the punishment of the wicked. Secondly, indirectly, by reason namely of something annexed to it: and in this way the saints will rejoice in the punishment of the wicked, by considering therein the order of Divine justice and their own deliverance, which will fill them with joy. And thus the Divine justice and their own deliverance will be the direct cause of the joy of the blessed: while the punishment of the damned will cause it indirectly.[38]

It is unlikely that a man of Nietzsche's learning was unaware of what Thomas was really teaching on this point, especially when he clearly states, just a page or so after the passage that Nietzsche cites, that to "rejoice in another's evil as such belongs to hatred."[39] Assessing the motives of one who is not present to defend himself

---

36. Pinnock, "The Conditional View," 138. Pinnock goes on to point out, rightly, that the idea of hell as a place of everlasting pain became the dominant one in Christian thought. Still, there was never any consensus that the saved would enjoy the sufferings of the damned (although Dante in his *Inferno* does take this position).

37. Crockett, "The Metaphorical View," 44.

38. Aquinas, *Summa Theologica*, 2973. Again, Father Lehrberger pointed this out in his lecture.

39. Ibid., 2973.

The Implausible Foundations of Nietzsche's Attack Upon Biblical Religion

is perhaps a less-than chivalrous thing to do, but one critic has remarked that "one gets the impression, when reading Nietzsche's slashing attacks against Christianity, that he is distorting the facts, giving them a crude twist that they may fit in with his own theories and preconceived ideas. Nietzsche can hardly be called a scientific thinker. His mind is too full of prejudice."[40]

Nietzsche's belief that Christians secretly, subconsciously rejoiced in the eventual demise of their opponents in the fires of perdition naturally leads into his next critique of Christianity, namely, that it is a religion of self-love. If God will destroy his enemies in hell, how great will be the reward of those who love him! Just as Nietzsche saw in Christianity an exaggerated, inordinate hatred of non-Christians, so he saw an unhealthy, obsessive self-love on the part of the followers of Christ. Listen to Nietzsche's comments on the subject:

> The reality is that here the most conscious *arrogance of the elect* is posing as modesty. One has placed *oneself*, the "community," the "good and just," once and for all on one side, the side of "truth"—and the rest, "the world," on the other . . . *That* has been the most fateful kind of megalomania that has ever existed on earth."[41]

The first thing that rings odd about this statement is the fact that the early Christians saw themselves, just as did the Old Testament Jews, as chosen by God, recipients of his divine grace. They did not see their salvation as something they were entitled to based upon their meritorious lives. In Romans, Paul wrestles with the fact that God's salvation does not seem to extend to everyone, for "Jacob I loved,

---

40. Thompson, *Nietzsche and Christian Ethics*, 29. Even when not writing about Christianity, Nietzsche was often taken to task for his less than rigorous approach to scholarship. His first work, *Birth of Tragedy*, was considered to be a failure by many in the scholarly community. One reason was that the work "was largely speculative and utterly devoid of footnotes." Quoted from Magnus and Higgins, "Nietzsche's Works and their Themes," 22.

41. Nietzsche, *The Anti-Christ*, 170. It should be kept in mind that it is not so much egotism per se that angered Nietzsche. After all, his *Ecco Homo* is nothing if not a celebration of the author's self-aggrandizing tendencies. His disgust with Christianity resulted from the fact that he thought it *masquerades* as a religion of meekness and humility.

but Esau I hated" (Rom 9:13). "Paul then responds to the question of whether this would be unjust (i.e., God choosing one person but not another for salvation) but, rather than offering morally sufficient reasons for these most fateful expressions of God's will, he juxtaposes the greatness of God's power and mercy with man's 'will or exertion' (Rom 9:16). Declaring that God 'has mercy upon whomever he wills, and ... hardens the heart of whomever he wills' (Rom 9:18)."[42] Paul then goes on to explain that the molded vessel has no right to ask the molder why it has been thusly fashioned. The predestinarian ideas that Paul espouses here were certainly not in theological vogue in nineteenth-century Germany where Nietzsche was raised. But the idea that God chooses who will and will not be saved recurs in other biblical books as well. In John 6:44, Jesus says, "[n]o one can come to me unless the Father who sent me draws him." Jesus expresses a similar sentiment in 17:9, when he tells his Father that "I am not praying for the world, but for those you have given me, for they are yours." The belief that God, not man, initiates salvation was further developed by St. Augustine a few hundred years later, and again by all of the Reformers in the sixteenth century.[43] Nietzsche is certainly right that some Christians have taken an unhealthy pride in their faith, assuming that their "good" works merit them a place in heaven at the expense of "sinners." But this shortcoming could not have characterized the majority of the first Christians who sprang from the roots of Jewish theological soil:

> Both Paul and the evangels are undeniably subject to the lure of the "moral world-order" of law and judgment, punishment and reward, but the fact nevertheless remains that they, with the ancient tradition of faith from which they originated, have also given expression to an

42. Lewis, C., "Nietzsche's Concept of Biblical Religion," 77.

43. Whereas the early Christians saw their election by God as a wonderful blessing springing forth from God's love which ennobled their lives, Nietzsche has the following comments on divine election: "They are miserable, no doubt of it, all these mutters and nook counterfeiters, although they crouch warmly together—but they tell me their misery is a sign of being chosen by God; one beats the dogs one likes best; perhaps this misery is also a preparation, a testing, a schooling, perhaps it is even more—something that will one day be made good and recompensed with interest, with huge payments of gold, no! of happiness. This they call 'bliss.'—Go on!" (*On the Genealogy of Morals*), 47.

elemental aspect of the attitude of worship that cannot be assimilated by the moral point of view. This powerful undercurrent of biblical faith arises from the primordial basis of the uniquely *religious*, the attitude of worship, wherein an original condition of sinfulness is conjoined with gratitude for a mysterious and salvific love. Neither the expectation of reward nor the fear of punishment can account for this enmity and this gratitude for deliverance from alienation and annihilation.[44]

Nietzsche did not understand how seriously the first Christians took the ideas of sin, and the cure for that sin—the unmerited love of God as manifested in Christ.

Finally, Nietzsche charged that Christianity is a religion that has traditionally appealed to the physically and morally weak, the impotent, fear-wracked members of Western society. Nietzsche thought that Christians have traditionally embraced the religion of the Crucified One because it "symbolizes the hope for final redemption from the human condition, the romantic wish for a life without suffering, resurrection into a *new* life."[45] Nietzsche sums up what he thought was the attitude of the early Christians as follows: "we weak ones are, after all, weak; it would be good if we did nothing *for which we are not strong enough*."[46] Such a religion as Christianity, Nietzsche maintained, was ultimately grounded in fear of suffering. "The fear of pain, even of the infinitely small in pain—*cannot* end otherwise than in a *religion of love*."[47]

This interpretation appears to be a very strange perception regarding a religion that is universally acknowledged to have its roots in martyrdom. It is true, as Nietzsche points out, that martyrdom in and of itself does not prove a cause to be true.[48] Men and women throughout history have died for all sorts of foolish, fallacious ideas and causes. But the case of Christian martyrs certainly proves one thing: that early Christians were not afraid of suffering. Of course, most Christians became martyrs through no choice of their own;

44. Lewis, C., "Nietzsche's Concept of Biblical Religion," 80–81.
45. Roberts, *Contesting Spirit*, 63.
46. Nietzsche, *On the Genealogy of Morals*, 46.
47. Nietzsche, *The Anti-Christ*, 154.
48. Ibid., 182–84.

the early church did not encourage its members to die needlessly. But, when persecution came, many Christians proved their mettle in a way that even Nietzsche, had he been a bit more honest with himself, should have admired. Church historian Eusebius writes of the persecuted members of the church in Palestine that some "were scourged with innumerable strokes of the lash, others racked in their limbs and galled in their sides with torturing instruments, some with intolerable fetters, by which the joints of their hands were dislocated. Nevertheless they bore the event."[49] Nor is the horror described by Eusebius an isolated event. In the first three centuries of Christianity, numerous Christians from Rome, Asia Minor, Gaul, and Africa suffered horribly. In fact, the "steadfastness of large number of Christians in persecution is in itself an interesting phenomenon that has received several explanations."[50] Such was the bravery of certain Christians when faced with torture and death that even pagans found much in them to admire. The pagan Galen for instance, was compelled to admit that "their contempt of death and of its sequel is patent to us everyday."[51]

Nietzsche, of course, was aware of the great sacrifices made by the early Christians[52], but he apparently saw Christian suffering as something that was accepted by Christians because they were too weak to do otherwise. In his view, Christians accepted suffering, pretending it was an honor bestowed upon them by God, while

49. Quoted in Stark, *The Rise of Christianity*, 163.

50. Hinson, *The Early Church*, 73. Interestingly, Hinson points out that the "martyrs included several persons of high social status, especially women, willing to expose themselves in defense of Christian friends" (73). This is ironic in terms of the manner in which Nietzsche often portrays women in his works, as beings of little substance, not to be taken all that seriously. Martyrdom would surely count as "manly" behavior in Nietzsche's eyes!

51. Quoted in Hinson, *The Early Church*, 134.

52. As I pointed out earlier in the chapter regarding Nietzsche's discounting of the biblical and the classical literature that counts against his thesis, the same can be said of his attitude toward the evidence supplied by the heroic early Christians. Nietzsche can be exasperating at times, and he has caused one scholar to remark that when "reading Nietzsche, one has the feeling continually that one is reading a prejudiced mind. . . . one always feels, when studying Nietzsche, that he is working on preconceived ideas which he is too stubborn to alter because he has an axe to grind" (Thompson, *Nietzsche and Christian Ethics*, 76).

in reality it only fed their subconscious feelings of resentment and stoked their desire for vengeance against their oppressors. But this explanation is highly unlikely. Why would persons as weak as Nietzsche thinks Christians were so gleefully accepting the persecution that they received? Is it realistic to assume that large numbers of persons would submit to horrendous suffering in order to seek some kind of "revenge" against their tormentors? I do not think human nature simply is constituted in this manner. Nietzsche thought that Christians accepted suffering because they had no other choice; it was part of their being. Concerning Christian suffering and humility, he said that "in reality they do what they cannot help doing."[53] Now, it could be the case that a religion that stresses the importance of suffering and submission would attract persons who have passive natures to begin with, but this hardly explains the bravery shown by the martyrs. The faint of heart would not have endured the torture chambers of the Roman Empire as resolutely as the first Christians did. Nietzsche's attack upon Christianity as a religion that initially appealed *only* to the weak and the cowardly will not stand.[54]

Theologically speaking, his thesis that the first Christians were moral, as well as physical, weaklings also seems quite odd. Nietzsche says of religion (although Christianity is certainly in the forefront of his mind), that "religion gives [Christians] an inestimable contentment with their situation and type, manifold peace of the heart . . . something of a justification for the whole everyday character, the whole lowliness, the whole half-brutish poverty of their souls . . . [Religion] makes, as it were, the most of suffering, and in the end even sanctifies and justifies."[55] If these words can be applied to the first Christians (and Nietzsche certainly thought that they

53. Nietzsche, *The Anti-Christ*, 170.

54. Nietzsche could have made the opposite case, namely, that Christianity was a religion of war and violence, as evidenced by the turbulent history of Europe after Emperor Constantine declared Christianity the state religion. A problem with Nietzsche's writings is that one is often unsure which Christianity he is attacking. Is it pre- or post-Constantinian Christianity? Is it Christianity in its Catholic form, its Protestant form, or both? "To Nietzsche the name 'Christianity' seems to stand for a single closely-knit system. But such an assumption will not bear a moment's scrutiny" (Thompson, *Nietzsche and Christian Ethics*, 47).

55. Nietzsche, *Beyond Good and Evil*, 73.

could), one must ask why such long-suffering persons would choose Christianity at all. Christianity was a religion that insisted that its members abstain from the pleasures that made the "half-brutish" culture of the ancient world bearable: the spectacle of the gladiatorial contests, drunkenness, and sexual promiscuity. Not only this, but Christianity added something to the matrix of human suffering that surely would not have appealed to the weak and beaten down: the concept of hell. Why would people who had so little to cheer them in this life embrace a faith that told them they could spend eternity in a place of fiery punishment far worse than the miserable existence they knew on earth? Nietzsche would say that the early Christians who labeled themselves as "good" saw hell as something reserved only for the "other," the wicked. But hell for early Christians was not a matter to be taken lightly. The apostle Paul warned his readers to "work out their salvation with fear and trembling" (Phil 2:12). And the Church Fathers are replete with examples of just how fine a line existed between the saved and the damned. Excommunication was a reality for those in the early church, and excommunication was tantamount to damnation. Those who had sinned in the eyes of the church had to "lament their sins with groaning and weeping; prostrate themselves before the elders of the church; and kneel before the congregation, entreating them to intercede with the elders for their restoration to communion."[56] By the nineteenth century, the Protestant version of state Christianity that Nietzsche knew was undoubtedly far smugger in its belief about the believer's salvation. Christianity was, in many instances, a matter of being baptized and attending church only on special occasions. But the Christian faith of the first believers was not like this, as Nietzsche surely knew. And for those early believers to embrace a religion that required scrupulous moral and ethical standards, lest they be found wanting and worthy of eternal punishment, gives the lie to Nietzsche's thesis that Christianity was, *a la* Marx, merely a remedy for a tired, downtrodden group who sought solace in the new religion.

In conclusion, Nietzsche's attack upon biblical religion, Judaism but primarily Christianity, appears to fail. It fails because he does not take into account evidence from the Bible, history (both Christian and pagan), and Christian theology that render his assaults ineffec-

56. Hinson, *The Early Church*, 84.

tive. One, the prophets of Judaism did not revalue their values, for everything they represented had already been revealed in the pre-prophetic stage of Israelite religion. Additionally, the "golden age" of the noble pagan that Nietzsche envisions never really existed. Two, there is little in the literature of Christianity, beyond a few examples, that supports the idea that Christianity originated as a religion based on *ressentiment*. Three, the early Christians did not see their new faith as an excuse to indulge in egotism. Rather, they celebrated the inscrutable ways of the God who saves the unworthy. And four, to claim that Christianity is built upon weakness and fear makes little sense, given what we know about the steadfast willingness of large numbers of Christians to endure torture and death for their new faith. They may have been misguided, but cowardly they were not.

PART TWO

What Can We Believe about the Resurrection of Jesus?

SINCE THE very inception of the Christian faith, it has been the resurrection that served as the apologetic focal point of the faith. The apostles preached, above all else, that they followed a risen savior, and the churches of Christendom, whatever their denomination, have always insisted that Christ is not just an historic figure, but a living Lord who has burst the shackles of death, thus foreshadowing the believers own eventual deliverance.

Yet after the Enlightenment, many Western scholars began to question the miraculous elements of the Bible, including that supreme miracle, the resurrection. As time progressed and what used to be called higher criticism of the Bible took its toll, many in the academy were no longer comfortable talking of a literal, historical resurrection. And so, alternative explanations were attempted to account for the fact that the gospel writers obviously believed that Christ had indeed been raised from the dead. Some thought that the resurrection was better taken in spiritual, non-literal terms. Others advanced the so-called swoon theory, which claimed that Jesus merely fainted on the cross, later to wake and "appear" to be resurrected. Another theory advanced was that, yes, the apostles "saw" the risen Jesus, but what they saw were only hallucinations, a result of wishful thinking and their mental inability to accept the reality that their beloved Teacher was indeed gone.

This theory has made a surprising comeback in recent decades, especially at the hands of Michael Goulder and German New Testament scholar Gerd Ludemann. Aside from the fact that the New Testament presents Christ in his resurrected body as having corporeal qualities, there are many obstacles to accepting the theory that the resurrection appearances were only the visions of unhealthy minds. I explore these obstacles in chapter 6, originally published in *Churchman*, Autumn, 2001.

Chapter 7 is a defense of the traditional Christian understanding of the resurrection, but from an unlikely source, the narrative theologian Hans Frei. Frei may seem like an odd choice for such an apologetic endeavor, for he has often been exasperated with scholars who seek to go beyond the narrative of the biblical stories to discover a "historical" core. Still, in his *The Identity of Jesus Christ*, as well as in other essays, he does indeed seem to be writing as an apologist, if a non-traditional one. In this essay, originally published in *Evangelical Quarterly* (Spring, 2004), I attempt to show why I think Frei can be labeled a resurrection apologist, and how his efforts could be strengthened in this area.

6

Were the Resurrection Appearances Hallucinations? Some Psychiatric and Psychological Considerations

DAVID STRAUSS hypothesized as far back as the nineteenth century that the resurrection appearances the disciples saw were nothing more than subjective visions, actually hallucinations.[1] Others followed Strauss's lead, and further developed his idea. However, none of these thinkers were able to establish a convincing case.[2] Still, the hallucination theory has never truly died. In fact, it remains an option for those who seek an alternative explanation to the Gospels' record of Christ's resurrection. This chapter will examine two modern-day proponents of the hallucination theory, Gerd Ludemann, and Michael Goulder. Specifically, I will critique the va-

---

1. That Strauss could not accept a literal resurrection is obvious from the manner in which he begins his treatment of the resurrection appearances: "The proposition: a dead man has returned to life, is composed of two such contradictory elements, that whenever it is attempted to maintain the one, the other threatens to disappear. If he has really returned to life, it is natural to conclude that he was not wholly dead; if he was really dead, it is difficult to conclude that he has really become living." Strauss, *The Life of Jesus*, 359. This naturalistic, anti-miraculous view of the world is usually at the bottom of any attempt to deny the bodily resurrection of Christ, right up to our own day. This is certainly the case of Michael Goulder, whose views will be examined in this chapter. Goulder is a former Anglican minister, who left the priesthood when he lost his faith in God.

2. Pannenberg, *Jesus—God and Man*, 95–96.

lidity of their claims in light of what psychiatry and psychology tell us about the nature of hallucinations, especially the nature of mass hysteria-induced hallucinations.[3]

A good starting point is the scriptural accounts of the resurrection appearances. In 1 Cor the apostle Paul summarizes those appearances. He states that the risen Christ appeared to, in chronological order: Peter, the twelve disciples, and "five hundred brothers," all of whom saw the risen One at the *same time*. Then Christ appeared to James, "all the apostles," and finally, Paul himself. (This list omits the women whom Christ appeared to in Matt 28, and John 20. These appearances have great apologetic value, since the testimony of women in first-century Palestine was considered worthless. Therefore, this can hardly be a fabrication the gospel writers concocted in order to help their cause, for it surely would have had the opposite effect.) The first thing that must be said is that the appearances are varied. That is, they occurred to different persons, at various times. Second, they are substantiated. Paul mentions the fact that of the five hundred, most are still alive. In other words, Paul is saying that if anyone doubts that Christ has really risen, there are hundreds of witnesses who will verify that he has indeed been seen

---

3. There is a good amount of debate, even among those who do not believe that Jesus' body was literally resurrected, as to the nature of the "appearances." Some believe the resurrection appearances were outright hallucinations, while others think that, although the disciples did not actually see the physical, resurrected Christ, God gave them personal, subjective visions of Christ that confirmed he was indeed alive in some spiritual sense. For the purposes of this rebuttal, I will take the position of the New Testament writers, who stress the fact that the apostles objectively saw the resurrected body of the Lord. "It must be remembered that to the apostles and their opponents alike, resurrection meant one thing—resurrection of the body" Bruce, *The New Testament Documents*, 66. I find the hallucination/subjective visions dichotomy a bit misleading, since the purpose usually seems to be to sneak around, as it were, the fact that Christ was resurrected bodily, as the New Testament insists. Those who take the subjective vision tack apparently think they can maintain the integrity of the New Testament resurrection reports, while at the same time reject the "unscientific" notion of a man rising corporeally from the dead. For instance, Ludemann makes this distinction between vision and hallucination, but the result of his theology is the same: Christ did not bodily rise from the dead. See Craig and Ludemann, *Jesus' Resurrection: Fact or Figment?* 53–54, 150–51. However, in the latter passage, Ludemann is open to the idea that Christ, from heaven, did indeed make appearances to his followers.

Were the Resurrection Appearances Hallucinations?

alive. For Paul, the resurrection was the event that proved the gospel to be true. If the resurrection did not occur, Paul was wasting his life preaching a false faith, and the faith of all Christian believers was in vain (1 Cor 15:12–19). Since Paul bases the validity of the entire Christian religion on the resurrection, it hardly seems likely that he would claim there were hundreds of witnesses to the event, if he could not produce them to silence a skeptical inquirer.[4]

Gerd Ludemann's position is that Peter was the first one to "see" the risen Christ, just as Scripture maintains. However, it was not really the risen Lord he saw, but merely a vision that was brought about by Peter's guilt complex, a complex that resulted from his denial of his Lord after Christ's arrest. Peter's vision in turn "became the initial spark which prompted the further series of visions mentioned by Paul in 1 Cor 15. The subsequent appearance of Christ can be explained as mass psychoses (or mass hysteria). This phenomenon was first made possible by Peter's vision."[5] Ludemann rules out the position taken by some, that although these were subjective visions, nonetheless they were God-initiated: "these were psychological processes which ran their course with a degree of regularity—completely without divine intervention."[6] Goulder's position is essentially the same as Ludemann's. That is, Peter was the first to have a "Jesus hallucination," brought on by the stress of Passion Week, or perhaps by the shame he felt because he had denied his Master, while the later resurrection appearances should best be considered the result of mass hysteria.[7] Both Ludemann and Goulder are clear that they do not believe there is any supernatural element present in any of the resurrection appearances.

Now, it is certainly *possible* that Peter's severe guilt caused him to have a hallucination of a risen Christ. Hallucinations can be

---

4. For some of the problems the early Christians would have had perpetrating a resurrection deception, see Bruce, *The New Testament Documents*, 66. And for one of the best defenses of the traditional understanding of Christ's bodily resurrection, as well as some devastating criticisms of the resurrection-as-visions theory, see the debate between evangelical scholar Craig and skeptic Ludemann, in *Jesus' Resurrection: Fact or Figment*, especially 46–51, and 163–206.

5. Ludemann, *What Really Happened to Jesus*, 130.

6. Ibid., 130.

7. Goulder, "The Baseless Fabric of a Vision," 51–55. Goulder makes the same point in *Jesus' Resurrection: Fact or Figment*, 96–98.

triggered by a number of different factors.[8] But the aim here is to examine the resurrection appearances-as-vision hypothesis to see if it is truly a *plausible* option. Ludemann's and Goulder's case stands or falls on whether or not *all* of the sightings of the risen Christ can be explained away in naturalistic terms as cases of mass hysteria. I do not believe that they can, but first, we must have a working definition of some key terms.

The following is a psychiatric definition of what constitutes a hallucination: "an individual seer must perceive an auditory or visual stimulus (or both), and believe that this stimulus really exists (i.e., that it is not imaginary or only in one's head). Second, a third party (read: clinical psychologist or psychiatrist) must be unable to detect a stimulus of any sort that corresponds to the seers [sic] perception."[9] Hallucinations are distinct from visions, for with visions there are stimuli present that a third party can observe.[10] Another thing which must be kept in mind is that "[h]allucinatory and related perceptual experiences are essentially private and subjective. That is, at the instant in time at which the experience occurs, no other person shares the same experience."[11]

Based on these definitions, it is quite surprising that so many persons would have the very same sort of hallucinations, namely, the dead Jesus presenting himself as alive, since hallucinations are, by definition, intensely private matters. Both Ludemann and Goulder seem to believe that the succession of visions of Christ only properly begins with Peter, while not addressing the visions that occurred with the women. However, as explained above, the appearances to the women are almost certainly historical. So, if the women first saw Christ, and only later did Peter see him, we have an example of three different persons having exactly the same hallucination. There was no time for mass hysteria to develop since Peter saw the resurrected Lord very shortly after the women. Plus, it is obvious from Scripture (Luke 24:10–11) that the women's testimony about what they saw

8. Slade and Bentall, *Sensory Deception*, 82–109.

9. Carroll, "The Cult of the Virgin Mary," 58.

10. Ibid. Many of the apparitions of the Virgin Mary thus qualify as visions, since many observers have reported seeing some type of "luminescence," although the seer actually sees, or thinks he sees, Mary.

11. Slade and Bentall, *Sensory Deception*, 16.

was not taken seriously, so there was no atmosphere of anticipation that could have served as the basis for Peter's vision. Given the fact that three different persons all saw the resurrected Lord, it is hard to discount the three sightings as hallucinations, since hallucinations are very much individual affairs.

But if these initial hallucinations are hard to explain, the dilemma becomes exponentially more complex when we turn to the matter of mass hysteria, upon which Ludemann and Goulder base the greater part of their respective cases. These scholars are saying, in effect, that the great majority of Jesus' appearances in the New Testament are examples of mass hysteria, hysteria that fed off the initial hallucination to Peter. To evaluate their claim, the nature of mass hysteria must be briefly examined. Mass hysteria does not usually involve visions at all. Rather, mass hysteria takes seemingly mundane events and attributes them to "mysterious, and to some degree anxiety-producing causes."[12]

Some examples, culled from various geographical locations over the past fifty years include such varied phenomena as "windshield pits, phantom anesthetists or slashers, and mutilated cattle."[13] A case has also been made for chronic fatigue syndrome, Gulf War syndrome, the recovery of repressed memories, satanic ritual abuse, and alien abductions. All are modern-day examples of mass hysteria, yet none of them involve hallucinations.[14]

As for those instances of mass hysteria that *do* involve visions of some sort, Goulder cites several examples: the statue of Mary at Knock moving, the phenomenon of UFOs, and "Sasquatch" sightings (Sasquatch, or Bigfoot is, of course, a huge ape-like being that supposedly haunts the western parts of the US).[15] Goulder maintains that these examples are analogous to the New Testament visions of the resurrected Jesus. However, I do not think these examples are at all comparable to the sightings of the risen Christ, for the following reasons.

With regard to the moving statue sightings at Knock, the first problem with Goulder's analogy is the fact that the statue of Mary at

12. Stewart, "Sasquatch Sightings," 289.
13. Ibid., 288–89.
14. Showalter, *Hystories*, 115–201.
15. Goulder, "The Baseless Fabric of a Vision," 53.

Knock actually *exists*. It is an object that can be seen by anyone who goes to Knock, not just those who may be suffering from "Roman Catholic mass delusion." It is quite a jump from thinking one has seen a veridical object (the Mary statue) move slightly to a full-blown hallucination of a dead person (the risen Jesus).

Actually, the miraculous happenings at Knock can be traced back to 1879 (Goulder is apparently referring to more recent sightings of the moving statue), when actual visions of Mary, as well as of St. Joseph and St. John, were reported by up to fourteen persons over a one-and-a-half-hour period.[16]

I assume Goulder would think that this is similar to what happened in the New Testament with the sightings of the risen Christ. However, a few things must be borne in mind. First, the visions of Mary were confined to a single location, whereas Christ appeared to multiple persons at various locations. Second, the seers at Knock did not report that Mary spoke to them,[17] whereas the risen Christ had quite a bit to say to his surprised disciples! Also, these Knock visions are best described as illusions, since there was some sort of mysterious bright light that seems to have served as an optical catalyst for the visions.[18] So, as with the more modern sightings of the moving statue at Knock, there was something "there" (in this case the bright light) which served to stimulate the seers' imagination. Again, the New Testament reports of a dead man appearing, talking, and even eating, seem to be quite a different manner.

Thus, the Marian visions and the moving statue at Knock can be understood as resulting from any number of factors: unexplained natural phenomena (the bright light) that are misconstrued; the way the sunlight, or shadows, fall in a certain way and; of course, the air of miraculous expectancy with which many Catholics visit shrines. (And bear in mind, there was no such expectancy that the dead Jesus would appear to his followers. But more on this below.) All of these factors could lead to a classic case of mass hysteria (and I believe this may be what happens with many of the Marian visions worldwide), but such hysteria would not be applicable to the resurrection appearances, where various, sometimes hundreds of people, who were

---

16. Carroll, The *Cult of the Virgin Mary*, 204–05.
17. Ibid., 205.
18. Ibid.

not miracle-hungry pilgrims, saw a dead man who had risen. It is far easier to misconstrue what is before our eyes than to suddenly "see" something that does not exist in reality.

Goulder also sees the UFO phenomenon as shedding light on the Christ appearances. The first thing to be said is that UFOs *may* exist—and, if they do exist, sightings of them certainly cannot be considered as examples of mass hysteria. I myself am a skeptic, but there is no way to disprove their existence. Goulder would only have a valid analogy here if we knew for certain that they do not exist. But, even if they do not exist, when people report UFO "sightings," they are often seeing something veridical, be it a comet, a shooting star, or some kind of man-made aircraft.[19] I myself, while in the Nevada desert, saw a red, dot-like object darting through the desert sky, with movements that were far too quick and erratic to be an airplane or helicopter. Of course, I am dubious that it was a saucer full of little green men, but I know I saw *something*. So, as with the Knock example, Goulder's UFO analogy fails, because he examines objects that probably objectively exist (be they UFOs, comets, or something else), and tries to compare them to hallucinations, which do not, save in the mind of the individual seer.

But it is with an outbreak of Sasquatch, or Bigfoot, sightings in North Dakota that Goulder believes he has the strongest analogy to what happened with the resurrection appearances.[20] Briefly, the sightings started in the fall of 1977 in South Dakota. A B-grade Bigfoot movie had been popular in the state that summer. Suddenly, sightings of the hairy beast began to be reported. It started slowly at first with a few Native American boys, but eventually hundreds reported having seen the monster. Goulder tells us that six factors can explain these sightings, and that these factors have close parallels to the sightings of the resurrected Jesus. However, at least two of his six points seem highly problematic. The first point I wish to address is his claim that there was an existing social/cultural framework into which fit the Bigfoot sightings. In parallel fashion, he says, the early Christians had a similar framework in which to place the resurrection appearances, namely, the general resurrection that sig-

---

19. For examples of how mundane objects are easily misinterpreted as UFOs, see Menzel and Taves, *The UFO Enigma*, 129–78.

20. Goulder, "The Baseless Fabric of a Vision," 53–54.

naled the dawn of God's kingdom. His second point is that spotting the creature brought instant celebrity status to the seer. Similarly, he claims, for the first Christians "seeing" the risen Jesus provided similar status, and also proved they were "right" about Jesus and his claims all along.[21]

It may be true that the Bigfoot seers had a framework within which to fit their sightings (e.g., the B-grade movie of the summer, the Native American Bigfoot fables that had long been in circulation, and the oft-repeated rumors of Bigfoot sightings which had originated in the Pacific Northwest). However, it is not true that the early Christians had anything like a social/cultural framework into which a "risen" Jesus could possibly fit. As Wolfhart Pannenberg has written: "The primitive Christian news about the eschatological resurrection of Jesus—with a temporal interval separating it from the universal resurrection of the dead—is, considered from the point of view of the history of religions, something new, precisely also in the framework of the apocalyptic tradition."[22]

The early Christians may have had an idea of the general resurrection of the dead, as Goulder maintains, but they certainly had no idea that they were to have a dying (much less rising!) Messiah. Even Strauss, the father of the resurrection-as-visions theory, admitted that there was no substantial Old Testament teaching that predicts such a messiah, and the disciples had to "stretch" their exegesis of the Old Testament in order to find the predictions that confirmed their experiences of the risen One.[23] Indeed, the Old Testament Scriptures speak of three different resurrections (resuscitations, really) that were accomplished by the prophets Elijah and Elisha (in one case, by the bones of Elisha). However, none of these cases led to any sort of supernatural consequences in the further life of the resuscitated persons."[24] And, it could be added, none of these served as any sort of harbinger of the messiah. Thus, the early Christians truly had no tradition with which to reconcile the resurrection of Jesus, be it an

---

21. Ibid.
22. Pannenberg, *Jesus—God and Man*, 96.
23. Strauss, *The Life of Jesus*, 370.
24. Lapide, *The Resurrection of Jesus*, 49.

Old, or New Testament, one. F.F. Bruce opines that the common Jewish beliefs of the day held no room for a crucified messiah.[25]

Nor was the belief prevalent that a resurrected messiah would, in turn, generate a mass resurrection of the dead. In fact, there were various views regarding the messiah. For some, he would be a mighty military leader who would deliver the Jews from Roman oppression. But, generally speaking, the messianic expectations of the early New Testament period were somewhat nebulous, although his acting with divine power on behalf of God seems to have been a common thread.[26]

Goulder's second comparison between the Bigfoot sightings and the early Christian community also fails. Certainly, those who "saw" Bigfoot at once became celebrities, especially since the media eventually descended upon the town. "Seeing Bigfoot became a way of gaining prestige and living in the limelight, at least temporarily."[27] But there are two reasons why this analogy cannot be applied to the resurrection appearances in the New Testament.

First, the Master had taught the value of humility to the early Christians, and so it is not likely that so many of them would have sought public acclaim and adulation in this manner. Even more damning to the analogy, though, is the fact that the Bigfoot sightings were rather playful; it is exciting to tell your friends that you have seen a monster! One could claim to have seen the creature without any negative repercussions. Not so with those who saw the risen Christ. For a Christian to proclaim that he or she had seen alive a man both the Roman and Jewish authorities despised and executed was to expose oneself to political and religious persecution. We know from the book of Acts the type of trouble one encountered once he or she made a public confession of faith in Christ (e.g., the stoning of Stephen in Acts 7).

Speaking of Roman and Jewish authorities, the power of authority comes to bear on the question of mass hysteria. It is symptomatic of mass hysteria cases that, when the community leaders cannot offer an adequate explanation of the phenomena, the hysteria tends

25. Bruce, *Defense of the Gospel*, 15–16.
26. Brown, *Introduction to New Testament Christology*, 159–61.
27. Stewart, "Sasquatch Sightings," 292. This article, by the way, provides much of the basis for Goulder's theory that the resurrection appearances were episodes of mass hysteria.

to grow even more out of control. In the case of Bigfoot sightings, the local authorities were at a loss to explain the panic, and so they actually increased the hysteria: "Their inability to provide reassuring explanations and answers increased the mysterious aspects of the sightings and actually, although not deliberately, gave credence to the extraordinary explanation . . . When control agents/agencies cannot adequately explain the case of something unknown, they unwittingly are placed in the position of being accomplices to those who 'believe' in the fantastic interpretation."[28]

The New Testament does not tell us precisely how the Jewish leadership responded to the reports of the appearances of Jesus,[29] although they surely heard about them (e.g., Peter and John's speech before the Sanhedrin in Acts 4). But one can imagine that they were not nearly so, shall we say, flabbergasted, as were the authorities in South Dakota. One can imagine the response of the Jewish leaders (especially the Sadducees, for they denied the reality of any type of resurrection), when confronted with Christians who claimed to have seen the "resurrected" Jesus. The Jewish leaders would have had many options. They might simply call the Christians liars, or they might say the visions were demonic; Christ himself was accused of being possessed by demonic forces (John 8:48–52). They could say the Christians were mad, the same charge that is sometimes leveled against Jesus in the Gospels. However, based on what Acts tells us about the kind of persecution the early church faced, it is very doubtful that the Jewish authorities would have displayed the type of puzzlement that was shown by the authorities in the case of Bigfoot sightings. Even if the Jewish leaders had accepted as factual the reports of the resurrection, they would not have encouraged the disciples in their messianic interpretation of the event.[30]

Finally, mass hysteria as a phenomenon in history must be looked at in terms of the fruit it has produced. Ludemann and Goulder, if they are to maintain the position that the resurrection appearances are nothing more than another example of mass hyste-

28. Ibid., 293.

29. The chief priests and elders do, however, concoct the story that the disciples stole the body of Jesus. This is done to explain away the fact of the empty tomb (Matt 28:12–15).

30. Lapide, *The Resurrection of Jesus*, 49.

ria, will have to address the following three items. First, it must be admitted that nothing good has ever come of cases of mass hysteria. In fact, they often have quite negative results. One need only think of the Salem Witch Trials, or the "communist" witch hunts of the 1950s. These are just two examples, but history is replete with cases of mass hysteria that end in disaster,[31] and it is not surprising that such delusions end poorly, for they are founded upon nothing but deception; falsehood rarely produces anything of lasting worth.

Second, mass hysteria episodes always die out. The most common reason is simply that interest in the phenomenon begins to diminish. The demise of the Bigfoot epidemic is probably paradigmatic for most cases of mass hysteria:

> In sum, the episode dies a "natural death." The failure of believers to produce even a shred of credible evidence regarding the existence of Bigfoot eventually caused interest and enthusiasm to wane. Outbreaks of collective delusion seem to have within them the "seeds of their own destruction." When the basic assumption of the episode (i.e., the existence of a monster) rests upon delusion evidence other than that of a circumstantial nature can never be presented [sic]. Eventually people tire in their efforts, their zeal diminishes and the episode quietly disappears.[32]

Third, cases of mass hysteria that are centered on a charismatic leader cannot survive that leader's demise. Mass hysteria fades away when it is centered on a "pathological fanatic," or messiah-like figure. The hysteria abruptly draws to an end when the source of hysteria is removed: "When the pathological leader is removed the pathological spell seems to disappear. Every mass delusion, however intense, disappears once its cause is eliminated."[33]

None of the above-mentioned reasons for the demise of cases of hysteria is remotely applicable in the case of Christianity. With regard to the first point, Christianity did not come to a bad end. In fact, just the opposite is the case. The disciples who saw the resur-

31. Showalter, *Hystories*, 4–5, 24–25.
32. Stewart, "Sasquatch Sightings," 302.
33. Meerloo, *Delusion and Mass Delusion*, 71.

rected Jesus bequeathed their religious convictions to their successors, who eventually conquered the Roman world for Christ, and eventually much of the globe. With regard to the second point, the same thing may be said. Interest in Christianity never waned, but rather grew, so much so that it is today the world's largest religion. With regard to point three, the death of Christianity's "messiah-like figure" certainly did not spell the demise of Christianity—indeed, it was the very catalyst, along with the resurrection appearances, that spurred the religion's amazing growth. In this context, even orthodox Jewish scholar Pinchas Lapide has said of the origin of the Christian faith that "No vision or hallucination is sufficient to explain a revolutionary transformation [in the disciples]. For a sect or school or an order, perhaps a single vision would have been sufficient—but not for a world religion which was able to conquer the Occident thanks to the Easter faith."[34]

To sum up, the resurrection appearances-as-visions theory is not persuasive, for the following reasons. One, hallucinations are by definition private mental affairs which are only experienced by the individual seer; that several persons would have the very same hallucination is not well supported by the medical literature on the topic. Two, to claim that the resurrection appearances were examples of mass hysteria flies in the face of what is generally known about the nature of mass hysteria. Three, the resurrection appearances could not have been cases of mass hysteria, for they did not end in disaster, the way that actual cases of mass hysteria always have. To suggest that the resurrection appearances were hallucinations might be understandable, indeed, inevitable, if one is working from a purely naturalistic framework, in which the very concept of bodily resurrection is an utter impossibility. But the objective evidence does not favor such an interpretation.

---

34. Lapide, *The Resurrection of Jesus*, 125–26

7

Hans Frei as Unlikely Apologist for the Historicity of the Resurrection

DESCRIBING THE late Hans Frei as an apologist for any aspect of Christianity, not to mention the resurrection, may strike many readers as rather incongruous. After all, in his magnum opus, *The Eclipse of Biblical Narrative*, Frei often seemed exasperated with scholars who had gone beyond the narrative of the biblical texts to find a "historical" foundation upon which to ground apologetic endeavors.[1] In fact, one of his former students has written that Frei was "concerned almost to the point of obsession with making it clear that he is not doing apologetics."[2] However, in his *The Identity of Jesus Christ*, as well as in various essays, Frei makes a case for the historicity of the resurrection that I believe can only be classified as apologetic. In this chapter, I hope to provide several reasons why this is so. Additionally, I will examine weak points in Frei's thesis, and suggest how it could be improved to provide a much more rigorous defense of the resurrection of Jesus Christ as a historical event.

---

1. Frei, *The Eclipse of Biblical Narrative*. Frei was equally critical of both apologists and biblical critics who employed the historical-critical method, because each was overly concerned with the alleged historical events that lay behind the texts. His description of the state of biblical scholarship in the eighteenth century is typical of his critique of all periods in the post-critical era: "neither religious apologists nor historical critics were finally able to take proper and serious account of the narrative feature of the biblical stories" (136).

2. Placher, "Scripture as Realistic Narrative," 37.

PART TWO: WHAT CAN WE BELIEVE ABOUT THE RESURRECTION OF JESUS?

Hans Frei's tenure as a Christian apologist began with his insistence that the Christian community, that is, the faith community, is the forum in which the Christian Scriptures should be interpreted. The idea that the Christian story *qua* narrative should be the provenance of the believing Christian community can be traced back to H. Richard Niebuhr's essay "The Story of Our Lives." From this modest beginning grew the modern narrative theology movement as we know it today.[3] Frei can be seen as one of the first non-fundamentalist theologians in the twentieth century to realize that the *believing* Christian community interprets the Christian Scriptures properly. Frei was reacting against the Enlightenment agenda that reduced the Bible to merely a document for analytical scrutiny by critically minded Christians, non-Christians, etc.[4]

Frei's position here is quite important, and I believe it further supports my contention that he was attempting to ground the Christian proclamation on an apologetic foundation, even if that foundation was inward-looking, rather than an attempt to appeal to non-Christians. "Frei has said in effect that the christological assertion of the community of faith must control the method of interpretation by which Scripture is read." Rather than allowing "higher" criticism or literary theory to dictate the terms by which the Christian Bible must be read, Frei assigned interpretive authority "to what the Christian community affirms about Jesus Christ. In this way the authority of Scripture in theological discourse is maintained, but that authority does not depend on a general literary theory."[5] In a sense, Frei returned ownership of the New Testament to those whose task it was to interpret it before the "eclipse of biblical narrative" occurred. He returned the Christians Scriptures to the Christian community, the only group that can interpret them as they were written to be interpreted: as *story*, not as a collection of isolated pericopes, different levels of literary strata that have been skillfully woven together by a redactor, etc. Frei, of course, was no fundamentalist who derided the tools of the historical-critical method, but he knew that the essence of the Christian faith was being obscured by this cold, analytic technique that robbed the Christian stories of their "story-ness." Because

3. Clark, D., "Narrative Theology and Apologetics," 499.
4. Sykes, "Narrative Accounts of Biblical Authority," 327.
5. Ibid., 329.

Hans Frei as Unlikely Apologist for the Historicity of the Resurrection

the rendering of the uniqueness of the identity of Christ was not simply a by-product of the Gospels but rather their very essence, "the sacrifice of story or narrative impinges on the authority of Scripture as well as the question of the unique identity of Jesus."[6]

Before Frei offered his defense of the resurrection, he established the historical reality of the person of Jesus Christ. Against those who would consign the passion/resurrection accounts to the realm of the non-historical, Frei says,

> We should ask, then, if the Gospel account of the resurrection can be understood to be a myth . . . the resurrection account (or, better, the passion-resurrection account as an unbroken unity) is a demythologization of the dying-rising savior myth. For, in contrast to the substance of myth, the passion-resurrection account concerns an unsubstitutable individual whose mysterious identity is not ineffably behind the story but is inseparable from the unsubstitutable events constituting it, with the resurrection as its climax.[7]

The passion/resurrection narratives cannot be myth, for they owe their entire existence to a concrete person: "The Gospel story is a demythologization of the savior myth because the savior figure in the Gospel story is fully identified with Jesus of Nazareth. The early Christians would substitute no other name."[8] Two things should be noted here. First, Frei sounds very much like C.S. Lewis at his most apologetic, who also saw the Christ event as a "demythologization of the dying-rising savior myth." For Lewis, Christ represented "myth made fact," that is, in Christ we have the reality to which dying/rising god stories were merely a preparation.

> The heart of Christianity is a myth which is also a fact. The old myth of the Dying God, *without ceasing to be myth*, comes down from the heaven of legend and imagination to the earth of history. It *happens*—at a particular date, in a particular place, followed by definable historical consequences. We pass from a Balder or an Osiris, dy-

---

6. Callahan, "Convergence of Narrative and Christology," 541.
7. Frei, *The Identity of Jesus Christ*, 139–40.
8. Ibid., 59.

ing nobody knows when or where, to a historical Person crucified.⁹

Second, Frei challenged the Bultmannian type of denial of the physical, literal resurrection of Christ. The historicity of the resurrection has taken somewhat of a beating in the last several decades; many scholars have been so reluctant to declare the resurrection a historical fact that they have sought refuge in the realm of a "history beyond history." That is, they maintain that the resurrection indeed happened, but not in the realm of observable, verifiable history. Of course, this is merely theological double-talk; there is no such realm, at least not that we know of. Past events either happened, or they did not. Indeed, the phrase "historical event" cannot even be understood apart from the idea that something actually occurred in space-time history. But, even if such a meta-historical realm does indeed exist, why would it be any easier for God to perform miracles there than in our own historical realm? If God cannot work miracles (e.g., if he cannot raise Jesus from the dead), then he cannot work miracles, regardless of the "world" in which he operates! Rudolf Bultmann was one of the most famous advocates of this supra-historical view of the resurrection. For Bultmann, "God is beyond space-time history. His acts are transcendent; they are above observable human history. . . . Miracles are not of this world. They are acts in the spiritual world. In brief, Bultmann has defined them out of existence."[10] But appeal to a make-believe realm of supra-history does nothing to settle the matter one way or another. Indeed, from an apologetic viewpoint, this retreat into the non-historical realm seems to be a tacit admission that the resurrection need not be taken too seriously, since it seems to be like so many other religious stories—purely mythical, regardless of the effect it may have had on the disciples.[11] Evangelical distaste

---

9. Lewis, C.S., "Myth Became Fact," 66–67.

10. Geisler, *The Battle for the Resurrection*, 90. For a good, succinct summary of Bultmann's views on the historical (or non-historical) character of the New Testament, see Michalson, "Rudolf Bultmann," 102–13.

11. Although Bultmann thought that it was possible for the resurrection to be a non-physical, non-objective event in history, the "event" of the resurrection nonetheless sparked the rise of the kerygma in the apostles. For his skepticism regarding the historicity of the gospel accounts, see his *The History of the Synoptic Tradition*.

for such a view is captured in the following words from Gregory Boyd and Paul Eddy: "A good deal of liberal theology is premised on the mistaken notion that people can embrace the symbolic meaning of an event while denying the event ever literally took place . . . Evangelicals have always regarded this line of thinking implausible, if not incoherent."[12]

For Frei, the stories about Jesus, especially the story of the resurrection, cannot be relegated to the realm of the non-historical precisely because Jesus is what Frei terms an "unsubstitutable" person. In other words, the stories about Christ are inconceivable unless the person at their center (i.e., Jesus) actually had the experiences that the Gospels record him as having. And it is in his resurrection that Frei says Christ is most "unsubstitutable." Frei writes that "What the accounts are saying, in effect, is that the being and identity of Jesus in the resurrection are such that his nonresurrection becomes inconceivable."[13]

Frei is not at his most lucid here, but the gist of his argument seems to be that, if the gospel writers, indeed the Christian community, are going to talk of Jesus Christ, it is necessary that he must be viewed as the Resurrected One, for this is who Christians claim him to be. To talk of a non-resurrected Christ might be to talk about an actual human being who lived in first-century Palestine, but this person bears no resemblance to the Lord Christians believe has conquered the chains of death. An analogy may prove helpful here. When we think of Hamlet, we necessarily think of a *mad* Hamlet. A sane Hamlet simply would not be Hamlet at all. When it comes to Jesus, we could easily think of him as hailing from a town other than Nazareth, since his birthplace is not fundamental to our understanding of his nature and mission. "To think of Jesus is to think of one who *is*, who is not dead but alive, not absent but with us always, to the very end of the age."[14] In fact, a case can be made that in Frei's understanding of the resurrection, we have a very philosophically sophisticated apologetic argument. Indeed, it is nothing less than "a kind of Ontological Argument: the concept "Jesus" analytically

12. Boyd and Eddy, *Across the Spectrum*, 71.
13. Frei, *The Identity of Jesus Christ*, 145.
14. Higton, "Frei's Christology," 89.

contains the idea of existence with us now, so Jesus *cannot be thought of as not present.*" [15]

If this is correct, Frei seems to have placed himself (as far as the issue of the resurrection is concerned) at least partially within the theological camp of no less an apologist than St. Anselm himself!

Rudolf Bultmann once remarked that, even if Christ's bones were to be discovered tomorrow in a cave in Israel, it would not negatively impact the Christian faith and kerygma. Of course, St. Paul had quite a different view of this matter. In 1 Cor 15:12–19, he clearly teaches that if Christ was not raised in bodily form, the Christian faith is a sham, and "we are to be pitied more than all men" (v19). Paul knew full well that the Christian faith was based upon objective evidence, and he appealed to it often in his letters. Frei, though obviously not as thorough an evidentialist as Paul, still realized that the resurrection of Christ is the central event in the Christian faith, and to talk of a non-resurrected Jesus is akin to saying nothing at all of the founder of Christianity.

So far, we have seen that Frei does two important things regarding the resurrection. First, he has given the authority for interpreting this event to the community of believing Christians. Second, it is their inability to conceive of him as not risen that renders ridiculous all talk of a non-resurrected Christ. Such a procedure surely can strengthen the faith of those within the church, but what about those outside the church? Does a resurrected Jesus whose own community is the only one who thinks he is alive carry any weight with those outside of the community? Frei is quite unwilling to say that there is any evidence for Christ's resurrection, aside from the "ontological argument" described above.[16] Consider what he says in the following passage regarding the possibility of making the transition from the truth of the resurrection narratives, to actual historical truth: "explaining how this transition becomes possible—to say nothing of demonstrating its actual occurrence—is what we claimed from the

---

15. Ibid., 89.

16. Although, in Frei's defense, it has been pointed out that "Frei is implying at least negative historical claims (the disciples did not steal the body; Jesus did not merely faint on the cross; it is not enough to say that his memory was wondrously preserved in the minds of his disciples, etc.)." Quoted from Placher, "Scripture as Realistic Narrative," 40.

Hans Frei as Unlikely Apologist for the Historicity of the Resurrection

beginning to be impossible, certainly in the context of our analysis of the unity of Christ's presence and identity, if indeed at all."[17] Or again, he states that there is "no argument from factual evidence or rational possibility to smooth the transition from literary to faith judgment. But this is really not surprising, for faith is not based on factual evidence or inherent historical likelihood."[18]

What is odd about the above statement is that the *narratives themselves* in the New Testament are used to undergird the historicity of Christ's resurrection from the dead in bodily form. For the New Testament writers, the resurrection of Christ was an objective event in time-space history that verified the claims of the new faith the disciples were preaching. In Acts 17:31, Paul, who is debating with the Athenians, explicitly states that there is objective evidence for his religion, since God "has given *proof* of this to all men by raising [Jesus] from the dead." The same apologetic technique is on display in Acts 26, when Paul appears before Festus and Agrippa. Here again, Paul is arguing the Christian case based on the evidence provided by the resurrection. Indeed, so central is the reality of the resurrection for Paul that he plainly says the Christian faith stands or falls based on the veracity of this event (1 Cor 15:12–19).

Thus it can be said that the New Testament, contra Frei, is strongly evidentialist in its approach to the faith. Yes, it teaches that the Christian life is one based on faith, but it is a faith based upon historically verifiable events.

These events can be summed up as follows. First, the tomb of Christ was empty. Had he not risen, hostile Roman and Jewish authorities could have easily produced the body, thus squelching any talk of a risen messiah. Such talk would have been blasphemy to the Jewish religious leaders, and potentially seditious as far as the Romans were concerned. The idea that the disciples stole and hid the body, then later claimed that Christ was resurrected, is ludicrous. The disciples suffered greatly for the gospel that they preached. They certainly gained no worldly benefits from preaching their message. Ultimately, tradition tells us, most of them died as martyrs. It is highly unlikely that twelve men would suffer and die for a religion they knew to be based on a lie.

17. Frei, *The Identity of Jesus Christ*, 147.
18. Ibid., 151.

Second, the resurrection must have actually occurred, for it is these appearances that obviously turned a rag-tag group of Jewish peasants into the mighty evangelists who began to preach the resurrection and divinity of Christ. How else to explain the fact that these simple men, who were so dejected when their Master was executed, suddenly became witnesses unto death for that same Master? That these resurrection appearances were only visions or hallucinations is entirely untenable, for no twelve men (not to mention the five hundred persons that Paul mentions!) can be expected to have the same hallucinations![19] Even orthodox Jewish scholar Pinchas Lapide is compelled to assert: "No vision or hallucination is sufficient to explain such a revolutionary transformation [in the disciples]. For a sect or school or an order, perhaps a single vision would have been sufficient—but not for a world religion which was able to conquer the Occident thanks to the Easter faith."[20]

Third, the story of the resurrection was preached in the presence of "hostile witnesses," that is, Jewish authorities who would have gladly discredited the story had they been able to do so.[21]

---

19. For a treatment of the problems inherent in the idea that several persons can experience the same hallucination or vision, see my "Resurrection Appearances Hallucinations? (227–38), where I show that clinical evidence for this position is severely lacking. I also point out serious problems with the idea that the resurrection appearances can be attributed to mass hysteria on the part of the disciples. Documented cases of mass hysteria differ greatly from the reports of the risen Christ we find in the New Testament. But some critics take a different approach regarding the appearances and claim that these reports can be dismissed because visions of deceased persons are fairly common among those who have recently suffered the loss of a loved one. However, as N.T. Wright has pointed out, people who "see" departed loved ones realize that what they are seeing is only a "vision," or a "ghost." Such visions never convince the seer that the loved one has been "resurrected." Thus we often hear such seers saying things like, "my *dead* father appeared to me last night," or "I saw the spirit of my dearly *departed* mother last night." Only in the case of Jesus do his postmortem appearances convince people that he is still alive (Dr. Wright made these telling comments during a lecture at Truett Seminary, Baylor University, October 2002).

20. Lapide, *The Resurrection of Jesus*, 49. As an Orthodox Jew, Lapide does not view Christ as the Jewish Messiah. However, he does believe that his resurrection proves that he is God's Messiah to the *Gentile* world.

21. For a fine treatment of this type of approach, see Montgomery, *Where is History Going?* 53–74.

Now, such evidence does not, of course, prove beyond a doubt that the resurrection happened. Still, for Frei to not even have *addressed* it is strange indeed. Had he faced it, and then offered a plausible refutation of it, his position would be far stronger. In the one place where he does seem to address this type of evidential argument for the resurrection, he seems to suggest that those who think the resurrection has good evidence in its favor are fundamentalists, who "believe that the New Testament accounts are an absolutely accurate record of the things that actually happened when Jesus was raised from the dead. They take accounts such as those of the empty tomb [and] the resurrection appearances of Jesus in the Gospels, and Paul's account of the resurrections appearances (1 Cor 15:3–8) to contain no contradictions among themselves and to constitute reliable evidence in favor of an earthly event, Jesus' resurrection."[22] But this is nothing more than an argument aimed at a straw man. Very few scholarly apologetic treatments of the evidence for the resurrection claim that the Gospels are a word-for-word description of what actually happened. Also, the fact that there are discrepancies between the gospel writers' resurrection appearance accounts are granted by most conservative scholars, because the issue at hand is the appearances themselves, rather than whether or not all four evangelists tell exactly the same story.[23]

Of course, those who in the past have tried to refute the good evidence in favor of the historicity of the resurrection have often faired poorly. Even so illustrious an atheist as Antony Flew badly stumbled when he attempted to debate evangelical Gary Habermas on the resurrection.[24] And atheistic philosopher Kai Nielson, when pressed by his opponent J.P Moreland to address the many evidences Moreland had laid out in favor of the resurrection, replied, "I don't know much about such things and to be perfectly frank, I'm not terribly interested in them." He then goes on to explain why, even if

22. Frei, *Theology and Narrative*, 202.

23. See, for example, Davis, *Risen Indeed*, and *Jesus Under Fire*, edited by Wilkins and Moreland. In fairness to Frei, both books were published after his works were written.

24. The debate can be found in Habermas and Flew, *Did Jesus Rise from the Dead?* For a similar debate, see the exchange between Craig and Crossan, *Will the Real Jesus Please Stand Up?*

Christ was indeed raised bodily from the tomb, it would only constitute a peculiar fact we cannot explain because we lack the scientific resources to do so.[25] Of course, if Christians are claiming that "such things" are one of the main reasons (the other being that faith is a gift of God through the Holy Spirit) people have faith in Christ to begin with, it is odd that an opponent would not do his or her best to demolish those things. To ignore them is to not seriously engage the issue at hand, and this is, unfortunately, the path Dr. Frei is guilty of taking.

But even if Frei was opposed to the traditional evidence that has been advanced to bolster confidence in the resurrection, it is truly shocking that he did not apply his own narrative technique to the *post*-resurrection stories about Christ that are preserved in the New Testament. Frei took great trouble to point out that in the passion/resurrection stories we have the surest proof that Jesus must have died and risen, because a dying/rising savior is what all Christians take Jesus to be; he cannot be understood apart from this. Well and good. But if the narratives in the Gospels that portray Christ as dying and returning to life are so normative for Frei, then what about the narratives in the book of Acts? Why are not these narratives treated with the same seriousness as those we find in the Gospels? In fact, in Frei's writing on the resurrection, we find him almost exclusively concentrating on the passion/resurrection narratives in the Gospels, but paying very little heed to what is found in the rest of the New Testament. Granted, he is focused on narrative, and once we move beyond the Gospels, there is little narrative to be had; Paul's works are all epistolary, as is most of the New Testament. But it cannot be denied that Acts is just as thoroughly a narrative work as the Gospels. In fact, Frei even seems to have recognized this at one point in *The Identity of Jesus Christ*, where he stated that Paul, on the Road to Damascus, heard the voice of Jesus. This heavenly voice, Frei admits, represents "the claim that the presence of Jesus after his death is fully identical with who he was and what he did in the flesh before his death. He is none other than Jesus of Nazareth. His presence is self-focused and not diffused."[26]

---

25. Nielson, *Does God Exist*, 66.
26. Frei, *The Identity of Jesus Christ*, 49.

Now, Paul heard this voice, and he realized who it was; it belonged to the one he had been persecuting, the one whose followers claimed had been resurrected. When the voice of the speaker identifies himself as "Jesus whom you persecute," (Acts 9:5) Paul seems to have instantly understood who this Jesus was. This Jesus could only be the "unsubstitutable" One who was said to be alive by his followers. Yet Frei insisted there is no evidence of the resurrection beyond the accounts in the Gospels. But if he is willing to lend credence to the gospel accounts, why not to Paul's conversion experience? After all, in order for Paul to hear the voice of a man who had been executed (not to mention Paul's blinding by Christ's supernatural presence), he had to presuppose that Jesus had been resurrected. This meant that Paul met the "unsubstitutable" One; the one whom he encountered had to be Jesus, for only Jesus has risen from the dead.

Furthermore, what about the other narrative episodes in the book of Acts? Acts simply would not be possible had it not been for the events recorded in the Gospels. In other words, the entire Acts of the Apostles is predicted upon the resurrection of Christ as described in the Gospels. Just as it is impossible for Christians to think of Jesus as not raised from the dead, so it is impossible to understand, say, Peter's speech in Acts; why would he claim that God had raised Jesus from the dead (4:10)? Because Peter knew that Christ had indeed been raised. In fact, all of Acts makes little sense if the resurrection was not a reality for the Christians who began to spread the new faith. For when they preached in the name of Christ, they preached about someone for whom it was impossible to say was anything less than the Resurrected One.

As explained above, Hans Frei seems to offer the Christian a good reason for believing that Christ rose from the dead (i.e., his unsubstitutability). Granted, the resurrection makes sense to the Christian, but would not the same hold true for a Muslim's view of Muhammad? That is, are not Muslims justified in thinking of Muhammad as God's last and greatest prophet, since for Muslims to think about Muhammad is to necessarily think of him in this "unsubstitutable" manner? Does Jesus as the resurrected, unsubstitutable One mean the event happened in time-space history? In an article critical of Frei, evangelical theologian Carl F. Henry sums up the dilemma for theologians who stress the narrative nature of Scripture to the exclusion of any ostensive referent in actual history. I quote him at length:

> Representations of biblical history by many narrative theologians leave one with the uneasy sense that their commendable reservations about the historical method are correlated with a view that important aspects of biblical history belong to a different historical category than the history that contemporary historians investigate. Biblical history indeed bulks large in redemptive acts, that is, in specialdeeds in which God is active for human salvation. But insofar as such acts are heldto be historical, must they not fall into the same category of history that legitimately concerns contemporary historical investigation?[27]

Henry's point here is, of course, that Christian faith, at least as the New Testament writers understood it, is based on the resurrection as an actual, space-time event. Indeed, the "NT itself affirms that historical disconfirmation of the resurrection would undermine the Christian faith."[28] The question is, did Frei conceive of the resurrection as something that happened in history, or is it merely a compelling story for those in the Christian community? Frei is notoriously hard to pin down on this issue; he never really tells us where the line between biblical narrative and "real" history starts (or ends?). It is as if Frei was so intent upon stressing the importance of reading the Bible narratively that he forgot that the biblical writers thought of themselves as writing true history.

Frei was certainly aware that the question of the resurrection's historicity is an important one. And when pressed on the issue, he said the following: "The New Testament authors, especially Luke and Paul, were right in insisting that it is more nearly correct to think of Jesus as factually raised, bodily if you will, than not to think of him

---

27. Henry, "Narrative Theology," 11.

28. Ibid., 7. Frei is aware of this, and agrees that although there is no historical proof that substantiates the resurrection, it is possible that negative evidence could be amassed that would disprove the reality of the resurrection. Exactly what would prove the resurrection to be ahistorical, Frei does not explain (*Theology and Narrative*, 86–87).

in this manner."[29] This is about as close to an affirmation of the historical nature of Christ's resurrection as one is likely to find in Frei's writings. And although this statement would probably not satisfy Henry, it certainly places Frei in the same camp as some of the most prominent evangelical apologists. For it seems to me that Frei is here stressing the probability, not the certitude, of Christ's resurrection. This approach was the one taken by evangelical theologian/apologist Edward John Carnell:

> Christian faith . . . cannot rise above rational probability. Probability is that state of coherence in which more evidences can be corralled for a given hypothesis than can be amassed against it . . . . Since Christianity is a way of life, and not an unabridged edition of the Pythagorean Theorem, it cannot enjoy the demonstrative certainty of the latter.[30]

The evidence for Christ's death and resurrection is strong, but it is not so strong as to make the resurrection an undeniable fact of history (but of course, how could one prove that any event that happened two thousand years ago is irrefutably true?). John Warwick Montgomery, one of the ablest evangelical defenders of the resurrection in the twentieth century, constantly stressed this point in his writings. Although he believes that the evidence for the resurrection is strong, he knows it is not irrefutable. But what of that? As Montgomery wisely points out, we live our lives based on probabilities, including many of the most important decisions we make.[31] Why should faith in the resurrection be any different?

So Frei apparently was inclined to see the resurrection *perhaps* as a real event in history, although he did not fully commit himself to its historicity. Henry criticizes this lack of commitment, chiding theologians like Frei for advocating "uncertainty over historicity."[32] Frei wrote a brief response to Henry's critique and attempted to explain his position. His answer to Henry is, basically, that he is attempting to secure a middle ground between "liberal" and "conserva-

29. Frei, *Theology and Narrative*, 86.
30. Carnell, *An Introduction to Christian Apologetics*, 113.
31. Montgomery, *Human Rights and Human Dignity*, 152–54.
32. Henry, "Narrative Theology," 13.

tive" views on the matter of God's revelation in history, but especially as it pertains to the divine revelation of God in Christ.[33] Henry, in his critique, was asking Frei to commit to an either/or dichotomistic view of Scripture. He thought that Frei (and other narrative theologians) should clearly state whether or not the biblical narratives had an objective basis in history, because "it is incumbent on those who claim that narrative story and [biblical] history are not incompatible to clarify which historical specifics are non-negotiable."[34]

But Frei would not be so easily pinned down. He wanted to move beyond the conservative/liberal theological impasse. He objected to Henry's attempts to force him into a narrative versus history position because, for Frei, terms like "historical reality" are not "as theory-free, as neutral as he [Henry] seems to think they are . . . If I am asked to use the language of factuality, then I would say, yes, in those terms, I have to speak of an empty tomb. In those terms I have to speak of the literal resurrection. But I think those terms are not privileged, theory-neutral, trans-cultural, an ingredient in the structure of the human mind and of reality always and everywhere for me, as I think they are for Dr. Henry."[35] Essentially, Frei is telling Henry that, if he must play by Henry's "rules," then yes, the resurrection was a historical event. However, he does not agree that Henry's rules are binding upon all Christians, because a term like "reference" (or even "truth") "in Christian usage is not a simple, single, or philosophically univocal category."[36] Frei is accusing Henry of assessing his thought in perhaps an overly simplistic manner, and maybe it is true that Henry does not capture all the nuances that Frei makes between different types of theological reality.[37] But Henry raises a

---

33. Frei, *Theology and Narrative*, 207–12. Interestingly enough, Frei says that his most famous work, *The Eclipse of Biblical Narrative,* was written more against liberals than conservatives. Frei knew that liberals had largely abandoned the "plain meaning" of the text because they had become consumed with historical-critical issues. Frei wanted to remind them that, in the Bible, "the text means what it says" (208).

34. Henry, "Narrative Theology," 13.

35. Frei, *Theology and Narrative*, 211.

36. Ibid., 210.

37. For more on the Henry/Frei matter, see Hunsinger, "What Can Evangelicals and Postliberals Learn?" 134–50.

question that Frei cannot avoid: are the truths found in the narrative portions of Scripture based on actual events of history? And if they are not, why should anyone take them seriously in terms of the truth they allegedly convey? Could not just as much truth be found in the Hindu Scriptures, which do not pretend to have the same type of historical foundation that the Christian Scriptures claim? To this Frei gave no real answer, and his position that truth is not "univocal" (whatever that may mean) is not helpful when faced with the type of unavoidable question asked by Henry.

Despite his refusal to provide a forthright answer to Henry, he does give an answer of sorts, and it reminds me of the "Reformed epistemological" approach that Alvin Plantinga would develop just a few years after Frei as an alternative to traditional evidentialist apologetics. For Plantinga, belief in God is "properly basic" so long as certain conditions are met. Those conditions arise within the Christian community itself (this, recall, is part of Frei's apologetic, too). That is, the Christian community largely determines the faith of its individual members. For those inside the Christian community, Christian faith is properly basic, and therefore as valid a belief as any other belief.[38] For Plantinga, the Christian community shares certain beliefs about God. These beliefs gave shape to that community, and provide the basis of its worldview. These beliefs are shaped by Scripture, but also by the experiences that Christians within the community share, such as "guilt, gratitude, danger, a sense of God's presence, [and] a sense that he speaks."[39] The Christian may not be able to convince everyone that his beliefs are true, but this does not render his faith invalid, according to Plantinga. One scholar sums up Plantinga's position as follows: "For example, I might *know* that I am hungry, even if I can't convince you through an argument. In the same way, the believer might know that God exists in some immediate or non-inferential way, but not be able to convince others of her knowledge."[40] Plantinga's point is that, for a Christian, the Christian worldview "makes sense" and seems to be a valid approach to life, even if one cannot "prove" that her faith is true beyond a doubt. Still, for the Christian, her belief can be termed properly basic, because it

38. Grenz, "Articulating the Christian Belief-Mosaic," 131–33.
39. Plantinga, "Reason and Belief in God," 81.
40. Hatcher, "Plantinga and Reformed Epistemology," 88.

does not rest upon any "foundational" belief. For Plantinga, belief in God is its own foundation, if you will.[41]

In Plantinga-like fashion, Frei maintained that he was not overly concerned with the type of historical issue Henry raises, because "belief in the divine authority of Scripture is for me simply that we do not need more. The narrative description there is adequate. "God was in Christ reconciling the world to himself" is an adequate statement for what we refer to, though we cannot say univocally how we refer to it."[42] This, much like Plantinga's position, deems the faith of the Christian community in and of itself sufficient; no "confirmation" of the faith is required from any source outside the narrative of the Bible. Aside from the charge of fideism that such a position is open to, the question must again be asked, *why* should the Christian community hold this faith? How does it know that Christ was the means whereby God reconciled the world to himself? Is Christ as the unsubstitutable One sufficient grounds for a life commitment? Or, must we assert with Henry that,

> The narrative approach therefore seems not fully befitting the historic Christian faith, nor fully serviceable to the need for an intellectually compelling argument with modernity. Readers may and often do find in the biblical narrative a means of grace that stirs the spirit, and also claims and evidences which involve a supernatural resolution of the human dilemma, and centered supremely in the resurrection of the crucified Jesus. But neither a transcendent revelatory content nor objective scriptural inspiration lends supernatural sanction to the biblical drama when read on narrative premises. One discerns here an enchantment with the affective, a flight from history to the perspectival that enjoins no universal truth-claims, a reflection of the revolt against reason, a

---

41. Here, Plantinga reminds me very much of the presuppositionalist approach to apologetics developed by Cornelius Van Til. For Van Til, too, Christian belief could not be deduced from any sort of argument. It simply is a God-given fact, and it provides the Christian with the correct way of viewing and interpreting the world. See, for instance, his *The Defense of the Faith*. For an assessment of his thought, by both fellow presuppositionalists as well as evidentialsts, see "My Credo."

42. Frei, *Theology and Narrative*, 210.

reliance in "symbolic truth" and imagination, an interest in earthly theatre more than in [historically] revealed theology.[43]

Henry, it seems, is right; the more the narrative aspect of Scripture is emphasized, the less attention is given to the historical aspect of Christianity. And since Christianity is a "religion of the book," a historically-based religion, Henry's comments must be taken seriously. This is especially true since, as Frei himself admitted, the culmination of the Christian story is the resurrection of Christ, and Frei almost begrudgingly admits that the resurrection is probably a historical event. But why could not Frei's powerful argument for the truth of the resurrection be combined with the traditional "evidences" for the resurrection's historicity? Why did Frei insist on choosing narrative to the exclusion of all else? His call to treat Scripture as narrative, that is, to take seriously the story of the Bible, was well founded. The Scriptures, especially the passion/resurrection narratives, lose all their transformative religious and moral authority when the biblical critic reduces them to isolated literary units. But why did Frei's position involve narrative and nothing but narrative? His thesis of Christ as the unsubstitutable One would have lost nothing of its power had he been open to other types of evidential support for the historicity of the resurrection. Indeed, this openness would have only made his position stronger. As Gabriel Fackre has written, "Story by no means excludes history. The Christian recital could not exclude empirical narrative or it would cease to be Christian, for its central events presuppose hard empirical claims—Jesus did live, Jesus did die on the cross."[44] As far as I know, Frei in his writings never said why a narrative approach must rule out all other types of approaches to Scripture. He saw narrative as a corrective to scholars who were consumed with historical issues, and in this he was correct. But why all historical issues must necessarily be eclipsed by narrative interpretation, he never explained. In fact, just before his death, in a lecture at Yale University, he seemed to have even less interest in historical referents. By the mid 1980s, he had absorbed enough of structuralists and post-structuralists thought that he apparently saw

43. Henry, "Narrative Theology," 19.
44. Fackre, *The Christian Story*, 27.

the text and what the text "referred to" as completely distinct from each other.[45]

In conclusion, it may be said that Frei as an apologist for the resurrection of Christ both succeeded and failed at the same time. Frei was right to insist that the reality of the resurrection is only probable; were it a certain fact, the New Testament's teaching on the necessity of faith would make little sense. But the New Testament does not encourage a fideistic sort of faith, either. It seems to me that Frei would have made his good case for the resurrection of Christ immeasurably stronger had he *combined* his idea of Christ as the unsubstitutable One, along with a proper respect for the apologetic arguments for the resurrection that are found in traditional evidentialist apologists. This would have allowed Frei to have the best of both worlds. He could have retained the idea (along with Plantinga) that the Christian community, not hostile biblical critics, should be the final arbiter of the Jesus stories. He could have maintained his unique concept of Jesus as the one who had to be raised based upon the utter uniqueness of his person (Frei's "ontological" argument). He could have kept the key idea (as found in Carnell and Montgomery) that belief in the resurrection must involve a degree of faith; it is not a tautological certainty. And he could have availed himself of the New Testament evidence for the resurrection, evidence that the biblical writers thought was so strong that they based their entire kerygmatic message upon it, as reflected not only in the Gospels but in the book of Acts as well. Still, despite his shortcomings, Hans Frei must, in the end, be regarded as no less than a powerful apologetic witness for the abiding truth of the resurrection event. For, in defiance of the "liberals," he offered an ontological Christ who could be understood *only* as risen Lord. Against narrative-undermining biblical critics, he asserted that only the Christian community could properly understand the story of Jesus. And he reminded the "fundamentalists" that the resurrection's truth is only probable but, when combined with personal faith, the result is a confident belief that Jesus was the unsubstitutable One who rose on Easter morning.

---

45. Lee, *Luke's Stories of Jesus*, 91–95. For those seeking a book-length, detailed analysis of Frei's work, this book will prove very useful.

Part Three

Christianity, Judaism, and the Holocaust

8

A New Testament Understanding of the Jewish Rejection of Jesus: Four Theologians on the Salvation of Israel

Is Christian theology inherently anti-Semitic? Are the fundamental teachings of the New Testament blatantly anti-Jewish? Is the church's historical oppression of Judaism responsible (at least in part) for the Holocaust? More importantly, does the Holocaust force Christians to re-think the matter of Jewish salvation? A growing number of scholars, both Jewish and Christian, are answering "Yes" to these questions, and are seeking alternative understandings of the Christian message which they believe will avoid the anti-Semitic trappings of the past.

The landmark work in this area is Rosemary Ruether's *Faith and Fratricide*. This book examines how Judaism has been demeaned and vilified by the New Testament, the Church fathers, and the states of Christian Europe. Ruether called for a radical new openness on the part of Christians toward Judaism in order to make amends for these sins: "Christians must be able to accept the thesis that it is not necessary for Jews to have the story about Jesus in order to have a foundation for faith and a hope for salvation."[1] The solution to Christian anti-Judaism, Ruether claimed, lies in a "revitalization of

---

1. Ruether, *Faith and Fratricide*, 256.

Christian absolutism which can accept the independent salvific validity of the Jewish tradition."[2]

Ruether's book has had a tremendous influence on the contemporary Jewish-Christian dialogue. The extent of this influence can be judged from the fact that Gregory Baum, who wrote a powerful apologetic work in 1968 vigorously defending the New Testament against the charge of anti-Semitism, penned the introduction to 1974's *Faith and Fratricide*. He there admitted that the apology he presented in his earlier work was untenable.[3] Baum stated he had come to believe that, in light of the history of Christian anti-Judaism, especially the Holocaust, Christian theologians must "look for a formulation of the Christian faith that does not negate Jewish existence."[4]

Baum is not alone in his abrupt change of position. For example, Krister Stendahl no longer believes that Paul's letter to the Romans teaches that Jews must receive Christ as their Savior in order to experience salvation.[5] There is a host of prominent thinkers, many of them Christian, who share Baum and Stendahl's views, and they continue to have an enormous effect on the ongoing Jewish-Christian dialogue.[6]

This article is an attempt to understand, from a decidedly New Testament perspective, some of the ways in which the Jewish people's rejection of the messiahship of Jesus Christ has been understood. My aim is to challenge the new orthodoxy that now prevails among many mainline Christian theologians regarding the matter of Jewish salvation. This new orthodoxy is largely a result of theological reflection upon the Holocaust. Due to the sheer horror of Jewish suffering, and Christian complicity in that suffering, many now consider any attempt to link Jewish salvation with the Christian Savior theologically untenable, if not dangerously anti-Semitic.

I wish to demonstrate that the traditional claim that Jesus is the Savior of the Jews is not anti-Semitic, and that it is in fact a requirement if an honest interpretation of the New Testament evidence is to

2. Ibid., 260.
3. Ibid., 1–22.
4. Ibid., 22.
5. Stendahl, *Paul Among Jews and Gentiles*.
6. Two representative works are Gager, *The Origins of Anti-Semitism*, and Pawlikowski, *Jewish-Christian Dialogue*.

be maintained. Christian theology must be based on revelation, not on human experience, however tragic and far-reaching that experience may be. To assume that Christian theology must change as a result of the Holocaust is to base our theological thought on the tragedy of human evil rather than on the revelation of God. And while the Holocaust is a particularly obscene example of human depravity, it is different only in degree, not in kind, from all the sins of mankind throughout the centuries. C.S. Lewis, responding to the alleged "new urgency" brought about by modern man's recognition of the riddle of evil, cogently remarks, "[W]hat new urgency? . . . it is no more urgent for us than for the great majority of monotheists all down the ages. The classic expositions of the doctrine that the world's miseries are compatible with its creation and guidance by a wholly good Being come from Boethius waiting in prison to be beaten to death and from St. Augustine meditating on the sack of Rome."[7] And while Lewis was not writing about the Holocaust *per se*, his comments are plainly relevant to our discussion. Terrible examples of evil have plagued mankind throughout the ages, but Christians never radically changed their soteriology as a result. Why should the Holocaust be treated differently? What the Holocaust *should* do, and largely *has* done, is to make Christians realize that their old anti-Semitic prejudices must go, that the vilification of Jews as "Christ-killers," etc., must be repudiated for the sin that it is. But this is far different from altering the central message of the New Testament: the gospel of salvation through Christ is for all, Gentile and Jew alike.

The first two theologians I address are Clark Williamson and Sidney Hall, both of whom can be considered contemporary representatives of the paradigm shift in Jewish-Christian relations that was inaugurated by Ruether some twenty years ago. They are both proponents of the so-called dual covenant theory, which holds that Christ is indeed the Messiah, but only for *Gentiles*, not for *Jews*. They differ somewhat in their reasons for advocating this view, but the Holocaust is the primary motivation in the thought of both men. The next two theologians I treat are Karl Barth and Jakob Jocz. They represent the more conservative, pre-Ruether view that Jesus cannot really be called the Christ if he is not truly Messiah for both Gentile and Jew. These two (especially Jocz) rely more heavily upon the New

---

7. Lewis, C.S., "Evil and God," 22.

Testament for the formulation of their views, but they differ greatly in their understanding of the way in which Jewish salvation through Christ occurs. Barth believes that the Jews will be saved *en masse* as a result of divine election. Jocz, on the other hand, seems to be more aware that the New Testament treats the matter of Jewish salvation in terms of divine election *and* personal choice. Jocz arrives at his position because he is willing to take seriously the apparent dichotomy between God's electing grace and the individual's freewill, which is evidenced in Rom 9–11. I believe that Jocz's view is to be preferred over those of Williamson, Hall, and Barth, because his position has the support of the New Testament.

In order to assess the positions of these four theologians and to show the superiority of Jocz's view of the matter, I will turn at the end to an examination of each scholar's view in light of what Paul says regarding Jewish salvation in Rom 9–11. Since this passage is the most comprehensive biblical treatment of the relationship between Jesus Christ and the Jews, any Christian understanding of this matter must honestly come to terms with what Paul says in these chapters.[8] E.P. Sanders has said regarding the salvation of the Jews via Christ, "it is only in Romans, and explicitly in Rom 9–11, that Paul directly addresses the question of the status of the Jews [regarding their relationship to Christ]."[9]

Clark Williamson has written extensively on the subject of anti-Semitism for many years, but his fullest treatment of the subject is found in *A Guest in the House of Israel: Post-Holocaust Church Theology*. For Williamson, the Holocaust was the culmination of nearly 2,000 years of Jewish persecution at Christian hands. Williamson does not believe that Christian anti-Judaism was solely responsible for the Holocaust, but that centuries of Christian anti-Semitism created the environment that made the Holocaust far more likely. Because Christian theology played a role in this awful event, it must necessar-

---

8. There are, of course, other New Testament passages that touch on the matter of Jewish salvation, especially in the Gospels. However, I believe that many of these assume a negative attitude toward the Jews only because *particular* Jews in the Gospels are hostile to Christ. See, for example, Von Wahlde, "The Johannine Jews," 33–60. However, none of these passages has the systematic quality, or the *balance*, of Rom 9–11. I will therefore assume throughout this chapter that this is the definitive biblical text concerning Jewish salvation.

9. Sanders, "Paul's Attitude," 178.

ily be radically amended, altered, and reformulated to ensure that it never again has a part in so great a human catastrophe. Williamson's battle cry throughout his book is that no "statement, theological or otherwise, should be made that would not be credible in the presence of the burning children."[10] For Williamson, any type of Christian theological statement is unacceptable if it in any way suggests that Judaism is inferior to Christianity, or that Jews must convert to the Christian faith. Such statements, he believes, helped pave the way to the Holocaust.

Williamson is concerned not only with eliminating harmful anti-Jewish ideas from current Christian thought, but also with reinterpreting the very Christian canon itself in order to remove the anti-Jewish tradition which has propagated anti-Semitism for centuries: "[t]he anti-Judaism in the [Christian] tradition, including parts of the tradition defined as canonical, must be eliminated and a new interpretation offered that seeks both to be more appropriate to the tradition and more plausible in a post-*Shoah* [Holocaust] situation."[11] The traditional Protestant reliance upon the *sola scriptura* principle can no longer be maintained in light of the terrible evil of the Holocaust which was, at least in part, caused by anti-Jewish statements in those Scriptures. Christianity is a *living* religion, Williamson maintains, and an absolute insistence upon the primacy of Scripture does not permit Christianity to properly respond to the exigencies of human existence, especially the Holocaust. Williamson writes that "we have stipulated one set of rules for doing Christian theology after Auschwitz: that we will beware any theological statement made after the *Shoah* that is unchanged from how it was made before [the *Shoah*]."[12]

By rejecting Scripture as the sole criterion for the basis of Christian theology, Williamson must find a new criterion that will enable him to respond to a post-Holocaust world. He finds this in what he terms "authentic" Christianity. The only passages of the New Testament that may be considered "authentic" are those that reveal "the gracious promise of God's love freely offered to each and all" and teach "the command of God that in turn we love God with all

10. Greenberg, "Cloud of Smoke," 23.
11. Williamson, *House of Israel*, 18.
12. Ibid., 20.

our selves and do justice to, that is, love, the neighbor as ourselves."[13] Any New Testament passage that provides a basis for Christian contempt of Judaism or suggests that Judaism is an "inferior" faith that has been superseded by a "superior" Christianity does not meet this standard and hence cannot be considered authentically Christian.

The word "freely" in the above quotation plays so prominent a role in Williamson's discussion of authentic Christianity because of his disdain for the many New Testament passages that are exclusivist in nature, teaching that salvation is possible only for members of the "new" covenant [Christians], not those belonging to the "old" covenant [Jews]. Not only are such passages inauthentically Christian, Williamson maintains, they actually promote the very thing Christians have always accused Jews of: reliance upon works-righteousness for salvation! "The claim that Jews lost the covenant because they were not worthy of it is simply works-righteousness... works-righteousness contends that God is not free to covenant with whomever God pleases but only with those who *deserve* to receive it."[14]

Obviously, Williamson rejects the traditional Christian doctrine of salvation through Christ alone, for this would imply that only Christians receive salvation, and that God is not free to extend his love to anyone outside of the Christian faith. Such traditional theology makes Jesus "a condition upon the grace of God, apart from which God is not free to be gracious."[15] In fact, Williamson goes so far as to claim that the Christ event cannot really be considered a "new" episode in salvation history as Christians have always claimed. Rather, what God did through Christ is merely a continuation of the salvific action he began with the Jewish people and continues with them to this very day: "Christ re-presents the same grace of God that had earlier been re-presented to the people of Israel and that continues to be re-presented in the synagogue. Hence, we must understand the grace of God in Christ in the light of God's continuous faithful dealing with the Israel of God."[16]

---

13. Ibid., 23.
14. Ibid., 114.
15. Ibid., 208.
16. Ibid., 258.

Williamson rejects any thought of a "new," "better," or "improved" covenant made possible by Christ. He even views the sacraments of baptism and Eucharist, the symbolic representations of the covenant established by Christ, as a mere continuation of God's grace, which had been extended to the Jewish people throughout the pages of the Hebrew Bible. The bread of the Eucharist is tied to Jewish tradition and cannot be understood apart from this tradition, because it "re-presents the bread the Hebrew people ate in the exodus from slavery in Egypt," while the rite of Christian baptism recalls "the waters of freedom through which the Israelites passed at the Exodus."[17] It is not that Williamson denies the efficacy of the sacraments for Gentiles: he fully affirms them. But he insists that nothing *new* or *superior* is made available through them: "Neither baptism nor the breaking of bread conveys any different or 'better' kind of grace than is available to the Jews through synagogue and family."[18]

It is no surprise that Williamson flatly rejects the idea of conversionary missions to the Jews. The whole notion of evangelizing Jews is "premised upon the theologically absurd notion that Jews are unacquainted with the God of the Bible."[19] Williamson also believes the New Testament offers no justification for any such mission, and he explains that those passages that speak of missionary activity (e.g. Gal 1:16; Rom 1:4–5; Luke 24:27; Acts 28:28; Matt 28:19–20) do so only in reference to Gentiles. There are no concrete passages that can be used to support missionary activities toward Jews: "The pertinent New Testament literature offers no warrant for such a mission."[20] Rather than viewing Judaism as an inferior religion, Christians must realize that Jews are their spiritual equals and that "Christian mission is a *shared* mission, one in which both the church and synagogue are called to be the witness of the God of Israel before the world and each other."[21] Williamson's solution to the problem of the Jewish rejection of Christ is plain and simple: he denies that they need to accept him in the first place, and rejects any passage of the New Testament that teaches otherwise.

17. Ibid., 258–59.
18. Ibid., 259.
19. Ibid., 250.
20. Ibid., 251.
21. Ibid.

Williamson is correct when he reminds Christians about their ancestors' shameful treatment of the Jewish people for almost two millennia. He is right to welcome the recent proclamations issued by various Christian denominations that repudiate the "teaching of contempt" about the Jews and recognize the value and integrity of their religious heritage. And he is certainly correct that Christian anti-Semitism played a role in the Holocaust. But do the sins of our Christian past mean that we must abandon the central message of the New Testament, namely the doctrine that salvation comes through Christ alone? I turn now to another theologian who seems to be more willing than Williamson to grapple with the New Testament's teaching about the primary role of Christ in the salvation of both Gentiles and Jews.

In *Christian Anti-Semitism and Paul's Theology*, Sidney Hall, despite his many similarities with Williamson, does not believe an approach like Williamson's is sufficient from a Christian perspective, for it ignores the Scriptures that lie at the very heart of the Christian tradition. Although he calls Auschwitz the "normative event for doing Christian theology," Hall, unlike Williamson, tries to account for the New Testament's insistence that all men, Jews included, must embrace Christ to receive salvation. However, he does this in such a way as to remain faithful to his belief that the Holocaust *demands* a new approach to Christian theology: "The death of innocent Jewish children must be an event that helps determine the character of particular doctrines of the Christian faith after Auschwitz."[22]

Hall devotes the main portion of his book to an exegesis of Romans. He admits that in Romans Paul does indeed demand that all must receive Jesus as the Christ, but he believes traditional interpreters have misconstrued Paul's meaning here. According to Hall, Paul does not demand that Jews embrace Christ as *their* Messiah, only that they recognize him as the Messiah for the Gentiles. The gospel is an original revelation only for Gentiles: "the good news already belongs to the Jewish people . . . Paul's good news was never intended to be bad news for Jews."[23] Hall, unlike Williamson, admits that God has done something new in Christ, but Paul, according

---

22. Hall, *Christian Anti-Semitism*, 141–42.
23. Ibid., 91.

to Hall, "insists Jews embrace the gospel *of* Christ, not that they embrace *Christ* [italics mine]."[24]

Those passages in Romans where Paul seems exasperated with Jews who rely on the law for salvation and reject Christ as Savior must be reinterpreted accordingly. "Paul's frustration is not over the Jewish people's inability to accept Jesus as their Messiah, but over some Jews who boast in Torah and their relation to God (2:17, 23; 3:27)."[25] The "hardening" of the Jews that Paul speaks of in chapter 11 has "nothing to do with their not becoming Christians."[26] Rather, it pertains to the only real criticism Hall believes Paul levels at the Jews in Rom: they are hardened to the idea that God could possibly offer covenant fellowship to anyone outside the law.[27] In fact, Hall believes the salvation of "all Israel" in 11:25 will come about when Jews finally cease boasting about their allegedly exclusive relationship with God and admit that he has decided to covenant with Gentiles as well as with Jews.[28]

Referring to the traditional interpretation of Rom 11:25, which holds that Jews will eventually be saved because they will accept Christ, Hall says a "Christ-centered thesis that in the end God will make Jews into Christians is inadequate and unacceptable. It retains an eschatological rejection and replacement theology of the Jews."[29] Despite his attempt to offer a Scripturally-based reinterpretation of a Christian theology of Judaism, Hall ends in a position akin to that of Williamson. Hall believes the idea of an eventual Jewish conversion to Christianity is in effect a denial of Judaism's continuing validity: "A theology accepting Jews as Jews now, but with an eschatological vision that accepts Jews only as Christians, is not a credible faith . . . Genuine pluralistic spirituality is a faith that permits one to maintain the integrity of one's own faith while respecting others in the integrity

24. Ibid., 92.
25. Ibid., 113.
26. Ibid., 120.
27. Hall believes that the "boasting" of some Jews over their special relationship with God via the law (rather than, say, the question of Jewish salvation) is the *most* serious problem Paul addresses in Rom. *Christian Anti-Semitism*, 93–100.
28. Ibid., 123–24.
29. Ibid., 118.

of their own faith."³⁰ Hall believes that his position, which he refers to as the "inclusive promise" of God, allows Christians and Jews to exist in an atmosphere of mutual respect. Christians partake of the promise through Christ, while Jews are included in the promise via faithful Torah observance.

As with Williamson, one can appreciate the fact that Hall is attempting to dismantle the legacy of Christian hatred toward the Jewish people that has marred Jewish-Christian relations for so long. His attempt to seriously wrestle with what Paul teaches about the Jewish law vis-à-vis salvation through Christ must also be applauded. But it is doubtful if his interpretation of Paul will prove acceptable to those who find in the New Testament (especially in Paul!) a rejection of the Jewish law in favor of the Christian gospel. I now turn to a theologian who is, in most respects, far more "traditional" than either Williamson or Hall. This may be due, in part, to the fact that he wrote before the era of the sea-change in Christian thought ushered in by serious reflection on the Holocaust.

In stark contrast to the views of both Williamson and Hall is the theology of Israel advocated by Karl Barth. Despite many charges to the contrary, Barth was not anti-Semitic. He insisted on the validity of the Jews' designation as the chosen people, he strongly supported the state of Israel, and he went as far as to say that "[a]ntisemitism is sin against the Holy Ghost."³¹

Barth told Pope John XXIII in a 1966 visit that, for Christians, "there is ultimately only one truly great ecumenical question: our relationship to Judaism."³² For Barth, Christianity was nothing but a "balloon trip [if] separated from the history of Israel."³³ Barth had no wish to denigrate or revile Judaism. He did, however, attempt to understand the Jewish rejection of Jesus from an uncompromisingly *Christian*, and *biblical*, point of view.

For Barth, the Jews were, are, and will remain the chosen people of God—nothing can alter this divinely ordained fact. So convinced of this is Barth that he considers the ongoing existence of the Jews, in the face of centuries of unparalleled persecution, to be the only

---

30. Ibid., 123.
31. Barth, *Church and the Political Problem*, 52.
32. Quoted in Jocz, *Christians and Jews*, 485.
33. Barth, *Dogmatics in Outline*, 75.

real "visible and tangible" proof of God's existence.³⁴ Barth is fond of quoting a conversation between Frederick the Great and his personal physician, Zimmermann: "'Zimmermann, can you name me a single proof of the existence of God?' And Zimmermann replied, 'Your majesty, the Jews!'"³⁵ Barth accepts this response, despite the fact that the Jews, God's special people, do not accept God's Messiah, Jesus Christ. Israel still "upholds the Synagogue . . . It acts as if it had still another special determination and future beside and outwith the Church."³⁶

Yet Barth does not simply dismiss Israel's disobedience as an act of unfaithfulness that results in a reciprocal rejection by God, as have many traditional Christian thinkers. Rather, Barth believes the Jews' disobedience is *temporary*, and that it fits within God's salvific plan for humanity, actually serving God's larger purposes: "Israel cannot alter the fact that even in this way [the rejection of Jesus] it discharges exactly the service for which it is elected."³⁷ Struggle as they may against God's purpose for them, their efforts can never revoke their election, nor foil God's intentions for them. The Jews belong in God's "elected community," and Israel "cannot escape its appointed service in it."³⁸ Here Barth breaks radically with those more traditional Christian thinkers who see in Israel's refusal to receive Christ a purely *human* refusal, a merely human blindness to the messiahship of Christ. For Barth, the Jews do not receive Jesus because God has *ordained* their rejection of him.

But for what purpose has God ordained this unbelief of the Jews? The reason, according to Barth, is to reflect the judgment of God, to exemplify the sorry state of humanity when it is in rebellion against God.³⁹ Barth interprets the long, sad history of Jewish suf-

---

34. Ibid., 75.
35. Ibid.
36. Barth, *Church Dogmatics* II.2, 208.
37. Ibid., 209.
38. Ibid., 208.
39. Barth's position is similar to Augustine's, who maintained that Jewish suffering since the fall of Jerusalem at Roman hands was a judgment upon them for their lack of faith in Christ, and that they served as a warning to all about the perils of rejecting the Christian Savior. However, Barth seems far more optimistic than Augustine about the ultimate salvation of the Jews. For a good summation

fering not so much as punishment for Israel's sins (though it is that, if the Old Testament is to be believed), but as something God has brought upon them not so much because of their *sin*, but because of their *election*. Barth writes that "it costs something to be the chosen people, and the Jews are paying the price."[40]

Israel's disobedience is really a sign of *humanity's* rebellion against God. The Jews have been "chosen" to represent the sinful state of all men: Israel has been elected "to reflect the judgment from which God has rescued man and which He wills to endure Himself in the person of Jesus of Nazareth."[41] Barth writes: "in the Jew we have revealed and shown to us in a mirror who and what we all are, and how bad we all are."[42] The Jews, then, are a microcosm of the human race, in its sinful rebellion against its Creator and in need of a Savior. Caution is needed here. Barth is not saying that Jews are especially sinful, or that they somehow "personify" evil: "The Jew as a Jew is neither better nor worse than other men . . . [the Jew represents] every man, without exception."[43]

The Jews do more than simply make the Gentile world aware of its sinfulness. The Jews point all humanity toward the only solution to Gentile *and* Jewish sinfulness: Jesus Christ. But in order to complete their role as a guidepost to the Gentiles, the Jews must finally receive Jesus as Savior. This is necessary "if men are to read and understand the sign and testimony which is given them in the existence of the Jews, and are actually to be convinced that they [Gentiles] too are the enemies of God."[44] The Jews do not fully convince the rest of the world of its need of God until the Jews themselves acknowledge their own need and enter the church. Then, the Gentile world will know that "on its own it can only plunge into ruin, that it cannot save itself from ruin."[45]

---

of Augustine's view, see Williamson's *House of Israel*, 115–17.

40. Barth, *Church Dogmatics* III.3, 220.
41. Barth, *Church Dogmatics* II.2, 206.
42. Barth, *Church Dogmatics* III.3, 221.
43. Ibid., 221.
44. Ibid., 223.
45. Barth, *Church Dogmatics* II.2, 207.

A New Testament Understanding of the Jewish Rejection of Jesus

In order for all of this to come about, there must obviously be a mass Jewish conversion to Christianity. Unlike Williamson and Hall, this poses no problem for Barth. In fact, it is absolutely essential to God's salvific plan for humanity. Like Paul, Barth does not pretend to know when this conversion will occur. It is an eschatological event for which the church can only patiently wait, confident that God will bring it about.[46] So confident is Barth of this eventual God-inspired conversion that he attaches absolutely no importance to Christian missionary activity toward the Jews.

Still, there is one great problem. Israel has not yet become faithful to her election. Israel is not yet an "active" participant in the church, although she is still part of it. She is not yet a full member in what Barth calls the "one community" of God, but even in her state of disobedience she remains a powerful witness to the sin of which all humanity is guilty before God. Barth looks forward to a time when the Jews will fulfill their election, when they will cease to be dormant members of the one community of God and accept full, active membership in this community. They will then serve as a "reminder of the settled, the canceled indictment, the forgiven sin, its witness [will] lend critical salt to the message of the accomplished reconciliation of the world with God without calling it into question."[47] Once this occurs, the "special honor of Israel [will] then consist in continually consoling and exhorting the Church by magnifying to it the judgment which has overtaken man . . . and therefore holding before it the cross of its Lord as its one and only hope, not to assail but to confirm the faith that the Church as such has to confess."[48]

Barth, like Williamson and Hall, repudiates Christian anti-Semitism. Like them, he insists that the Jews remain God's chosen people. But unlike Williamson and Hall, he reminds us that the Jewish rejection of Jesus is God's mysterious work (in accordance with Paul's teaching in Rom 11:25). However, he has little to say about the role of *personal choice* in the matter of Jewish salvation (which is certainly taught in Rom 9–11). I turn now to a theologian who, in my opinion, is to be preferred over Barth, because he builds his theology around the dual theme of divine election/personal

---

46. Ibid., 213.
47. Ibid., 208.
48. Ibid.

choice, which Paul teaches are both essential in the matter of Jewish salvation.

Jakob Jocz was a Jew by birth, a Christian by choice. All of his books are concerned with the relationship between Judaism and Christianity, specifically the relationship between Jews and Jesus. Like Barth, he wrote before the advent of the change in theological attitudes caused by reflection on the Holocaust (most of his books were published in the 1950s and 60s). Also like Barth, he is insistent upon the Jews' designation as God's chosen people. To deny this is a virtual historical impossibility for Jocz: there "is an aspect of Jewish history which remarkably corroborates the faithfulness of God. No theologian can seriously write about this people without paying attention to the miracle of its survival."[49] As with Barth, the Jews for Jocz were and remain God's chosen, and they cannot alter this fact, despite their efforts: "Israel's history is the supreme proof that there is no escape from a God-given task."[50] The Jews' rejection of Jesus cannot change what God intends for them, and those who have throughout the Christian era advanced the idea that Christians are the "new," "spiritual" Israel, which replaces the "old," "false" Israel, receive no support from Jocz. The very concept of a "new" Israel has no New Testament basis, Jocz claims: "there can be no plural to Israel. The idea of another Israel is utterly alien to the N.T., as alien as the idea that beside the God of Israel there can be another God."[51]

While Jocz rejects the idea that Christians have replaced Jews as God's chosen, he is well aware that there is indeed one great difference between them: Christians know Jesus as Messiah, while Jews do not, to their great loss.[52] On this point, Jocz is not willing to retreat. In fact, to compromise on this clear distinction between Christian and Jew is to court disaster for Christianity. It is "a matter of fact that a bridge theology spanned between the two faiths always means a compromise for the Church on the basic issue, namely the Lordship of Jesus Christ."[53] As much as Christians may wish not to offend Jews, they cannot give ground on this crucial issue: "for

49. Jocz, *A Theology of Election*, 97.
50. Ibid., 108.
51. Ibid., 120.
52. Ibid., 132.
53. Jocz, *Christians and Jews*, 34.

the Church to reduce her high christology in order to accommodate the Synagogue would spell dissolution. She stands or falls with the confession that Jesus is Lord."[54]

Such compromise inevitably leads to the "dual covenant" theology espoused by Williamson and Hall, and Jocz does not believe such compromise is an acceptable position for Christians. Surely it is not acceptable if the New Testament is to be taken seriously. The Christian Scriptures know nothing of two Messiahs, nor of two separate ways to salvation. Jocz writes that the "Gospel is only Good News if the offer of God's grace extends to all men [Jews included.]"[55] If Christ is indeed the Messiah, as Christians believe, then he is Messiah for all, and this means there can be no ambivalence on the question of a conversionary mission to the Jews. Not only *should* the church engage in such a mission; it *must* do so. Mission to the Jews is the "inevitable result of the claim that Jesus is Lord."[56]

But when presenting the gospel to the Jews, the church must never lose sight of the fact that it also, no less than Israel, is in dire need of that very gospel. In other words, the Christian church and Israel are both, at the same time, what Jocz terms church and mission: "in the Bible Israel is at the same time both Church *and mission*. Israel is Church as God's people of election; but Israel is also mission as part of the rebellious world in need of conversion."[57] According to Jocz, not only Israel, but also the Christian church, is portrayed this way in Scripture, and he cites as an example Paul's Corinthian correspondence. The Corinthians are the "church" in that they have been saved through grace, yet they are still "mission" because they remain "confused, struggling sinners" who need to be chastised by the apostle.[58]

Jocz's point is that *"only a repenting Church can be a missionary Church."*[59] The Christian community can effectively present the gospel to the Jews if it does so with an attitude of humility, fully aware

54. Ibid., 33.
55. Ibid., 44.
56. Ibid.
57. Ibid., 2–3.
58. Ibid., 4.
59. Ibid., 5.

that it is spiritually no better than Israel, and that it is guilty of all the sins of which Israel is guilty.[60] Some would say that a church that did not do all it could to prevent the Holocaust has no moral credibility, indeed, no moral right, to preach to the Jewish people. But Jocz says just the opposite is true—the nature of the gospel demands that just such a sick, unworthy church must present the message of sin and forgiveness to the Jews: "[I]t is a sick and humiliated Church which has to face the Jewish people and face up to it . . . In this encounter the Church can never assume an air of superiority, but can only in humble penitence try to hear again what she says to others."[61]

By approaching the Jews in such a manner, the church not only improves her chances of conversionary success, she also discovers for herself the true nature of the gospel, namely, that it is entirely a matter of grace. Christians and Jews are equally guilty in the eyes of God, and both find their hope only in Christ. Jocz would say that Christian complicity in the Holocaust, far from disqualifying Christians from presenting the gospel to the Jews, *better* qualifies them for the task, for it makes them realize that they dwell in sinful solidarity with those whom they know so desperately need to hear the gospel. There "is nothing that historic Israel is guilty of, that the Church is not."[62]

When it comes to the question of Jewish salvation, Jocz radically departs from Barth. Whereas Barth saw corporate Israel saved *en masse* (if not now, then sometime in the future) due to their special status as God's chosen people, Jocz strongly rejects such an idea. He does not accept the premise that membership among God's elect is based on only racial/ethnic heritage. Only individuals, not racial or ethnic groups, can experience salvation, according to Jocz. He says this is one of Paul's central points in Romans, and to claim that an individual is assured salvation as a matter of birthright would "make nonsense of faith" in the Pauline understanding of salvation.[63]

Jocz insists that salvation can occur for Jews "only by returning, by believing, by submitting to the regenerating power of the Holy

---

60. Ibid., 12.
61. Ibid., 13.
62. Jocz, *A Theology of Election*, 131.
63. Ibid., 139.

Spirit of God."[64] It must be stressed here that Jocz is not advocating Pelagianism; he is fully aware that human salvation is both initiated and completed by God.[65] Yet he stresses the importance of the individual Jew's personal response to Christ because he believes it is necessary to refute the idea that Jews will somehow "magically" be saved at the eschaton, simply by virtue of their Jewish heritage. This accounts for Jocz's insistence on the need for Christian missions to the Jews (something to which Barth gives no attention). "Israel as a people cannot hear the word of the Cross; it can be heard only personally by the individual Jew."[66]

The concept of personal faith in Christ is so important to Jocz's doctrine of Israel that he rejects outright the Barthian assumption that the unbelief of the Jews is in any way compatible with the divine plan. Unlike Barth, Jocz says that Israel's unbelief is related not to its *election*, but to its *humanity*. He thinks not in terms of collective "Israel's unbelief but human unbelief."[67] God does not will Jewish unbelief in Christ any more than he wills Gentile unbelief. Nor is Jewish unbelief any different than Gentile unbelief: by not receiving Christ, both Jew and Gentile rebel against God.[68] Whereas Barth divided the Christian church and the Jewish synagogue into two historically distinct camps, Jocz rejects such a demarcation based on racial distinction, for "the Church is frequently Synagogue and the Synagogue is sometimes Church."[69] That is, Jews and Gentiles reveal themselves to either be within or without the elect of God by their response to Christ.

Jocz acknowledges that Israel as a collective entity, as the chosen race of God, as a people elected to do his will, *is* a biblical concept, especially in Rom 9–11. How does Jocz reconcile this fact with his insistence on the importance of the individual's response to Christ? He explains that the key lies in a proper understanding of what the New Testament, especially Romans, means by election. "St. Paul

---

64. Ibid., 12.
65. Ibid., 109.
66. Ibid., 191.
67. Jocz, *Jewish People and Jesus Christ*, 321.
68. Jocz, *A Theology of Election*, 7.
69. Ibid., 134.

uses election in a twofold manner: sometimes he speaks of election in personal terms and sometimes in collective. The two are not the same. Israel's election is in respect of revelation; individual election is in respect of salvation."[70]

While Jocz admits that Paul is rather ambiguous regarding these two meanings of election, he insists that Rom 9–11 cannot truly be understood unless this distinction between the two aspects of election is maintained.[71] In Romans, Paul attempts to balance two different, yet related, concepts: his belief in Israel's corporate election as the chosen people of God, and his belief that each person, Jew or Gentile, is elect only if he comes to have personal faith in Christ. Both ideas are necessary, Jocz maintains, in order to make the Christian concept of salvation possible. For if corporate election did not occur, the individual would, in Pelagian fashion, elect himself; only an elect community can make possible individual election, and the personal choice it involves. The community, be it historic Israel or the Gentile Christian community, is elect in terms of the *revelation* it receives from God; this revelation in turn makes possible individual Jewish or Gentile salvation.[72]

It is at this point that Jocz introduces an eschatological component to his theology. While individual salvation occurs in the present, the salvation of "all Israel," which Paul refers to in Rom 11, is an eschatological event; it cannot be understood in the same way as the conversion of individual Jews. The salvation of "all Israel" will occur in the future, although the "remnant," or individual Jewish Christians, such as Paul, are saved in the present.[73]

By "all Israel," Jocz understands Paul to mean all those Jews and Gentiles who will eventually constitute the one true people of God. For Jocz, all Israel is "the Church of God in her completion, the Church in heaven."[74] The salvation of individuals is an ongoing process, but the full salvation of all Israel "is an ideal to pray for, to

---

70. Ibid., 111.
71. Ibid., 111.
72. Ibid., 138.
73. Ibid., 111.
74. Ibid., 139.

strive after, to try to realize."⁷⁵ In order to bring about this one united Israel, Christians can only continue to proclaim to the Jews (and to remember themselves!) the one thing that will make the true Israel a reality: the cross of Christ. I turn now to a brief analysis of Rom 9–11 as a basis for understanding and evaluating the four positions set forth in this article, with a view toward showing the superiority of Jocz's position.

Any theological attempt to explain such matters as the Jewish rejection of Jesus or the nature of Jewish salvation will hardly be credible, at least from a New Testament standpoint, if it cannot claim the support of Paul's teaching in Romans. I hope to show two things. First, that an interpretation of Rom 9–11 that sees Christ as Savior for Gentiles *and* Jews is in no way anti-Semitic. And second, that the interplay between divine sovereignty and personal choice found in Romans indicates that Jocz's theology of Jewish salvation is preferable to those of Williamson, Hall, and Barth.

To put it bluntly, the dual covenant theory maintained by both Williamson and Hall finds no support in these chapters, as just a few examples will make clear. In fact, the theory encounters an immediate, insurmountable problem in the opening verses of chapter nine, namely, Paul's somber, heartbroken attitude regarding his Jewish brethren: "I have great sorrow and unceasing anguish in my heart. For I wish that I myself were cursed and cut off from Christ for the sake of my brothers, those of my own race, the people of Israel" (9:2–4). While it is true that Paul does not specifically state that Jewish unbelief in Jesus is the cause of his anguish, Heikki Raisanen rightly remarks that "no other reason makes sense." If it were only a matter of the Jews' failure to understand that God had decided to include Gentiles in his salvific intentions (so Hall), then Paul's deep anguish seems hard to explain.⁷⁶ Why would Paul be willing to abandon his own salvation because of a mere theological misunderstanding on the part of his fellow Jews? John Piper notes that Paul's willingness to sacrifice himself must mean that his unbelieving brothers are "in a plight as serious as the one he is willing to enter for their sake."⁷⁷ Raisanen bluntly declares that Paul's attitude here

75. Ibid., 139.
76. Raisanen, "Paul, God, and Israel," 180.
77. Piper, *The Justification of God*, 29.

"presupposes that his kinsmen are for the moment outside the sphere of salvation."[78]

If Paul maintains this attitude toward Jews who have not received Christ, then clearly Paul does not consider the law to be sufficient for salvation, contrary to both Williamson and Hall. Paul makes this point in 9:30–32, where he contrasts Gentiles, who find righteousness through faith, with Jews who cling to the law and fail to find it. Paul agonizes over non-Christian Jews because he believes the law cannot do for them what the redemptive power of the gospel can. As Charles Talbert declares, "human nature is assumed by Paul to be in bondage to sin, a bondage from which only God can deliver one. Humans are, as a result of their sin, faithless in any relation [including a Torah-observance relation!] with God, a faithlessness from which only God can deliver."[79]

Faced with such evidence, Williamson can only designate as "inauthentically Christian" those passages in Scripture that demand that Jews respond to Christ. Hall, on the other hand, is forced to develop a radical reinterpretation of the Pauline gospel that owes far more to his desire to develop an acceptable post-Holocaust theology than to a fair assessment of Paul's teaching.

If Williamson and Hall's position does not adequately address what Paul teaches concerning Jewish salvation, what of Barth's view that the Jews, *en masse*, will be saved at some moment in the eschatological future?[80] Barth surely cannot claim Paul's support for his view. There is near-unanimous consent among scholars that Paul did not think salvation was guaranteed for all Jews by virtue of their ethnic origin.[81] Paul makes this quite clear in Rom 9:6–9. In fact, Paul broke from the traditional Jewish understanding of his day, which maintained that all Jews were destined for salvation on the basis of birth.[82] Barth's position that salvation is something all Jews will arrive at *necessarily*, by divine *fiat*, is at odds with the struggle Paul evinces

78. Raisanen, "Paul, God, and Israel," 180.
79. Talbert, "Paul on the Covenant," 304.
80. While Barth never explicitly states that he believes every person of Jewish descent will be saved, this seems to be his meaning in, for example, *Church Dogmatics* II.2, 238–39.
81. Hvalvik, " 'Sonderweg' for Israel," 100.
82. Talbert, "Paul on the Covenant" 304.

in Rom 9–11. Paul believes the Jews, God's chosen people, have, for the most part, become enemies of the gospel.

This apparent contradiction in Paul can be best explained by Jocz's position that there are really two types of election described in Romans: the Jewish community is elect in terms of *revelation*, while individual Jews (and Gentiles) are elect in terms of *salvation*. Admittedly, there is a tension between these two themes that Paul never resolves completely,[83] but Jocz's theory goes a good part of the way toward relieving it. His belief in the two types of election enables him to fully affirm a passage like Rom 9:4, which calls the Jews the recipients of the covenants, the law, and the promises of God. It also allows him to take seriously the Pauline doctrine of salvation through Christ alone, which shows no partiality toward Jews (e.g. Rom 10:12).

There is a problem with Jocz's understanding of the duality of election, however. It seems to work well only if one's salvation depends *solely* on one's personal response to Christ. But in Rom 9–11, there is clearly more than human freewill involved; the thorny issue of predestination throws a great theological wrench into Jocz's understanding of Paul's teaching. John Piper rightly points out that in Rom 9, membership among Israel's elect is based *only* on the electing will of God, not on the actions of the individual.[84] In fact, Piper makes the case that it is precisely by invoking the doctrine of predestination that Paul can be confident that God's promises have not failed, despite the contrary response of most Jews to the gospel.[85] In chapter 11, the predestinarian overtones are even stronger. Paul says that God himself is responsible for "hardening" Jews against Christ (11:25). Jocz's position has little room for such divine hardening: Jewish unbelief for him is a matter of sinful, *human* rejection of God.

Karl Barth's position, on the other hand, is much more amenable to the predestinarian currents in Paul's thought. For Barth, God is in control of the Jewish rejection of Jesus, and ultimately it is God's responsibility to resolve the problem of the people who have rejected their own Messiah. At the end of chapter 11, one gets

83. Johnson, E., "Jews and Christians," 119.
84. Piper, *The Justification of God*, 202.
85. Ibid., 202.

the impression that Paul, too, assigns final responsibility for human salvation to God: "For God has bound all men over to disobedience so that he may have mercy on them all" (11:32). Elizabeth Johnson agrees, concluding that the matter of Jewish salvation is "God's problem, and Paul is willing to let God solve it."[86]

Despite the strong predestinarian elements in chapters 9 and 11, it would be wrong to assume that it is the sole basis of Paul's argument. For in chapter 10, faith in contrast to works-righteousness, not divine election, is Paul's criterion for determining salvation.[87] It has been said that chapter 9 looks at the matter of Jewish salvation from *God's* vantage point, while chapter 10 looks at it from *Israel's* point of view.[88] Even Piper, despite his insistence that Paul's approach to the Jewish problem is thoroughly predestinarian, still believes there is more to Paul's position than predestination alone. He warns against succumbing to "the naïve and usually polemical suggestions" that prayer and evangelism are pointless.[89] Barth's theology of Israel, followed to its logical conclusion, would inevitably fall prey to such dangers. There is no mistaking Paul's message in Rom 9–11, as well as his other writings, as inextricably bound up with preaching and missionary activity.[90] Paul asks in Rom 10:14, "how can they hear without someone preaching to them?" If Jewish salvation is *entirely* in the hands of God, as Barth claims, Paul's language here would make little sense.

Obviously, Barth's stress only on God's role in Jewish salvation is not sufficient. It makes no allowance for the importance of personal response to the gospel, which Paul insists is necessary for salvation (10:9–13, 11:20, 23). Still, in Rom 9–11, Paul seems to be saying that God *initiates* one's response to Christ.[91] Therefore Paul's teaching on predestination should humble us, moving us to recognize that we have no choice but to cast ourselves upon God's mercy.[92]

86. Johnson, E., "Jews and Christians," 120.
87. Watson, *Paul, Judaism and the Gentiles,* 164–65.
88. Heil, *Romans—Paul's Letter of Hope,* 70.
89. Piper, *The Justification of God,* 205.
90. Barrett, *Reading Through Romans,* 62–63.
91. Heil, *Romans—Paul's Letter of Hope,* 77.
92. Piper, *The Justification of God,* 205.

Nowhere is God's mercy more apparent than in the Savior whom Paul urges everyone, Jew and Gentile alike, to confess.

Even Jocz is compelled to write, regarding the interplay between individual response to the gospel and God's electing grace, "even man's 'Yes' can only be a humble 'Yes,' a sponsored 'Yes,' prompted and encouraged by the Holy Spirit of God."[93] And although Jocz may make this admission somewhat grudgingly, his position is preferable to Barth's, since it allows for the priority of God's electing will, while at the same time preserving the importance of personal response. Thus can Paul in chapter 11 speak of Israel's rejection of Christ as both divine hardening (11:25) and a lack of Jewish faith (11:20)? If Rom 9–11 is indeed the clearest New Testament statement regarding the matter of Jewish salvation, then surely Jocz's position is superior to those of Williamson, Hall, and Barth, for Jocz's theology is faithful to the teaching of Christianity's greatest apostle.

Christians should follow Paul's teaching in Romans honestly. They should, along with Williamson and Hall, repudiate the sin of anti-Semitism. They must affirm, with Williamson and Hall (and Paul!), that the Jews are and remain God's special people. Let Christians also recognize, along with Barth, that the "hardening" of the Jews is God's mysterious work; it certainly should not lead Christians to believe that they are in any way "spiritually superior" to Jews. After all, it is because of this hardening that the gospel became available to Gentiles (11:25). Christians are, as Williamson puts it, "guests in the house of Israel." Christians can only stand in puzzlement—and gratitude—at the inscrutable will of God. But Christians must also insist, along with Jocz, that Jesus Christ is Messiah for all, Gentile and Jew, and that personal response to him is essential for receiving the mercy God intends for his elect. Even the demonic evil of the Holocaust does not alter this.

---

93. Jocz, *A Theology of Election*, 146.

9

Should the Holocaust Force Us to Rethink Our View of God and Evil?

BY ALL accounts, the Holocaust was a nearly unimaginable example of human depravity that caused an unimaginable amount of human suffering. The so-called problem of evil, which had vexed theists for so long, was perhaps never as startlingly apparent as it was in the gas chambers and the ovens of the Nazi death-camps. Ever since that horrendous event, many Jews have found it impossible to hold onto a faith that, for them, vanished in the ovens of Auschwitz. This position is exemplified in the fiction of Holocaust survivor, Elie Wiesel. The following lines from his short autobiographical novel well capture the spirit of much contemporary Jewish thought, both popular and scholarly, regarding the Holocaust. Wiesel describes his reaction to the pious prayers of his fellow inmates in the death-camps:

> ... why should I bless Him [God]? ... Because He had had thousands of children burned in His pits? Because He kept the crematories working night and day, on Sundays and feast days? Because in His great might He had created Auschwitz, Birkenau, Buna and so many factories of death? How could I say to Him: "Blessed art Thou, Eternal, Master of the Universe, Who chose us from among the races to be tortured day and night, to see our fathers, our mothers, our brothers end in the crematory?

Should the Holocaust Force Us to Rethink Our View of God and Evil?

Praised be thy Holy Name, Thou Who hast chosen us to be butchered on Thine altar?"[1]

Many Christian thinkers have followed suit, and, after reflecting upon the Holocaust, are prepared to recast essential Christian doctrines in response to the horrors of the death-camps. I hope to address Jews and Christians who hold such views because they feel compelled to do so, in light of the tragedy of the Holocaust. My contention is that the real problem at hand is not the Holocaust *per se*, but rather the apparently pointless evil that falls on humanity in general. I aim to show that such Holocaust-inspired revisionist theology is not only unfaithful to Scripture, but especially fails to address adequately the real problem at the heart of the Holocaust, as well as many other human tragedies. That problem is the seemingly random evil that plagues humanity in a world that, according to Scripture, was created by an all-loving, omnipotent God. Unless we allow, as does the author of the book of Job, that evil ultimately is an impenetrable mystery, which must be accepted in humble faith, no revisionist theology of human suffering is satisfactory.

Long before the Holocaust, Christian (and non-Christian) thinkers anticipated the themes that run through much of post-Holocaust Jewish theology. This of course reinforces my position that it is the *general* problem of evil, not the *specific* example that the world witnessed in the Holocaust, that is at the root of the problem. One need only think of Dostoyevsky's *Brothers Karamozov*. In it, the atheist Ivan, does not reject God because he finds God's existence implausible, as would a Hume, who rejects God on philosophical grounds, or a modern-day evolutionary reductionist, who simply sees no need for an imagined deity when science alone can account for all things in our universe. No, Ivan can accept the idea of God's existence, but that existence is not compatible with the *world* God has made. He tells his brother Aloysha, "It's not that I don't accept God, you must understand, it's the world created by Him I don't and cannot accept."[2] It is the world with all its apparent needless suffering, especially the suffering of young children, which causes Ivan to reject the Christianity of his brother Aloysha. He goes on to recount

---

1. Wiesel, *Night*, 64.
2. Dostoyevsky, *The Brothers Karamozov*, 279.

atrocities committed by Turks in Bulgaria, who toss "babies up in the air and [catch] them on the points of their bayonets before their mothers' eyes."³ Ivan understands that adults are sinful, and he is able to accept a God who punishes them for their sins, but such atrocities committed against those who have not yet had time to earn the title "sinner" are impossible to reconcile with his Christian brother's idea of a loving God. Ivan's solution to the dilemma is, of course, atheism, but it is not really a solution at all, at least not for the Jew or Christian who believes in an omnipotent God and is struggling to reconcile that belief with human suffering. (Even for Ivan, atheism is no real solution, for it indirectly brings about the murder of Ivan's father at the hands of Ivan's half-brother, Smerdyakov, who uses Ivan's radical notions as justification for his crime.)

When we turn to the theological realm, we find a much different view of the relationship between God and evil in the classic theodicy of John Hick, *Evil and the God of Love*. After surveying traditional explanations of evil vis-à-vis God as espoused by such representative thinkers as Augustine and Calvin, Hick finds them unacceptable. Again, it is the awful reality of evil, the same stumbling block that prevented Ivan from accepting the "God of Love" his brother so firmly trusted. "The enigma of evil presents so massive and direct a threat to our faith that we are bound to seek within the resources of Christian thought for ways, if not of resolving it, at least of rendering it bearable by the Christian conscience."⁴ Hick rejects the "Augustinian" theodicy (which places the blame for evil on Satan and/or fallen man) and instead offers an "Irenaean" theodicy that he refers to as "soul-building." Basically, Hick's premise is that God allows evil in order that his creatures may develop moral and spiritual strength by being tested by life's hardships. Of course, this theodicy fails to take into account all of the suffering that appears to serve no useful "soul-building" purpose. Suffering often destroys, rather than builds up, its victim, and those closest to him or her.⁵ In addition,

---

3. Ibid., 283.
4. Hick, *Evil and the God of Love*, ix.
5. Hick, of course, understands this, but believes that even "destructive" suffering will eventually be replaced by "positive" suffering "in other spheres beyond this world," so that such an individual can reach the "perfection intended for him by God" (*Christianity at the Center*, 91).

it need hardly be mentioned that Hick's position finds little support in the Hebrew or Christian Scriptures, so it is little wonder that his theodicy has not found more support among traditional Jews or Christians.[6] That we are perfected and "made ready" for heaven via the soul-building process, rather than through the cross of Christ, is enough to render Hick's theodicy untenable to biblically-oriented Christians.

Current theistic treatments of suffering have been somewhat more realistic than Hick's, for they take into account the fact that suffering often serves no discernible purpose. For example, Wykstra has proposed what he calls the "Parent Argument" to explain the existence of evil, writing that "our discerning most of God's purposes [when He permits evil to occur] are [sic] about as likely as the infant's discerning most of the parent's purposes [when the parent does things which seem inexplicably cruel to the child, even though they are for the child's benefit]."[7] Wyskstra goes on to state that "if our universe is created by God it is expectable that it would be deep; this is of course reason to think that if there are God-purposed goods, they would often be beyond our ken."[8] Alston writes in a similar vein when he argues that God may have a myriad of reasons for permitting evil occurrences that seem pointless to us: "[p]erhaps, unbeknownst to us . . . suffering is necessary, in ways we cannot grasp, for some outweighing good of a sort with which we are familiar, e.g., supreme fulfillment of one's deepest nature. Or perhaps it is necessary for the realization of a good of which we as yet have no conception."[9] Of course, the objections to the type of theodicy Wykstra and Alston advance are many. The thoughtful theist will surely wonder why the omnipotent God of the Bible cannot bring about the good he desires without permitting evil at all, or at least without permitting *so much*

---

6. This is not to say that the Bible sees no value in suffering. On the contrary, the apostle Paul often speaks of the necessity, even the positive quality of suffering (i.e. Rom 5:3–4, 2 Cor 1:5–7). But suffering, apart from Christ's work on the cross, is never presented as the means whereby Christians find salvation. This is the primary weakness of Hick's theodicy from a biblically-based Christian viewpoint.

7. Wykstra, "Rowe's Noseeum Argument from Evil", 129.

8. Ibid., 140.

9. Alston, "The Inductive Argument from Evil," 109.

evil. And here, Ivan Karamazov again comes to mind, for what good can possibly result from the torture and murder of children? True enough, the apostle Paul's well-known statement, that God works all things together for good for those who love him, might be marshaled in defense of the writers' position. But this one statement is not detailed enough to ground a theodicy upon, and Scripture does not lend anything like unequivocal support to the idea that suffering *always* produces benefits in the long run. Thus the anguished cry of the psalmists, who ask why God permits suffering and oppression to continue. Therefore, a biblical theist (not to mention an atheist!) certainly is entitled to find this view less than satisfying, especially when confronted with evil in his or her own life. God may indeed use suffering to bring about good, but from our finite vantage point, this must forever remain speculation, not an explanation, for the evil we encounter in the world.

Clearly, the problem of evil that was so vividly made manifest in the Holocaust is not a new problem. It is an age-old problem: why does God allow innocent people to suffer at the hands of evil men, or at the whim of a seemingly indifferent world? In the case of the Holocaust, this puzzle was all the more baffling since the victims were God's chosen people, while the perpetrators were devilish madmen who committed their crimes under the aegis of a perverted Christian cross, the Nazi swastika. As early as the mid-sixties, the Holocaust was already becoming the pivotal event in Jewish history in regards to how Jews should view God. Rabbi Richard Rubenstein could already make the following statement: "We stand in a cold, silent, unfeeling cosmos, unaided by any purposeful power beyond our own resources. After Auschwitz, what else can a Jew say about God?"[10] Rubenstein expressed alarm that so many of his fellow Jewish theologians had not realized that the event of Auschwitz had forever altered, indeed destroyed, the faith of the Jews which for 4,000 years had sustained them through untold persecutions and suffering: "How can Jews believe in an omnipotent, beneficent God after Auschwitz?"[11] Traditional Jewish theology had often sought to explain Jewish sufferings in light of the wrath of a holy and just God who was punishing his rebellious people for their sins. To view the

10. Rubenstein, *After Auschwitz*, 152.
11. Ibid., 153.

Holocaust as yet another in a series of catastrophes imposed upon the hapless Jews by their God is "too obscene" for Rubenstein to accept.[12]

But if Rubenstein had cause to wonder why more Jewish theologians had not come to view Auschwitz in the same way he did, the tide of opinion has drastically changed. Today, of course, it is commonplace for Jewish theologians to redefine God, as well as what it means to be Jewish, in light of the Holocaust. During a four-day symposium on Jewish-Christian relations in New York City, Irving Greenberg said of the Holocaust that "[t]he cruelty and the killing raise the question whether even those who believe after such an event dare talk about God who loves and cares without making a mockery of those who suffered."[13] Greenberg believes that it is the scope, the sheer magnitude of the evil that the Holocaust manifested, that forces theists to re-examine their traditional view of God. In the Holocaust, "Limits were broken, restraints shattered, that will never be recovered, and henceforth mankind must live with the dread of a world in which models for unlimited evil exist."[14]

But it is not only Jewish theologians who now think this way. Christian thinkers, especially those engaged in the Jewish-Christian dialogue, have also adopted the Holocaust as the focal point for meaningful theological reflection. Clark Williamson is a Christian representative of this line of thought. And although he does not address the problem of evil *per se*, he is typical of many Christian thinkers for whom the Holocaust demands great theological change. He has written on the subject on anti-Semitism for many years, and treats the subject of Christian anti-Semitism, and the Jewish-Christian encounter in general, in his book, *A Guest in the House of Israel: Post-Holocaust Church Theology*. The very name of the work implies that Christian theology vis-à-vis Judaism must take on a new face in a post-Holocaust world. Williamson writes that, "We have stipulated one set of rules for doing Christian theology after Auschwitz: that we will beware any theological statement made after the *Shoah* [Holocaust] that is unchanged from how it was made

---

12. Ibid.
13. Greenberg, "Cloud of Smoke," 14.
14. Ibid., 14.

before [the *Shoah*]."[15] Williamson is not just talking about Jewish theological statements regarding Jewish views of God. Christian theology, too, must be radically altered to take into account the events of the Holocaust. For Williamson, the Holocaust was an event of such awful magnitude that even the most fundamental doctrines of the Christian faith (including the messiahship of Christ) must be rethought and, if need be, radically reinterpreted. Part of the reason for this is a certain amount of Christian complicity in the Holocaust: two millennia of Christian anti-Semitism, while not causing the Holocaust directly, certainly helped pave the way for that tragic event. But it is the Holocaust *itself*, and the sheer magnitude of the suffering it caused, that forces Williamson to radically reinterpret Christian dogma. Williamson's desire to combat anti-Semitism is laudable. His recognition of the Christian complicity in anti-Semitism is a hard truth of which all Christians must be made aware. But his willingness to sacrifice the essentials of the Christian faith in response to the evil that occurred in the Nazi death camps cannot be accepted by Christians for whom the New Testament still retains normative authority. Scripture, not experience (horrendous though that experience may be), must be the Christian's guide on matters of doctrine.

I wish in no way to underestimate the horror of the Holocaust. It was, without a doubt, one of the most demonic expressions of human evil the world has yet witnessed. As a Christian, it is all the more disturbing for me when I realize that the Nazis perpetrated their crimes in "Christian" Germany, and that the rest of the "Christian" world basically ignored what was happening in Germany until it was too uncomfortable to do otherwise. In fact, the Holocaust was, in some ways, the tragic culmination of centuries of Christian anti-Semitism, as Williamson's book correctly points out.

What I do want to suggest is that the Holocaust, while certainly one of the most appalling examples of evil yet seen, is really no different, in terms of human suffering, from many other great tragedies that have befallen humanity. For example, one need only think of the Black Death, which killed one-third of Europe's population in the Middle Ages, or the religious wars which ravaged the continent in the years following the Reformation. The sheer loss of life in both of these catastrophes is certainly comparable with the loss of life in

15. Williamson, *House of Israel*, 20.

the Holocaust. More current examples include the Taiping Rebellion of the 1850s that killed 20 million, or Stalin's purges that in one decade alone (1929–1939) also destroyed as many as 20 million lives. The Chinese civil war which raged in the 1930s and 40s consumed somewhere between 34 and 62 million lives.[16]

And, lest anyone object that these tragedies concerned the Gentile world, whereas the Holocaust was an unprecedented example of *Jewish* suffering, a quick review of the long, sad history of the Jewish people suggests otherwise. Paul Tillich once remarked that the Holocaust (Hebrew *Shoah*, or "destructive storm") "is only one storm in the whole history of Jewish life. You must teach it as part of the other persecutions: the Inquisition, the Middle Ages—they are all part of the story."[17] The "story," of course, began long before the Inquisition or the Middle Ages; the Hebrew Bible itself is ample witness to the tragic history of Jewish sufferings. Karl Barth notes that the tribulations of the Jews are "described by almost every book of the Old Testament."[18] Of course, neither Tillich nor Barth had any desire to underplay the sufferings caused by the Holocaust; they merely pointed out that persecution and suffering have always been at the core of Jewish existence, and that the Holocaust needs to be seen within that context, rather than as an aberration with no antecedents in Jewish history.

A brief examination of some statistics from Jewish history may help to put the Holocaust in its proper historical perspective. For example, the Assyrian Conquests (734–701 BC), while not as costly as the Holocaust in terms of the actual number of Jews killed, nevertheless were "nearly as demographically repercussive in percentage terms [that is, Jews killed and/or uprooted from their land] as the Sho-ah."[19] A similar case can be made for The Babylonian Conquest

---

16. Katz, *The Holocaust in Historical Context*, 66–67.

17. Quoted in Friedlander, "Final Conversation with Paul Tillich."

18. Barth, *Dogmatics in Outline*, 78. Barth is often criticized for attributing Jewish suffering to their unfaithfulness to God, but here he is only following in the footsteps of the Jewish prophets of Scripture, who constantly berate their fellow Jews for their lack of faith and predict dire consequences if they do not repent.

19. Katz, *The Holocaust in Historical Context*, 68–73.

(59–86 BC).[20] When we come to the Jewish revolt against Rome, which culminated in the destruction of Jerusalem in 70 AD, the actual number of Jews killed is far higher, which Roman historian Tacitus numbers at 600,000, while Jewish historian Josephus places the number at 1.1 million.[21] Of course, the sheer number of Jews who perished in the Holocaust was higher than in any of these earlier tragedies, but is there really any meaningful qualitative difference between the one million Jewish victims of Rome and the six million Jews who died in the Holocaust? Numbers alone cannot establish the Holocaust as unique in the history of Jewish tragedy.[22] Are we going to affirm that God is just if he allows six innocent persons to die, but condemn him as unjust (and revise our theology accordingly) if he permits six, sixty, or six million to perish?

If none of those events described above led to the abandonment of traditional views of God and evil, why should the Holocaust? It is certainly true that our century has seen a great amount of evil, and the Holocaust, along with the battlefield slaughter of two world wars, is largely responsible for this. But, surely this is not so different from what has occurred in previous centuries. C.S. Lewis, responding to the alleged "new urgency" brought about by modern man's recognition of the riddle of evil, cogently remarks, "*what* new urgency? . . . it is no more urgent for us than for the great majority of monotheists all down the ages. The classic expositions of the doctrine that the world's miseries are compatible with its creation and guidance by a wholly good Being come from Boethius waiting in prison to be beaten to death and from St. Augustine meditating on the sack of Rome."[23] For all the talk of a new theological age being ushered in by the Holocaust, for all those who claim that nothing in theology can ever again be the same after Auschwitz, Lewis's statement that "[t]he present [evil] state of the world is normal"[24] may be of little comfort, but it is clearly the truth.

---

20. Ibid., 73-76.
21. Ibid., 76-77.
22. Ibid., 83–84.
23. Lewis, C.S., "Evil and God," 22.
24. Ibid., 22.

Should the Holocaust Force Us to Rethink Our View of God and Evil?

When one ponders the enigma of evil from a biblical perspective, the book that comes to mind is, of course, Job. For centuries, Job has provided Jews and Christians with, if not an explanation for evil, at least a picture of a world where God is fully in charge, despite evidence that may sometimes seem to imply the contrary. Yet Rabbi Rubenstein has said that "[t]he agony of European Jewry cannot be likened to the testing of Job."[25] He says this because the evil of the German death camps seems so purposeless that to see God's hand in it defies credulity. But cannot the same be said for the case of Job? Contrary to what Rubenstein says, what happened to Job *is* analogous to what happened to six million Jews during World War II. In both instances, people were made to suffer horribly, and in both cases, the point of this suffering is impossible to discern. After Job's troubles have befallen him, God speaks to him from the whirlwind, but what kind of answers does God give? Does he explain why evil and suffering occur? Does he explain why he, as an all-powerful God, allows such things? No. He does, however, impress upon Job the limits of Job's *understanding* of such things. What Job does learn here is that the ways of God are beyond the understanding of men, and that sometimes men and women of faith can only accept, in ignorance and humble piety, the ways of God toward his creatures. Thus, the only "answer" that the author of Job gives to the dilemma of evil is really no answer at all, but rather an admission of the limits of human understanding. After God chastises Job, Job confesses that "I spoke of things I did not understand, things too wonderful for me to know" (42:3), and "I despise myself and repent in dust and ashes" (42:6).

Of course, the case can be made that the sufferings of Job were only the sufferings of one man (and, of course, his children who were killed) and the sufferings of one man, however horrific, cannot be compared to the sufferings of six million. But this is a spurious argument.[26] If God allows one to suffer unjustly, or millions to suffer

---

25. Rubenstein, *After Auschwitz*, 153.

26. This point is well-made by C.S. Lewis in the following quotation, which is not concerned with the Holocaust *per se*, but with the general idea that human suffering is somehow worse when many persons, rather than one, suffer: "[t]here is no such thing as a sum of suffering, for no one suffers it. When we have reached the maximum that a single person can suffer, we have, no doubt,

163

unjustly, the basic problem is the same—an all-loving, all-powerful God who allows what seems to be unmerited suffering. One could also say the despite Job's sufferings, all was made well in the end, for Job was compensated by God for all of the pain and loss he incurred. But is this really true? Can the pain of losing one's children be remedied simply by having more children? And what about the fundamental question of God allowing Job's unwarranted suffering in the first place? And, if we grant that sufferings in the past are overshadowed by blessings to come, then surely many who suffered during the Holocaust have sine been "reimbursed," for many of those who lived through the ordeal are now happily married, have large families, material blessings, etc. Simply put, a purely "rational" God who behaves only in ways that are acceptable and understandable to us is not the God we find described in either the Hebrew or the Christian Scriptures. His ways are not our ways, the Hebrew Scriptures tell us. In the end, the Holocaust, like any instance of evil or suffering that has no apparent good purpose, can dishearten even the most devout among us. But I think a saner, certainly more honest (and certainly more biblical) approach is to simply admit that we do not know why such things happen. Redefinitions of who God is and how he operates do nothing to solve the problem. Our theology must be based on revelation, not speculation or experience.

Interestingly enough, the criterion of human *experience* (rather than divine revelation), which so many theologians have used as the basis for reassessing their understanding of God and evil in the wake of the Holocaust, does not seem to apply in the same way to the establishment of the state of Israel in the late 1940s. While numerous theologians have revised their theology due to the Shoah, there seems to be far less of a corresponding appreciation of the benevolence of God as manifested in the creation of the modern Jewish state. But the revisionists are here confronted with a problem: if human experience is to determine what we believe about God, then surely the creation of a Jewish homeland after 2,000 years of Jewish homelessness and persecution must be taken more seriously. Add to this the fact that Israel has repelled every military attack leveled against it, often with

---

reached something very horrible, but we have reached all the suffering there ever can be in the universe. The addition of a million fellow-sufferers adds no more pain" (*The Problem of Pain*, 116).

Should the Holocaust Force Us to Rethink Our View of God and Evil?

near-miraculous efficiency against overwhelming odds. These events, it seems to me, are just as momentous as the Holocaust, yet they have not resulted in the same kind of sea-change in the theological thinking as has the Holocaust.

In the New Testament, Paul tells us that God works all things together for good for those who love him; the Scriptures seem to affirm in several places that God is in control of all that occurs, be it good or evil.[27] Just how this can be squared with the traditional doctrines of God's omnipotence and omnibenevolence cannot always be understood, but only accepted in the humble faith that is the very essence of biblical theism. A recent article rightly points out that, to be a biblical theist, is to accept the mystery of suffering: "if theism is true we would expect that there would be inscrutable evil. Indeed, a little reflection shows there is no reason to think we could so much as grasp God's plans here, even if he proposed to divulge them to us."[28] It is faith in the face of such inscrutable evil that has sustained the Jewish people through 4,000 years of assorted tragedies, and it is this faith that still sustains many of them, despite the horrors of the Shoah. In fact, the history of Jewish faith in their God has been nothing short of amazing. The Jews collectively have never abandoned their faith in the God of Scripture, despite the tragedies of 4,000 years of history. The amazing perseverance of this small group of people, despite the evil machinations of some of history's greatest powers, has, of course, been pointed out before, and it led Barth to declare this Jewish tenac-

---

27. Dominant since the time of Augustine, this traditional Christian view concerning evil has recently been challenged by Gregory Boyd, in *God at War*. Boyd maintains that the viewpoint of Scripture, as well as of the early church fathers, is that all evil in the world can ultimately be attributed to Satan and the realm of the demonic. Thus, evil forms no part of God's "grand design" for the universe. Rather, evil is something God is actively combating. Boyd's book is very persuasive at points, especially when he presents his case for what he terms the "warfare worldview" of Scripture (i.e., God, the cause of all good, vs. Satan, the cause of all evil). Modern Christians need to be reminded that this worldview is indeed part of the Bible, and that it is especially prevalent in the New Testament, where Christ is often presented as the destroyer of the devil's works. However, for our purposes here, Boyd's thesis does not alter the fundamental question of why God permits such appalling evil. Surely God is more powerful than Satan, and thus could put an end to him, and his evil deeds, at any time. Surely God could have at least "temporarily restrained" him to prevent the Holocaust!

28. Plantinga, "Epistemic Probability and Evil," 76.

ity as the *one* sure proof of God's existence. Barth liked to quote a conversation between Frederick the Great and his personal physician, Zimmermann: " 'Zimmermann, can you name me a single proof of the existence of God?' And Zimmermann replied, 'Your majesty, the Jews!' "[29] These words could have just as easily been uttered after, rather than before, the Holocaust occurred.

Earlier I quoted Rabbi Rubenstein: "We stand in a cold, silent, unfeeling cosmos, unaided by any purposeful power beyond our own resources. After Auschwitz, what else can a Jew say about God?"[30] But surely this statement could have been made, just as appropriately, after the Assyrian or the Babylonian Conquests, or after the Romans destroyed Jerusalem in 70 AD. It could have been made, just as appropriately, when any terrible tragedy befalls any one of us in our daily lives. And perhaps the best answer to this question, whenever it be asked, is that given by Job: "Though he slay me, yet will I hope in him" (13:15). This was Job's faith as he suffered his unwarranted afflictions, and it has been the faith of untold numbers of Jews and Christians through the ages, whether facing religious persecution or facing the general sorrow and suffering that comes upon us all at one point or another. The answer God gives from the whirlwind may not be especially satisfactory, especially when we are faced with horrible evil and suffering which seem entirely pointless. But this has always been a problem for the religious Jew and Christian (indeed, it has always been the strongest weapon in the atheist's arsenal). But it is intellectually dishonest to act as though this problem was not just as intractable millennia before the Holocaust occurred, and that it would not be just as vexing had the Holocaust never happened.

---

29. Barth, *Dogmatics in Outline*, 75.
30. Rubenstein, *After Auschwitz*, 152.

10

Are We Asking the Wrong Questions about the *Shoah*? Eliezer Berkovits as Post-Holocaust Jewish Apologist

THE JEWISH theological reflection upon the Holocaust, which began in the 1960s, has become paradigmatic for understanding the religious significance of that awful event. The works of writers like Elie Wiesel, Richard Rubenstein, and Irving Greenberg, although differing on various points, have helped to create what could almost be termed an "orthodox" view of the Holocaust. This view is centered on the idea that the Holocaust was utterly unique in terms of Jewish suffering. So unique was this evil that concepts that had always been central to Judaism, such as God, the covenant, and the Jews as the chosen people, are now seriously questioned, if not jettisoned altogether. The one major Jewish thinker who stands apart from this revisionist trend is Eliezer Berkovits. Berkovits admits the horror of the Holocaust, and is in full sympathy with those who lived through it and found that they could no longer affirm their Jewish faith. However, he offers an alternative view of the Holocaust, one that sees the suffering of the Jews at Nazi hands as a continuation of the oppression Jews have always suffered in the world. Because he sees the *Shoah* as quantitatively, but not qualitatively, different than other Jewish disasters, he is able to maintain faith in the God of Judaism; he is able to insist that the covenant is still in force; and he can still see the Jews as a chosen vessel who have a divine purpose to fulfill in history. This chapter will examine how Berkovits is able to do this, and how he, therefore, presents a powerful post-holocaust apologetic for traditional Jewish faith.

By all accounts, the Holocaust was an event of horrific proportions. The estimates that six million Jews were exterminated (not to mention thousands of gypsies, Slavs, and homosexuals) far exceed the death toll for any other single event in history. That so many Jews could be slaughtered within the span of just a few years boggles the mind, and prompts the question: "where was God?" Why did God allow such a huge number of people to be killed? For the religious Jew, the question is all the more poignant, since Jews had always seen themselves as occupying a special place in the divine plan. Elie Wiesel's classic survivor's account of his death-camp experiences captures the faith-shattering emotions engendered by the so-called final solution:

> ... why should I bless Him [God]? In every fiber I rebelled. Because He had had thousands of children burned in His pits? Because He kept the crematories working night and day, on Sundays and feast days? Because in His great might He had created Auschwitz, Birkenau, Buna, and so many factories of death? How could I say to Him: "Blessed art Thou, Eternal, Master of the Universe, Who chose us from among the races to be tortured day and night, to see our fathers, our mothers, our brothers, end in the crematory? Praised by Thy Holy Name, Thou Who hast chosen us to be butchered on Thine altar?"[1]

Wiesel here captures not only the disgust of a human being who is witnessing unimaginable cruelty, but also the pain of a once-devout Jew who can no longer maintain his pre-Holocaust faith. Undoubtedly, Wiesel speaks for a diversity of Jews who find faith difficult, perhaps impossible, after Auschwitz; those who experienced the camps firsthand; those who are not survivors, but who lost relatives there; and those who are too young to have experienced personal loss, yet who still see the Shoah as a theological hurdle to faith that they cannot surmount. Richard Rubenstein, though not a survivor, has given theological support to the ideas that Wiesel expresses in *Night*. Rubenstein echoes Wiesel's sentiments when he

---

1. Wiesel, *Night*, 64.

remarks that the Holocaust has taught us that we "stand in a cold, silent, unfeeling, cosmos, unaided by any purposeful power beyond our own resources. After Auschwitz, what else can a Jew say about God?"[2] Irving Greenberg, in a famous statement, offers perhaps the most challenging objection to all those who think that Jewish (and Christian) thinkers can carry on in a post-Holocaust world in the same theological vein as before the Jewish slaughter. He writes that no "statement, theological or otherwise, should be made that would not be credible in the presence of the burning children."[3] And it is not just Jewish thinkers who see the Shoah as forever altering religious belief. Consider a prominent Christian thinker's musings on the Holocaust, and how similar they are to Greenberg's: "we have stipulated one set of rules for doing Christian theology after Auschwitz: that we will beware any theological statement made after the *Shoah* that is unchanged from how it was made before [the *Shoah*]."[4]

Berkovits is in no way critical of this type of reaction to the Shoah, especially on the part of survivors. In fact, He shows great deference to their sufferings, and makes the salient point that only the survivors can speak about loss of faith after the Holocaust with any degree of credibility. "They [the survivors] who lost their faith there may well turn to our radical theologians [Berkovits obviously has those in the Rubenstein camp in mind here], saying: 'How dare you speak about loss of faith, what do you know about losing faith, you who have never known what we have known, who never experienced what we have experienced?' "[5] But Berkovits is equally critical of non-survivors who all too easily maintain their post-Holocaust faith, thereby insulting the "holy disbelief" of those whose trust in God was forever shattered: "In the presence of the holy faith of the crematoria, the ready faith of those who were not there, is vulgarity."[6] Thus, Berkovits knows that his own faith, as a non-survivor, can never be of the same intensity as that of a survivor. And he does not dare to consider criticizing the loss of faith by those who survived Auschwitz.

2. Rubenstein, *After Auschwitz*, 152.
3. Greenberg, "Cloud of Smoke," 23.
4. Williamson, *House of Israel*, 20.
5. Berkovits, *Faith After the Holocaust*, 5.
6. Ibid., 5.

PART THREE: CHRISTIANITY, JUDAISM, AND THE HOLOCAUST

Despite the theologically precarious position he is in as a non-survivor, Berkovits is intent on attempting to interpret the Holocaust in a way that will still make sense from a traditional Jewish faith perspective. The first step in his apologetic task is to place the Holocaust in its proper historical light. Whereas most Jewish post-Holocaust theologians see the Shoah as both quantitatively *and* qualitatively unique, Berkovits does not. He rightly sees that the problem of the Holocaust is really a manifestation of that age-old dilemma, the problem of evil. This problem has been especially acute for Jewish thinkers, since the Jews have experienced tragedy out of all proportion to their small numbers. And, when seen in this context, one can affirm with Berkovits that "we have had innumerable Auschwitzes: There [sic] were the two destructions of the Temple of Jerusalem and the concomitant dispersions of Israel; there was the destruction of the great Spanish Jewry; there were the massacres during the Crusades and the Black Death; the Chmelnicki massacres and, nearer to our own days, the Petlura pogroms."[7] To help put the Holocaust in the proper context of the history of Jewish suffering, some figures may prove helpful. For instance, the Assyrian Conquests (734–701 BC), while they did not kill as many Jews as did the Holocaust, nevertheless were "nearly as demographically repercussive in percentage terms [that is, Jews killed and/or uprooted from their land] as the Sho'ah."[8] The Babylonian Conquest (597–586 BC) can be seen in a similar vein.[9] If we examine the Jewish revolt against Rome, which ended with the destruction of Jerusalem in 70 AD, the number of Jews killed is a staggering 600,000; Jewish historian Josephus places the number at 1.1 million.[10] When one considers the large numbers of Jewish victims of past atrocities, it is obvious that numbers alone cannot make the Holocaust unique in the history of Jewish suffering.[11]

Berkovits rightly points out that the problem raised by these tragic events is precisely the same one as that raised by the Holocaust,

7. Ibid., 90.
8. Katz, *The Holocaust in Historical Context*, 73. See also pages 68–72.
9. Ibid., 73–76.
10. Ibid., 76–77. Josephus's figures are often called into question, but the fact remains that the fall of Jerusalem undoubtedly involved an agonizingly large amount of Jewish deaths.
11. Ibid., 83–84.

namely, why does God allow innocent suffering? The post-Holocaust theologians have based their case for the uniqueness of the Shoah largely on the sheer volume of its victims. But this is a spurious argument. Berkovits asks, was "the problem of faith in a personal God less serious during the Black Death than it is today because then only half of the half million Jews of Europe perished and not six million as in our days?"[12] Obviously, the Holocaust raises an old question, that of theodicy: how can Jews affirm the existence of an all-loving, all-powerful deity in the face of catastrophic, undeserved suffering? And the question does not become more pronounced simply because the number of victims increases. This holds true for examples of Jewish, as well as non-Jewish, suffering. This point is well-made by C.S. Lewis, who was not addressing Jewish suffering *per se*, but rather the idea that the magnitude of suffering increases exponentially based on the amount of victims: "[t]here is no such thing as a sum of suffering, for no one suffers it. When we have reached the maximum that a single person can suffer, we have, no doubt, reached something very horrible, but we have reached all the suffering there ever can be in the universe. The addition of a million fellow-sufferers adds no more pain."[13]

But was the Holocaust different in *certain* respects from other examples of Jewish suffering? Was this not the first (or at least the most successful) systematic, methodical attempt to wipe out a "race" of human beings? It was, but this can be largely attributed to twentieth-century technology. Hitler was the first anti-Semite in history who had access to the tools that made the mass-destruction of Jews so easy: modern media that spread his anti-Jewish propaganda, poison gas, industrialized crematoria, and an efficient system of trains that facilitated transportation of the victims to the camps. If previous persecutions of Jews did not lack the sinister efficiency of Hitler's final solution, it was only because the means he used were not available until modern times. Had such means been available during the anti-Jewish pogroms of earlier centuries, surely they would have been used, given man's general inhumanity toward his fellows, and his specific hatred of the Jew.

12. Berkovits, *Faith After the Holocaust*, 90.
13. Lewis, C.S., *The Problem of Pain*, 116.

PART THREE: CHRISTIANITY, JUDAISM, AND THE HOLOCAUST

But perhaps the Holocaust is unique from the point of view of the Nazis, and their reasons (or lack thereof) for what they did? Michael L. Morgan, commenting upon Hannah Arendt's treatment of twentieth-century totalitarianism (of which the Nazis were the most glaring example), interprets her as suggesting that the Holocaust could be seen as "the commitment to and verification of unrestricted domination, and this means pointless but total annihilation of people."[14] Commenting upon Arendt's belief that the camps were the first example of "radical evil," Morgan writes that the actions of the Nazis were often "beyond understanding and explanation; that is, they cannot be explained by reference to the agent's normal motives—greed, anger, lust for power, and so forth. In other words, a particular SS guard did not beat an inmate because he hated him or wanted something from him."[15] But the actions of the Nazis *did* have a purpose. In their warped imaginations, the Jews were the source of Germany's troubles, and by destroying them Germany (and the world) would be saved from their pernicious influence. True enough, the behavior of many of the guards often took on a "routine" quality, thereby exemplifying what Arendt has called the "banality of evil." But this does not mean that the Nazi leaders who were responsible for assigning the guards their wicked tasks did not have a purpose in mind when they formulated the final solution. It is inconceivable that they would have undertaken such a massive program of human extermination had there not been, in their minds, a very good reason for doing so. We certainly have trouble coming to grips with the evil motives behind the Holocaust, but that does not mean that motives did not exist.

If the Holocaust was not the absolutely unique, faith-shattering event that most post-Holocaust thinkers claim that it was, there should be ample evidence among those who experienced the Nazi atrocities that this is so. In fact, a plethora of testimony is available concerning the large number of Jews who kept their faith in the death-camps right until the very end, as Berkovits has shown. That he is the only major post-Shoah thinker to have produced a book chronicling this is indicative of what seems to be an anti-faith bias inherent in much Jewish Holocaust thought. Berkovits remarks that

14. Morgan, *Beyond Auschwitz*, 15.
15. Ibid., 18.

the "widespread religious life of the Jews under German domination [in the camps] which we are describing in theses pages has been the most neglected subject of the entire Holocaust literature."[16] Berkovits's book contains numerous examples of pious Jews who, despite the impending doom they faced in the camps, still tried to practice their faith as closely as the unfavorable circumstances allowed.[17] As stated above, Berkovits is not so naïve as to think that no Jew lost his or her faith as a result of their experiences in the camps, and he fully understands why this could have happened. To this he assigns the title of "holy disbelief." But Jews have emerged from every other disaster in their long, sad history with their faith more or less in tact, so it is not surprising that many should continue to believe in the God of the covenant even after His silence during the bleak years of the Nazi atrocities. Cases of lost faith have been well documented by numerous writers. Berkovits's book proves that for many Jews in the camps, their faith "actually strengthened them, revived them, and gave them new energies to endure the cruelties of the camp."[18]

A major mistake that many Jewish as well as Christian interpreters of the Holocaust make is to assume that faith is automatically an experiential matter, that it waxes or wanes based upon what one experiences during life. This is certainly true some of the time, but often, "the faith of the questioner often remains unaffected despite the Heaven's silence."[19] This is because the nature of biblical faith is not based upon existential experience, but upon *divine revelation in history*. This is especially true of the Jewish religion. Jewish faith is nothing else if it is not a faith grounded in history. That history concerns the propositional revelation of God to his people. This includes

---

16. Berkovits, *With God in Hell*, 49. It is indicative of the state of post-Holocaust studies that this volume is out of print, while a book like Wiesel's *Night* has not only undergone several printings, but has become standard reading for many high school and college students.

17. Ibid., 3–4. Rabbi Leo Baeck's experience of faith in the camps is described on pages 11–12, where he explains that, during secret religious services, the "faces of these Jews were illuminated by an unearthly radiance, as one was talking to them about matters of the spirit and the eternal questions, about God, about Jews and the world, about the eternity of Israel. I sensed a light in that darkness, the light of the Torah."

18. Ibid., 12.

19. Ibid., 119.

God choosing them to be a holy nation unto himself, and giving objective proof of his existence and concern for his people through historical events like the Exodus and Sinai. Berkovits remarks that throughout "our history we were a people that derived its national identity from its commitment to the transcendental dimension of the covenant with God."[20] Berkovits believes that this covenant, rooted firmly in history, transcends any later faith crisis that may arise out of a particular situation. "Notwithstanding Auschwitz, the life of the patriarchs is still with him [the Jew]; the Exodus did not turn into a mirage; Sinai has not come tumbling down; the prophets have not become charlatans; the return from Babylon has not proved to be a fairy tale."[21] He uses the example of Abraham's near-sacrifice of his son to further draw out the implications of his thinking here. Abraham knew that God was a reality in his life. He knew that God had revealed himself, and that he had displayed his providential care for Abraham. Yet here was this same God asking Abraham to do the most monstrous thing that could be asked of a father, to sacrifice his very son (the son who was a living symbol of the covenant God had made with Abraham!). This demand of God, this inscrutable order that Abraham shed his son's blood is incomprehensible to Abraham; it violates everything he feels as a father, and everything he hopes his God represents. But this confusion does not negate what he already *knows* about God. He knows that God is real, and that there is a covenant between them. Because certain things happened in the past, they cannot be undone by something in the present, however inexplicable it may be. Thus Berkovits pictures Abraham as saying to God: "What You are asking of me is terrible. I do not understand You. You contradict Yourself. But I have known You, my God. You have loved me and I love You. You are breaking Your word to me. What is one to think of You! Yet, I trust You; I trust You."[22] And, Berkovits points out, this trust that Abraham so stalwartly displays is not some type of Kierkegaardian "leap of faith." It is simply "a continuation of the life of the covenant. The very essence of trust consists not in 'leaping,' but in standing firm."[23]

20. Ibid., 149.
21. Berkovits, *Faith After the Holocaust*, 134.
22. Berkovits, *With God in Hell*, 124.
23. Ibid., 124.

Are We Asking the Wrong Questions about the Shoah?

Having said this, Berkovits does not for a moment assume that such covenant faithfulness renders God's purposes easier to comprehend, or to bear. For those who maintained their faith in the Nazi camps, the "monstrosity remained monstrous; the inhumanity remained foul injustice tolerated by God."[24] But the Jew knows he is in a covenant with God. Even if he has not had the privilege of a "personal" revelation from God like Abraham did, he still knows that Abraham had this revelation, and that as one of Abraham's descendants, the revelation is his as well. He "experiences the continuity of the eternal covenant between God and Israel in the continuity of the historic reality of the people of Israel . . . He stands in the Presence at all times together with all the generations of Israel and he hears the Voice in the midst of God's exasperating silences."[25]

At the heart of Berkovits's post-Holocaust apologetic is the *Hester Pamin*, the "Hiding of the Face" of God.[26] This is an essential idea for Berkovits, because in the Holocaust, God did indeed hide his face; Wiesel's boy on the scaffolds did not see the divine countenance as the noose was placed about his neck. Berkovits asserts that not only did God hide during the Holocaust, but has in fact often hidden himself from his covenant people. History, as well as the scriptural record, contains ample proof of this. However, Berkovits has been criticized for making too much of *deus abscondis* in Jewish thought and tradition. In a lengthy treatment of Berkovits, Zachary Braiterman insists that Berkovits places too much emphasis upon the *Hester Pamin* tradition in Judaism, while at the same time sacrificing the Jewish emphasis on the God who intervenes in the affairs of his people. He accuses Berkovits, in both *Faith After the Holocaust* and *With God in Hell,* of rewriting Jewish tradition. In fact, he goes so far as to accuse Berkovits of employing "considerable guile" to create an "antitheodic formulation of faith and covenant [that has more in common with] Rubenstein's negations than with traditional Jewish pieties."[27] This strikes me as a very odd comparison. Rubenstein

24. Ibid., 124–25.
25. Ibid., 125.
26. Berkovits, *Faith After the Holocaust,* 101.
27. Braiterman, *(God) After Auschwitz,* 112–13. Braiterman accuses Berkovits not only of incorrectly interpreting the Hebrew Scriptures on this point, but various Jewish scholarly traditions as well. Due to space constraints and my lack

does not jettison just traditional attempts at theodicy; he abandons *all* traditional Jewish religious thought forms, opting instead for a neo-pagan interpretation of existence. The "god" that he manages to preserve is not the personal God of the Hebrew Bible, but something more akin to Christian theologian Paul Tillich's Ground of Being.[28]

And is the term anti-theodicy really applicable to Berkovits's work? I would suggest that what Berkovitz has done is to attempt a *theodicy* in the traditional sense. That is, he has tried to "justify the ways of God to man," or at least to explain why, from a Jewish perspective, the Shoah does not have to be a faith-ending event for all Jews. One component in this theology is the factor so many theodicists have employed throughout the ages: the freewill of man. The Holocaust, Berkovits points out was, in the final analysis, the demonic, systematic destruction of Jewish lives by men who willingly and without reservation engaged upon their satanic work. There is nothing radical in this. That God has created man with freewill, and that man frequently uses his freewill to cause sorrow and suffering, has been the most common explanation for the existence of evil in the theodicies of most thinkers, Jewish and Christian, down through the ages.[29] So, right from the start, I believe that Braiterman has misstated his case against Berkovits. Berkovits does not come close to advocating the near-nihilism of Rubenstein, and his attempts to explain the Holocaust seem to be more in line with traditional theodicy, rather than anti-theodicy. But what of Braiterman's claim that Berkovits has twisted Jewish texts to suit his own vision of post-Holocaust theology?

Berkovits appeals to the Hebrew Scriptures to find evidence that God has often "hidden his face" during the turbulence of Jewish history. Using examples from the books of Psalms, Jeremiah, and Isaiah, Berkovits finds evidence that he believes suggests that the

---

of expertise with non-biblical Jewish texts, I will only examine the matter as it pertains to the Hebrew Bible.

28. For a good summary of Rubenstein's theological position, see Morgan, *Beyond Auschwitz*, 91–108. It is sometimes difficult to determine just how Rubenstein's position differs from outright atheism.

29. Although Berkovits rightly sees the misuse of human freewill as at the heart of the Holocaust, he also lays a great amount of blame on Christianity, which he believes paved the way for the crimes of the Nazis. More on this point will follow later in the chapter.

Hester Pamin is "a divine attribute, [an] essential feature of God's permanent relation to human existence itself and to the world."[30] Berkovits posits the hiding of the face as an essential attribute of God because human history, so full of suffering and misery, seems to demand it. It takes no great theological acumen to realize this; it is obvious even to a child.[31] That God does not always intervene in his creation is clear from our own experience, as well as from Scripture. Even so great a prophet as Jeremiah could ask, "Why does the way of the wicked prosper? Why do all the faithless live at ease?" (12:1). Berkovits says that Jeremiah raises the question of why God allows the wicked to succeed, whereas Habakkuk raises the question of innocent suffering: "Your eyes are too pure to look on evil; You cannot tolerate wrong. Why then do you tolerate the treacherous? Why are you silent while the wicked swallow up those more righteous than themselves?" (1:13). And Psalm 44 contains the following lines: "Awake, O Lord! Why do you sleep? Rouse yourself! Do not reject us forever. Why do you hide your face and forget our misery and oppression?" (44: 23–24). Based on these verses, Berkovits seems quite justified in rejecting what he calls the Jewish "radical" (i.e., post-Holocaust) theologians who claim that the Shoah has introduced a new aspect of Jewish suffering heretofore unknown: "[t]he men of faith in Israel knew very well of the problem. They experienced it in their own lives on their own bodies. How often did they cry out in their agony over the terrible experience of God's absence!"[32] This point is echoed by C.S. Lewis, who was writing in response to what some twentieth-century theologians took to be the "new urgency" of the problem of evil in modern times: "*what* new urgency? . . . It is no more urgent for us than for the great majority of monotheists all down the ages. The classic expositions of the doctrine that the world's miseries are compatible with its creation and guidance by a wholly good Being come from Boethius waiting in prison to be beaten to death and from St. Augustine meditating on the sack of Rome."[33]

But it is of course the book of Job that provides us with the most glaring example of the hidden God. True enough, the reader

30. Morgan, *Beyond Auschwitz*, 114.
31. Berkovits, *Faith After the Holocaust*, 92.
32. Ibid., 97.
33. Lewis, C.S., "Evil and God," 22.

of the book knows God is not hidden—we see him at work, behind the scenes, giving Satan permission to torment Job. But Job does not see this! As far as Job is concerned, he is suffering unjustly, and there is not a word from God as to why, at least not until the very end of the book. And even then, the answer that God gives Job can easily be seen as less than theologically satisfying. As I have pointed out elsewhere, God's "answer" to Job can only be taken to mean that, ultimately, the question of evil, and why God so often allows it, can only remain an inscrutable riddle.[34] If this is so, why does Braiterman insist that Berkovits has revised Jewish tradition on this point? To his credit, Braiterman admits that some of Berkovits's critics have not grasped the complexity of his thought when they criticize him for not emphasizing more the idea that the God of Scripture is a saving, rather than a hiding, God.[35] And Braiterman is surely right when he suggests that most of the books of Jeremiah and Isaiah are taken up with the issue of Israel's sinfulness, rather than God's hiddenness. And he is probably correct when he insists that Berkovits tends to downplay the judgment upon sinful Israel in these works.[36] Berkovits's reluctance here is understandable, given the fact that he is deeply concerned, as are all post-Holocaust theologians, to avoid even the suggestion that the Holocaust was in some way a just punishment for Jewish sins; the Christian view of the Jews as the "witness people" has wreaked enough havoc without a Jewish theologian making things worse![37]

But I believe Braiterman overstates his case. Berkovits does not have to prove that the hidden God is the overarching theme of Scripture in order for his theodicy to succeed. He only has to show that there are places in the Hebrew Scriptures where God obviously

34. For more on this matter, see my "Should the Holocaust?" 117–28.
35. Braiterman, *(God) After Auschwitz*, 119.
36. Ibid., 128.
37. Here Berkovits breaks with certain ultra-Orthodox Jews who insist on seeing the Holocaust as punishment for Jewish sins. Berkovits rightly points out that it is hard to imagine what possible sin the Jews could have committed that would require them to be slaughtered by the millions. To ascribe the Holocaust to God as a punishment upon Jews is, for Berkovits, "an absolute impossibility . . . a desecration of the Holy Name . . . when we explain the Holocaust as a result of Divine decision we factually describe God in diabolical terms. It is a terrible desecration." Quoted from Shweid, *Wrestling Until Day-Break*, 336.

is absent, and does not intervene to save his people (was not God hiding when the temple fell in 597 BC, and again in 70 AD?). Such examples, coupled with the irrefutable evidence all Jews (Gentiles, too) have of living in a world where things often do not make sense theologically is quite enough to render Berkovits's theodicy of the hidden God viable. In fact, a strong case has been made that, not only were the people of Old Testament times well aware that evil sometimes triumphs over good, but that they often *expected* this to happen. This was due to the mythological framework in which the writers of Hebrew Scripture thought and wrote. For them, the world was a hostile place, one in which God was constantly at war with the powers of chaos: "There was [in Old Testament times] and still is something hostile to God at a cosmic level, infecting the cosmos at a structural level, which he has battled and must continue to battle to establish and preserve his good creation . . . Put in a nutshell, the Old Testament assumes a type of warfare worldview and thus views the very creation and preservation of the earth as something that has to be fought for."[38]

Are the Jews the chosen people of God? If not, then their long history, as recorded in their Scriptures, seems to make little sense. For on virtually every page it is proclaimed: the Lord has chosen them to be a holy people; they alone out of all the nations of the earth has He chosen. If this idea of chosenness is not correct, then the Hebrew Scriptures would seem to make little sense, for they are predicated upon this idea. In fact, a case could be made that they should be rejected as historical and theological fabrication. But, if the Jews are indeed the chosen ones, what precisely does this mean? Many post-Holocaust theologians are understandably uncomfortable with this idea of the Jews as the special people of God. For one reason, because it seems to fly in the face of the Shoah experience; how could God allow His special ones to suffer so much? But, and I think more importantly, because it provides the fodder that Christian anti-Semitism

---

38. Boyd, *God at War*, 92. A large part of Boyd's thesis rests upon the idea that there are demonic forces in the world that God must continually battle. Berkovits probably would not accept this idea, as it is largely influenced by Boyd's Christian approach to Scripture. Still, the fact that the Hebrews saw the world as a hostile, evil-filled environment lends support to Berkovits's position that God's hiddenness in the midst of evil was something the people of the Old Testament had no trouble accepting.

has fed upon for centuries. Briefly summed up, the all-too-common Christian view of the Jews has been as follows.[39] The Jews were the chosen ones; they had been privy to the revelations and promises to God; they alone knew that God would one day send a messiah. Yet, when that messiah came, in the person of Jesus of Nazareth, the Jews rejected him. Many Christians have interpreted the destruction of the temple in Jerusalem in 70 AD as just punishment for their rejection of Jesus.[40]

Then of course there is the concept of the Jews as a "witness people," a race whose constant sufferings is ample testimony to the fact that they have rejected God's Messiah and are therefore paying the price. Thus, the Jews are "supernatural"; they alone were chosen by God and they alone are bearing the punishment for rejecting his Son. This type of thinking is summed up well in the following passage from Pascal:

> Those who find belief difficult seek a reason in the disbelief of the Jews: "If it was all so clear, say they, why would they not believe?" And they would almost have them believe, so as not be held back by the example of their refusal. But it is just this refusal which is the foundation of our belief. We should be much less inclined to believe if they were on our side. We should then have a far more ample pretext. It is a wonderful thing to have made the Jews great lovers of things foretold, and great enemies of their fulfillment.[41]

39. This view represents, unfortunately, the manner in which Christians have often seen the Jews. However, I do not believe that the New Testament documents require such a view. For instance, the Gospel of John has often been considered one of the most anti-Jewish documents in the Christian Scriptures, due to the negative connotations associated with the phrase "the Jews," which appears over and over again in John. However, John's use of "Jews" is almost always aimed at specific Jews (often Jewish religious authorities), not the Jewish people *en masse*. See, for example, Von Wahlde, "The Johannine Jews," 33–60.

40. From an anti-Jewish Christian perspective, the idea that the fall of Jerusalem is punishment for the Jews' denial of Jesus makes far more sense than the belief that the Holocaust was punishment for that same rejection. After all, the destruction of Jerusalem happened only a few decades after the crucifixion, while the Holocaust came so late in history as to make the supposed "punishment" too far removed from the "crime" to have any merit.

41. Quoted in Cohen, *The Natural and Supernatural Jew*, ix.

Are We Asking the Wrong Questions about the Shoah?

Many post-Holocaust Jewish theologians are concerned with this idea because, they believe, even in the thought of well-meaning Christians, the idea of the Jews as a supernatural witness people can produce tragic results. This is best exemplified by Richard Rubenstein's meeting with Dr. Gruber, a German school dean and pastor who was imprisoned by the Nazis for his efforts to save Jews during the Holocaust. Dr. Gruber risked his own life, as well as the lives of his family, by resisting the Nazis. Rubenstein never doubts that Gruber is a man of good will and great personal courage. But, he sees in the pastor's theological thinking a problem that has its roots in the biblical idea of the chosenness of Israel. Gruber was obviously no anti-Semite, and he does not specifically say that the Jews deserved the Holocaust for their denial of Jesus. Nevertheless, he views the Holocaust as punishment, for whatever reason, inflicted upon the Jews by God. Rubenstein states that Gruber's "thinking was thoroughly drenched in New Testament and prophetic categories that there is little reason to believe that he would have disagreed with Dr. Servatius [who saw the Holocaust as recompense for the Jews act of 'deicide']. Stated with theological finesse it comes to pretty much the same thing as the vulgar thought that the Christ-killers got what was coming to them."[42]

But Rubenstein is not simply accusing the dean of attributing to the Jews the theologically incorrect crime of deicide.[43] He makes the salient point that the dean, indeed, all Christians, could not have begun to see the Jews as supernatural if the Jews themselves had not portrayed themselves in this matter: "Can we really blame the Christian community for viewing us through the prism of a mythology of history when we were the first to assert this history ourselves?

42. Rubenstein, "The Dean and the Chosen People," 285.

43. The New Testament clearly teaches that all have sinned, and fall short of the glory of God. An idea that is foreign to the New Testament is that the Jews alone were/are responsible for Jesus' death. Jesus' death is there portrayed as necessitated by the sins of *all* humanity. True, there is the passage in Matthew (27:25), where the Jewish crowd cries out, "Let his [Jesus'] blood be on us and our children." However, these are the words of a mob of Jewish peasants, and can hardly be equated with a serious Christian theological statement that all Jews are guilty for his death. Of course, this one passage has all too frequently been singled out by the less theologically astute among the Christian community as a pretext for anti-Semitism.

As long as we continue to hold to the doctrine of the election of Israel, we will leave ourselves open to theology expressed by Dean Gruber, that because the Jews are God's Chosen People, God wanted Hitler to punish them."[44] Of course, Rubenstein is referring to the Hebrew Scriptures themselves, which proclaim on virtually every page the chosenness of the Jews. And, up until the Holocaust, many Jewish thinkers still confidently maintained this position. In fact, as late as 1962, Arthur A. Cohen published a major work that wrestled with the distinction between the Jews "natural" and "supernatural" vocations.[45] Rubenstein is probably correct that the Christian perception of the Jews in other-worldly terms led to their vilification, as exemplified in the concept of the witness people, or the legend of the wandering Jew. It is understandable that Rubenstein wants to remove this type of thinking from Jewish and Christian consciousness. But what if the Jews truly *are,* in some sense, supernatural? If they are somehow different from the rest of humanity, this needs to be honestly recognized and addressed, not conveniently ignored because it has the potential to cause harm.

Berkovits strongly disagrees with Rubenstein that the Jews should be seen as "normal" human beings, and he believes he has ample evidence to support his contention. A great deal of his post-Holocaust apologetic is built upon the idea that the Jews are indeed different from the rest of humanity, different because God has chosen them to be so. First, Berkovits employs the idea of the Jew as different to explain why the Jews, this tiny group of people who never had what the world would call great power or influence, has continually been the victim of hatred and oppression. Berkovits realizes that this can largely be attributed to the fact that Jews simply did not "fit in" with society as a whole; their insistence on their unique religion and lifestyle made them easy scapegoats for the non-Jewish masses.[46] But surely this alone, Berkovits knows, cannot account for the maniacal hatred to which the Jews have so often been exposed. This can be explained, he thinks, because, quite simply, "whether we accept it or not, we are not a 'normal' people in the sense of the rest of the nations. We can make no greater mistake than to try to normalize our

44. Rubenstein, "The Dean and the Chosen People," 287.
45. Cohen, *The Natural and the Supernatural Jew,* 283–314.
46. Berkovits, *God, Man, and History,* 141.

Are We Asking the Wrong Questions about the Shoah?

condition."⁴⁷ For Berkovits, this non-normal status explains why the Jews have often been persecuted with such hatred by a God-hating world. The Nazi persecution against the Jews was fiercer, more ruthless, and more systematic, than any previous pogrom against Jews precisely because the Nazis were a demonic force in opposition to God. The Nazi atrocities had "a quality of the transcendental about it; it was metaphysical barbarism. It was not just inhuman; it was satanic."⁴⁸ Thus, Berkovits sees the inhuman Germans attacking the supernatural Jews, but why? Because the Nazis were afraid of the Jews. Not afraid of their military or political might, of course, but afraid of what they represented spiritually. The Jews, quite simply, were a reminder here on earth, a sign of God's existence. The so-called final solution was not just a plan to rid the world of Jews; it was to purge any proof, any reminder, of God from the earth. If the Nazis believed the Nietzschean myth that God was dead, then they had to kill the one group of people who had always been a visible reminder of God's presence—the Jews. The Nazis could not truly implement their godless vision for the world until God's witness people were destroyed.⁴⁹ Berkovits contends that his point is proven not only by the Nazis, but by Communist Russia as well. Why is it that the Communists were far more anti-Jewish than they were anti-Christian? "If it were only a matter of the antagonism of an atheistic society to religion, there should be no difference between communism's rejection of Christianity and that of Judaism."⁵⁰

But why are the Jews such a convincing proof of God's existence? Why did even Karl Barth, who has upset many Jews because he held, at least in part, to the idea of the Jews as a witness people, believe that the Jews so undoubtedly proved God's existence? Barth was fond of quoting a conversation between Frederick the Great and his personal physician, Zimmermann: " 'Zimmermann, can you name me a single proof of the existence of God?' And Zimmerman replied, "Your majesty, the Jews!' "⁵¹ Zimmerman was referring to the

---

47. Berkovits, *Crisis and Faith*, 135.
48. Berkovits, *Faith After the Holocaust*, 117.
49. Ibid., 117–18.
50. Ibid., 118.
51. Barth, *Dogmatics in Outline*, 75.

fact that the Jews have survived, against impossible odds, for thousands of years, and that this survival is inexplicable apart from God's intervention in history. This is precisely the position that Berkovits holds. "The survival of the Jew, his capacity for revival after catastrophes such as had eliminated mighty nations and empires, indicate the mysterious intrusion of a spiritual dimension into the history of man."[52] Quite simply, it does not "make sense" that the Jews should still be alive in the millions. Everything about human history, its economics, its psychology, its politics, it could all be explained on purely natural grounds, where it not for the Jew! The Jew throws a theological monkey wrench into everything, and robs secular man of the God-less worldview he (and especially the Nazis) fought for. This is why, for Berkovits, Jews prove God's existence, while Christians do not. "Half a billion Christians [the number is now closer to one billion] all over the world prove nothing about God's presence in history. They are too many, too influential, too pervasive. They are a this-worldly power in the context of power history. The same is true of any other of the great world religions."[53]

For Berkovits, the Jews do more than prove God's reality by the tenacity of their existence. Through their almost constant experience of *Galut* (exile) they, in a sense, mirror the experience of God himself, who has been "exiled" by the sinful desires of his creatures, who would rather live in the world without his divine presence. Here Berkovits introduces his idea of the duality of exile. There is what he terms the "national exile," which manifested itself in such events like the fall of Jerusalem in 70 AD, or the expulsion of the Sephardic Jews from Spain. But there is another dimension to exile, and it is what Berkovits terms the "cosmic exile." It is on this level that the experiences of the Jews mirror that of God himself. For when men conduct their lives so that greed, personal pleasure and egotism rule the day, then "God's own purpose finds itself in Exile in the history of mankind. So long as the divine plan remains unrealized in history, the history of mankind tells the story of—what Jewish tradition calls— *Galut haShekhinah*, the Exile of the Divine Presence. God Himself is, as it were, a refugee in the world of men."[54] For Berkovits, the

52. Berkovits, *With God in Hell*, 83.
53. Berkovits, *Faith After the Holocaust*, 114.
54. Berkovits, *Crisis and Faith*, 154–55.

twentieth century seems to have been the culmination of mankind's rejection of God. The Holocaust is for him not only the pinnacle of human wickedness, but proof that the European Christian civilization that incubated the ideas that helped lead to the Holocaust is spiritually bankrupt.[55] For Berkovits, the tragedy of the Holocaust is not only the millions of Jews who perished in the death-camps. He also sees the Holocaust as ushering in the end of Christian civilization. After the Holocaust, the Jews find themselves in a world that has failed, both morally and spiritually. Berkovits sees post-Holocaust Jews as standing in judgment upon Christianity and its civilization, and finding both wanting.[56] So thoroughly does Berkovits perceive the failure of Christianity that even the idea of Jewish-Christian dialogue is a fruitless encounter. This is largely because there "is nothing in Christianity for them [Jews]. Whatever in Christian teaching is acceptable to them is borrowed from Judaism."[57]

Berkovits sees no hope in the shambles of post-Holocaust, post-Christian Europe and America, but he does hold out great hope for the Jews, (and through the Jews, for the rest of humanity). That hope is inextricably tied to the state of Israel. For him, Israel is not just a

55. Chapter two of Berkovits's *Faith After the Holocaust* contains the most bitter denouncement of Christianity that I have encountered in any Jewish-thinker writing about the Holocaust. Much of what Berkovits says here is accurate; that Christian anti-Semitism helped pave the way for the Nazis has been documented to such an extent that it is now an incontrovertible fact. Still, Berkovits often descends into a sarcastic, almost hateful tone that is inappropriate in scholarly discourse. And, he makes statements regarding Christianity that are gross exaggerations. For instance, he claims that Christianity "has no use for this world and no respect for it," and that Christianity "treats man as a worthless creature" (55). Christianity does indeed see the world as marred by the sin of the fall, and it does view man as a sinner who cannot be redeemed apart form God. But Berkovits's comments are caricatures of the Christian position, rather than accurate theological statements.

56. Ibid., 40–42.

57. Ibid., 44. See also pages 45–50. Berkovits is primarily opposed to Jewish-Christian dialogue because he does not believe it would be of benefit to Jews. Additionally, he does not think such dialogue would increase religious tolerance on either side. Of course, Berkovits wrote this in 1973, before the Jewish-Christian dialogue was in full bloom. He could scarcely have imagined how beneficial the dialogue would prove, especially in terms of helping *Christians* to better understand and respect Jews. Indeed, the dialogue has helped to eliminate much of the Christian prejudice that Berkovits railed against.

deserved sanctuary after the horror of the Shoah, but something essential to Jewish existence itself. In fact, he even goes so far as to say that Judaism, without Israel, has no purpose in the world. Without Zion, Judaism is merely one among many world religions. The state of Israel is "Judaism's raison d'etre, i.e., fulfillment in history."[58] All of the suffering of the Jews down through history, he states, only makes sense in light of the sufferers' expectations that one day, the Jews would be at home in Zion.[59] So important is Israel in his thought that he sees the entire history of Judaism as pointless without the messianic hope embodied in the Promised Land. If the Jews have no messianic hope anchored in Israel, then "two thousand years of *Galut* [exile] have been a deplorable episode, due to unfortunate circumstances, and the sooner it is forgotten the better for all."[60] Here Berkovits goes far beyond the other post-Holocaust theologians. Some, like Rubenstein, refuse to see in the establishment of the state of Israel anything indicative of the divine will. Others, like Fackenheim, would see Jewish support for Israel as part of the 614th commandment that requires Jews to fight for their survival in posthumous defiance of the Nazis.[61] Irving Greenberg speaks of a "voluntary covenant" that, in the post-Holocaust world, Jews are free to enter into if they wish; the covenant cannot be viewed as obligatory for Jews after the Shoah.[62] But for Berkovits, the covenant is something imposed upon Jews from above. They can dislike it, they can fight against it, but they can no more "withdraw" from it than they can cease to be Jewish. And this covenant, which is unbreakable and forever binding, finds its culmination in the state of Israel, which is the teleological purpose of Judaism. The Holocaust does not necessitate this; Israel has always been Judaism's destiny. The Shoah has, however, made the importance, the urgency, of Zion that much clearer.

What exactly is the messianic fate that awaits the Jews in their biblical homeland? Berkovits never really clarifies what he specifi-

58. Ibid., 151.
59. Ibid.
60. Ibid., 152.
61. For a good summary of Fackenheim's thought on this point, see Morgan, *Beyond Auschwitz*, 157–58.
62. Ibid., 135–40.

cally believes on this point. However, it is not just Jewish salvation he has in mind. Somehow, the Jewish people and the state of Israel are intimately connected with what he terms "universal salvation."[63] Does this salvation involve a personal messiah? Berkovits occasionally hints that it may,[64] but he never really develops this idea. It seems that, for him, the messiah can be equated with the messianic ideal in general. Of what messianic salvation will consist, Berkovits is again somewhat vague. But, because Jewish destiny "has been linked to *Galut haShekhinah,* [exile of the divine presence]" Berkovits seems to suggest that, once the Jews are fully at home in Israel, once Jerusalem has truly become the holy city that the prophets predicted, then God himself can return from "His man-created exile."[65] Then, presumably, he will hide his face no longer.

In conclusion, Eliezer Berkovits clearly stands apart from the other post-Holocaust Jewish thinkers. For them, the Shoah was an event that forever altered the content of traditional Jewish faith. However, Berkovits sees the Holocaust in its proper historical context, and realizes that the suffering the Jews endured in the death-camps, though worse than anything preceding it, does not alter the substance of Jewish faith. This is because Jewish faith is based upon God's historical revelation to, and covenant-making relationship with, his people. This same God sustained many Jews during the darkest hours of the Holocaust, just as he has always preserved them throughout their tragic history, when by all secular appraisals they should have ceased to exist long ago. The Jews are indeed a special people, Berkovits believes, and God has finally returned them to their promised homeland. Now, it is only a matter of discovering how God will use his people to help bring about the redemption of humanity of which the prophets spoke so long ago.

---

63. Berkovits, *God, Man, and History,* 154.
64. Berkovits, *Faith After the Holocaust,* 151–52.
65. Berkovits, *Crisis and Faith,* 160–61.

Bibliography

Abdalati, Hammudah. *Islam in Focus.* Indianapolis: American Trust Publications, 1975.
Abu-Hamdiyyah, Mohammad. *The Qur'an—an Introduction.* New York: Rutledge, 2000.
Ahmad, Mirza Ghulam. *The Philosophy of the Teachings of Islam.* UK: Islam International Publications, 1996.
Ahmad, Ziauddin. *Islam Universal Religion.* Karachi, Pakistan: Royal Book Company, 1989.
Akhtar, Shabbir. *A Faith for All Seasons: Islam and Western Modernity.* London: Bellew Publishing, 1990.
Alston, William P. "The Inductive Argument from Evil." In *The Evidential Argument from Evil,* edited by Daniel Howard-Snyder. Bloomington: Indiana University, 1996.
Aquinas, Thomas. *Summa Theologica.* Vol. 3. New York: Benziger Brothers, Inc., 1948.
Armour, Rollin. *Islam, Christianity, and the West: A Troubled History.* Maryknoll, NY: Orbis Books, 2002.
Bahnsen, Greg. "A Critique of the Evidentialist Apologetic Method of John Warwick Montgomery." Accessed August, 2007. Online: http://www.cmfnow.com/articles/PA016.htm.
Ball, D.A. "The Crucifixion and Death of a Man Called Jesus." *Journal of the Mississippi State Medical Association* 30 (1989) 77–83.
Barrett, C.K. *Reading Through Romans.* London: Epworth, 1963.
Barth, Karl. *Church Dogmatics.* Vol. 2, pt. 2. Translated by G.W. Bromiley et al. Edinburgh: T. & T. Clark, 1957.
———. *Church Dogmatics.* Vol. 3, pt. 3. Translated by G.W. Bromiley and R.J. Ehrlich. Edinburgh: T. & T. Clark, 1960.
———. *The Church and the Political Problem of Our Day.* New York: Scribner's, 1939.
———. *Dogmatics in Outline.* Edited and translated by G.T. Thompson. London: SCM Press, 1949.
Berkovits, Eliezer. *Crisis and Faith.* New York: Sanhedrin Press, 1976.
———. *Faith After the Holocaust.* NY: KTAV Publishing House, Inc., 1973.

Bibliography

———. *God, Man, and History.* Middle Village, NY: Jonathan David Publishers, Inc., 1959.
———. *With God in Hell.* New York: Sanhedrin Press, 1979.
Boyd, Gregory A. *God at War: The Bible and Spiritual Conflict.* Downers Grove, IL: InterVarsity Press, 1997.
———. *Satan and the Problem of Evil.* Downers Grove, IL: InterVarsity Press, 2001.
Boyd, Gregory A., and Paul R. Eddy. *Across the Spectrum: Understanding Issues in Evangelical Theology.* Grand Rapids: Baker Academic, 2002.
Braiterman, Zachary. *(God) After Auschwitz: Tradition and Change in Post-Holocaust Jewish Thought.* Princeton: Princeton University Press, 1998.
Brown, Raymond E. *An Introduction to New Testament Christology.* Mahwah, NJ: Paulist Press, 1994.
Bruce, F.F. *The Canon of Scripture.* Downers Grove, IL: InterVarsity Press, 1988.
———. *The Defense of the Gospel in the New Testament.* Grand Rapids: Eerdmans, 1959.
———. *The New Testament Documents: Are they Reliable?* Leicester, England: InterVarsity Press, 1943.
Brueggemann, Walter. *The Prophetic Imagination.* Philadelphia, PA: Fortress Press, 1985.
Bultmann, Rudolf. *The History of the Synoptic Tradition*, translated by J. Marsh. New York: Harper and Row, 1963.
———. "New Testament and Mythology." In *Kerygma and Myth: A Theological Debate,* edited by Hans Werner Bartsch, translated by Reginald H. Fuller. London: SPCK, 1953.
Callahan, James Patrick. "The Convergence of Narrative and Christology: Hans W. Frei and the Uniqueness of Jesus Christ." *Journal of the Evangelical Theological Society* 38 (1995) 531–47.
Carnell, Edward John. *An Introduction to Christian Apologetics.* Grand Rapids: Eerdmans, 1956.
Carroll, Michael P. *The Cult of the Virgin Mary: Psychological Origins.* Princeton: Princeton University Press, 1986.
———. "The Virgin Mary at LaSalette and Lourdes: Whom did the Children See." *Journal for the Scientific Study of Religion* March (1985) 56–74.
Clark, David K. "Narrative Theology and Apologetics." *Journal of the Evangelical Theological Society* 36 (1993) 499–515.
Clark, Kelly James. "Reformed Epistemology Apologetics." In *Five Views on Apologetics,* edited by Steven B. Cowan. Grand Rapids: Zondervan Publishing House, 2000.
Cohen, Arthur A. *The Natural and Supernatural Jew.* New York: Pantheon Books, 1962.
Copleston, Frederick. *Friedrich Nietzsche: Philosopher of Culture.* London: Search Press, 1975.

Bibliography

Craig, William Lane, and Gerd Ludemann. *Jesus' Resurrection: Fact or Figment?* edited by Paul Copan and Ronald Tacelli. Downers Grove, IL: InterVarsity Press, 2000.

Craig, William Lane, and John Dominic Crossan. *Will the Real Jesus Please Stand Up?* edited by Paul Copan. Grand Rapids: Baker Books, 1998.

Crockett, William V. "The Metaphorical View." In *Four Views on Hell,* edited by William Crockett. Grand Rapids: Zondervan Publishing House, 1992.

Davis, Stephen T. *Risen Indeed: Making Sense of the Resurrection.* Grand Rapids: Eerdmans, 1993.

Dawood, N.J. *The Koran.* London: Penguin Books, 1988.

Dostoyevsky, Fyodor. *The Brothers Karamozov.* Translated by Constance Garnett. New York: Random House, 1950.

Duffy, Michael F., and Willard Mittelman. "Nietzsche's Attitudes Toward the Jews." *Journal of the History of Ideas* 49 (1988) 301–17.

Edwards, W.D. et al. "On the Physical Death of Jesus Christ." *JAMA* 255 (1986) 1455–63.

Evans, C. Stephen. *Pocket Dictionary of Apologetics and Philosophy of Religion.* Downers Grove, IL: InterVarsity Press, 2002.

Fackre, Gabriel. *The Christian Story: A Narrative Interpretation of Basic Christian Doctrine.* Vol. 1. Grand Rapids: Eerdmans, 1996.

Feinberg, Paul D. "Cumulative Case Apologetics." In *Five Views on Apologetics,* edited by Steven B. Cowan. Grand Rapids: Zondervan, 2000.

Frame, John M. *Apologetics to the Glory of God.* Phillipsburg, NJ: P and R Publishing, 1994.

———. *Cornelius Van Til: An Analysis of his Thought.* Phillipsburg, NJ: P and R Publishing, 1995.

———. "Presuppositional Apologetics." In *Five Views on Apologetics,* edited by Steven B. Cowan, pp. 207–255. Grand Rapids: Zondervan, 2000.

———. "Van Til and the Ligonier Apologetic." *Westminster Theological Journal* 47 (1985) 279–99.

Frame, John and Steve Hays. "Johnson on Van Til: a Rejoinder." *Evangelical Quarterly* 76 (2004) 227–239.

Frei, Hans W. *The Eclipse of Biblical Narrative.* New Haven: Yale University Press, 1974.

———. *The Identity of Jesus Christ.* Philadelphia, PA: Fortress Press, 1975.

———. *Theology and Narrative.* Oxford: Oxford University Press, 1993.

Friedlander, Albert H. "A Final Conversation with Paul Tillich." In *Out of the Whirlwind.* Urj Press, 1999.

Gager, John G. *The Origins of Anti-Semitism.* New York: Oxford University Press, 1983.

Gardell, Mattias. *In the Name of Elijah Muhammad: Louis Farrakhan and the Nation of Islam.* Durham: Duke University Press, 1996.

Geehan, E.R., editor. *Jerusalem and Athens.* Philadelphia, PA: Presbyterian and Reformed Publishing Co., 1971.

Bibliography

Geisler, Norman L. *The Battle for the Resurrection*. Nashville: Thomas Nelson Publishers, 1989.

———. "Islam." In *Baker Encyclopedia of Christian Apologetics*, edited by Norman Geisler. Grand Rapids: Baker, 1999.

George, Timothy. *Is the Father of Jesus the God of Muhammad?* Grand Rapids: Zondervan, 2002.

Goulder, Michael. "The Baseless Fabric of a Vision." In *Resurrection Reconsidered*, edited by Gavin D'Costa. Oxford: England, 1996.

Greenberg, Irving. "Cloud of Smoke, Pillar of Fire." In *Auschwitz: Beginning of a New Era?* edited by Eva Fleischner. New York: KTAV Publishing House, 1977.

Grenz, Stanley J. "Articulating the Christian Belief-Mosaic: Theological Method After the Demise of Foundationalism." In *Evangelical Futures*, edited by John G. Stackhouse, Jr. Grand Rapids: Baker Books, 2000.

Habermas, Gary R. "Did Jesus Perform Miracles?" In *Jesus Under Fire: Modern Scholarship Reinvents the Historical Jesus*, edited by Michael J. Wilkins and J.P. Moreland. Grand Rapids: Zondervan, 1995.

———. "Evidential Apologetics." In *Five Views on Apologetics*, edited by Steven B. Cowan. Grand Rapids: Zondervan Publishing House, 2000.

Habermas, Gary R., and Antony Flew. *Did Jesus Rise from the Dead?* edited by Terry L Miethe. San Francisco: Harper & Row, 1987.

Hall, Sidney G. *Christian Anti-Semitism and Paul's Theology*. Minneapolis: Fortress Press, 1993.

Hamilton, John D.B. "Vengeance, Rage and Reconciliation: Homer and an Ancient Greek Perspective." Accessed August 2007. Online: http://www.holycross.edu/departments/crec/forgiveness/hamilton.pdf.

Hatcher, Donald. "Plantinga and Reformed Epistemology: A Critique." *Philosophy and Theology* 1 (1986) 84–95.

Heil, John Paul. *Romans—Paul's Letter of Hope*. Rome: Biblical Institute Press, 1987.

Henry, Carl F.H. "Narrative Theology: An Appraisal." *Trinity Journal* 8 (1987) 3–19.

Hick, John. *Christianity at the Center*. New York: Herder and Herder, 1970.

———. *A Christian Theology of Religions: the Rainbow of Faiths*. Louisville: Westminster/ John Knox Press, 1995.

———. *Evil and the God of Love*. San Francisco: Harper and Row, 1977.

———. *God Has Many Names*. Philadelphia, PA: Westminster Press, 1980.

———. *An Interpretation of Religion*. Yale University Press, 2005.

———. *The Metaphor of God Incarnate*. Louisville: Westminster/John Knox Press, 1993.

———. "A Pluralistic View." In *Four Views on Salvation in a Pluralistic World*, edited by Dennis L. Okholm and Timothy R. Phillips. Grand Rapids: Zondervan, 1995.

Higton, Mike. "Frei's Christology and Lindbeck's Cultural-Linguistic Theory." *Scottish Journal of Theology* 50 (1997) 83–95.

Hinson, E. Glenn. *The Early Church: Origins to the Dawn of the Middle Ages.* Nashville: Abingdon Press, 1996.

Horndern, William. *A Layman's Guide to Protestant Theology.* New York: Macmillan, 1955.

Hunsinger, George. "What Can Evangelicals and Postliberals Learn From Each Other? The Carl Henry—Hans Frei Exchange Reconsidered." In *The Nature of Confession,* edited by Timothy R. Phillips and Dennis L. Okholm. Downers Grove, IL: InterVarsity Press, 1996.

Hvalvik, R. "A 'Sonderweg' for Israel: A Critical Examination of a Current Interpretation of Romans 11.25–27." *JSNT* 38 (1990) 87–107.

Jocz, Jakob. *Christians and Jews: Encounter and Mission.* London: SPCK, 1966.

———. *The Jewish People and Jesus Christ.* London: Eyre and Spottiswoode, 1961.

———. *A Theology of Election.* New York: Macmillan, 1958.

Johnson, Elizabeth. "Jews and Christians in the New Testament: John, Matthew, and Paul." *Reformed Review* 42 (1988) 113–28.

Johnson, John J. "Are We Asking the Wrong Questions About the Shoah? Eliezer Berkovits as Post-Holocaust Jewish Apologist." *Conservative Judaism* 57 (2004) 65–86.

———. "A Case for 'Reformed Evidentialism.'" *Churchman* 117 (2003) 7–32.

———. "Is Cornelius Van Til's Apologetic Method Christian, or Merely Theistic?" *Evangelical Quarterly* 75 (2003) 257–68.

———. "Hans Frei as Reluctant Apologist for the Resurrection." *Evangelical Quarterly* 76 (2004) 135–51.

———. "How a Muslim Could Employ Van Til's Apologetic System." *Global Journal of Classical Theology* 5 (2006). Accessed August 2007. Online: http://www.trinitysem.edu/journal/5-3/TOC v5n3.htm.

———. "The Implausible Foundations of Nietzsche's Attack upon Biblical Religion." *Evangelical Journal* 23 (2005) 82–94.

———. "Is John Hick's Concept of the 'Real' an Adequate Criterion for Evaluating Religious Truth-Claims?" *Themelios* 27 (2002) 45–57.

———. "A New Testament Understanding of the Jewish Rejection of Jesus: Four Theologians on the Salvation of Israel." *Journal of the Evangelical Theological Society* 43 (2000) 229–46.

———. "Should the Holocaust Force us to Rethink our View of God and Evil?" *Tyndale Bulletin* 52 (2001) 117–28.

———. "Were the Resurrection Appearances Hallucinations? Some Psychiatric and Psychological Considerations." *Churchman* 115 (2001) 227–38.

Kaiser, Walter C. *The Old Testament Documents: Are They Reliable and Relevant?* Downers Grove, IL: InterVarsity Press, 2001.

Katz, Steven T. *The Holocaust in Historical Context.* Vol. I. New York: OUP, 1994.

Kee, Alistair. *Nietzsche Against the Crucified.* London: SCM Press, 1999.

Bibliography

Knudsen, Robert D. "Progressive and Regressive Tendencies in Christian Apologetics." In *Jerusalem and Athens,* edited by E.R. Geehan. Philadelphia, PA: Presbyterian and Reformed Publishing Co., 1971, 275–76.

Lapide, Pinchas. *The Resurrection of Jesus.* Translated by Wilhelm C. Linss. Minneapolis: Augsburg Publishing House, 1983.

Lee, David. *Luke's Stories of Jesus: Theological Reading of Gospel Narrative and the Legacy of Hans Frei.* Sheffield, UK: Sheffield Academic Press, 1999.

Lewis, Charles. "Nietzsche's Concept of Biblical Religion." In *Studies in Nietzsche and the Judaeo-Christian Tradition,* edited by James C. O'Flaherty et al. Chapel Hill: The University of North Carolina Press, 1985.

Lewis, C.S. "Evil and God." In *God in the Dock,* edited by Walter Hooper. Grand Rapids: Eerdmans, 1976.

———. "Myth Became Fact." In *God in the Dock,* edited by Walter Hooper. Grand Rapids: Eerdmans, 1970.

———. *The Problem of Pain.* New York: Macmillan Publishing, 1962.

———. *Surprised by Joy.* New York: Harcourt, Brace, and World, 1955.

Lieb, Michael. *Children of Ezekiel.* Durham: Duke University Press, 1998.

Lincoln, C. Eric. *The Black Muslims in America.* Grand Rapids: Eerdmans, 1994.

Ludemann, Gerd. *What Really Happened to Jesus.* Translated by John Bowden. London: SCM Press, 1995.

Magnus, Bernd, and Kathleen M. Higgins. "Nietzsche's Works and their Themes." In *The Cambridge Companion to Nietzsche,* edited by Bernd Magnus and Kathleen M. Higgins. Cambridge: Cambridge University Press, 1996.

Martin, Michael. *Atheism: A Philosophical Justification.* Philadelphia, PA: Temple University Press, 1990.

Martin, Walter. *The Kingdom of the Cults.* Minneapolis: Bethany House Publishers, 1985.

Mawdudi, Abul A'La. *An Introduction to the Koran.* Jamaica, NY: Islamic Circle of North America, 1982.

McDermott, Gerald R. *Can Evangelicals Learn from World Religions?* Downers Grove, IL: InterVarsity Press, 2000.

McDowell, Josh. *Evidence that Demands a Verdict: Historical Evidences for the Christian Faith.* San Bernardino, CA: Here's Life Publishers, 1979.

McGrath, Alister E. *Bridge-Building: Effective Christian Apologetics.* Leister: InterVarsity Press, 1992.

Meerloo, A.M. *Delusion and Mass Delusion: Nervous and Mental Disease Monographs.* No. 79. New York: Smith Ely Jelliffe Trust, 1949.

Menzel, Donald H., and Ernest H. Taves. *The UFO Enigma.* Garden City, NY: Doubleday, 1977.

Michalson, Carl. "Rudolf Bultmann." In *Ten Makers of Modern Protestant Theology,* edited by George L. Hunt. New York: Association Press, 1958, 102–13.

Montgomery, John Warwick. "How Muslims do Apologetics." In *Faith Founded on Fact.* Newburgh, IN: Trinity Press, 1978.

———. *Human Rights and Human Dignity.* Edmonton: Canadian Institute for Law, Theology, and Public Policy, Inc., 1986.
———. "Once Upon an A Priori." In *Jerusalem and Athens,* edited by E.R. Geehan. Philadelphia, PA: P and R Publishing, 1971.
———. *The Shape of the Past: An Introduction to Philosophical Historiography.* Ann Arbor: Edward Bros., 1962.
———. *Where is History Going?* Grand Rapids: Zondervan Publishing House, 1969.
Morgan, Michael L. *Beyond Auschwitz: Post-Holocaust Jewish Thought in America.* New York: Oxford University Press, 2001.
Nash, Ronald H. *The Gospel and the Greeks.* Richardson, TX: Probe Books, 1992.
Neilson, Kai. *Does God Exist: The Debate Between Theists and Atheists.* Amherst, NY: Prometheus Books, 1993.
Neumann, Harry. "The Case Against Apolitical Morality: Nietzsche's Interpretation of the Jewish Instinct." In *Studies in Nietzsche and the Judaeo-Christian Tradition,* edited by James C. O'Flaherty et al. Chapel Hill: The University of North Carolina Press, 1985.
Nietzsche, Friedrich. *The Anti-Christ.* Translated by R.J. Hollingsdale. London: Penguin Books, 1990.
———. *Beyond Good and Evil.* Translated by Walter Kaufmann. New York: Vintage Books, 1966.
———. *Ecce Homo.* Translated and Edited by Walter Kaufmann. New York: Vintage Books, 1967.
———. *On the Genealogy of Morals.* Translated by Walter Kaufmann. New York: Vintage Books, Inc., 1967.
Pannenberg, Wolfhart. *Jesus—God and Man.* Translated by Lewis L. Wilkins and Duane A. Priebe. Philadelphia, PA: Westminister Press, 1964.
Pawlikowski, John T. *Christ in the Light of the Jewish-Christian Dialogue.* New York: Paulist, 1982.
Pinn, Anthony B. *Varieties of African-American Religious Experience.* Minneapolis: Fortress Press, 1998.
Pinnock, Clark. "The Conditional View." In *Four Views on Hell,* edited by William Crockett. Grand Rapids: Zondervan Publishing House, 1992.
———. *A Wideness in God's Mercy: The Finality of Jesus Christ in a World of Religions.* Grand Rapids: Zondervan Publishing House, 1992.
Piper, John. *The Justification of God.* Grand Rapids: Baker, 1983.
Placher, William C. "Scripture as Realistic Narrative: Some Preliminary Questions." *Perspectives in Religious Studies* 5 (1978) 30–39.
Plantinga, Alvin. "Epistemic Probability and Evil." In *The Evidential Argument from Evil,* edited by Daniel Howard-Snyder. Bloomington: Indiana University, 1996.
———. "Reason and Belief in God." In *Faith and Rationality: Reason and Belief in God,* edited by Alvin Plantinga and Nicholas Wolterstorff. Notre Dame: University of Notre Dame Press, 1983.

Bibliography

———. *Warranted Christian Belief.* New York: Oxford University Press, 2000.
Raisanen, Heikki. "Paul, God, and Israel: Romans 9–11 in Recent Research." In *The Social World of Formative Christianity and Judaism,* edited by Jacob Neusner et al. Philadelphia, PA: Fortress, 1988.
Roberts, Tyler T. *Contesting Spirit: Nietzsche, Affirmation, Religion.* Princeton: Princeton University Press, 1998.
Rubenstein, Richard L. *After Auschwitz.* Indianapolis: The Bobbs-Merrill Company, 1966.
———. "The Dean and the Chosen People." In *Holocaust: Religious and Philosophical Implications,* edited by John K. Roth and Michael Berenbaum. NY: Paragon House, 1989.
Ruether, Rosemary. *Faith and Fratricide.* New York: Seabury, 1979.
Rushdoony, Rousas John. "The One and the Many Problem—the Contribution of Van Til." In *Jerusalem and Athens.* Edited by E.R. Geehan. Philadelphia, PA: Presbyterian and Reformed Publishing Co., 1971.
Salaquarda, Jorg. "Nietzsche and the Judaeo-Christian Tradition." In *The Cambridge Companion to Nietzsche,* edited by Bernd Magnus and Kathleen M Higgins. Cambridge: Cambridge University Press, 1996.
Sanders, E.P. "Paul's Attitude Toward the Jewish People." *USQR* 33 (1978) 175–87.
Sandmel, Samuel. *We Jews and Jesus.* New York: Oxford Univ. Press, 1965.
Schaeffer, Francis. *Trilogy.* Wheaton, IL: Crossway Books, 1990.
Showalter, Elaine. *Hystories: Hysterical Epidemics and Modern Culture.* New York: Columbia University Press, 1997.
Shweid, Eliezer. *Wrestling Until Day-Break: Searching for Meaning in the Thinking on the Holocaust.* Lanham, MD: University Press of America, 1994.
Slade, Peter D., and Richard P. Bentall. *Sensory Deception: A Scientific Analysis of Hallucination.* Baltimore: The John Hopkins University Press, 1988.
Solomon, Robert C. "Nietzsche *ad hominem*: Perspectivism, Personality and *Ressentiment.*" In *The Cambridge Companion to Nietzsche,* edited by Bernd Magnus and Kathleen M Higgins. Cambridge: Cambridge University Press, 1996.
Sproul, R.C. et al. *Classical Apologetics.* Zondervan: Grand Rapids, 1984.
Stark, Rodney. *The Rise of Christianity: A Sociologist Reconsiders History.* Princeton: Princeton University Press, 1996.
Stendahl, Krister. *Paul Among Jews and Gentiles.* Philadelphia: Fortress, 1976.
Stewart, James R. "Sasquatch Sightings in North Dakota: An Analysis of an Episode of Collective Delusion." In *Exploring the Paranormal: Perspectives on Belief and Experience,* edited by George K. Zollschan et al. Garden City Park, NY: Avery Publishing Group, 1989.
Strauss, David F. *The Life of Jesus.* Vol. 3. Bristol, UK: Thoemmes Press, 1998.
Sykes, John. "Narrative Accounts of Biblical Authority: The Need for a Doctrine of Revelation." *Modern Theology* 5 (1989) 327–42.
Talbert, Charles. "Paul on the Covenant." *RevExp* 84 (1987) 299–313.

Thompson, R. Motson. *Nietzsche and Christian Ethics.* New York: The Philosophical Library, Inc., 1951.

Van Til, Cornelius. *The Defense of the Faith.* Philadelphia: Presbyterian and Reformed, 1955.

———. "My Credo." In *Jerusalem and Athens,* edited by E. R. Geehan. Philadelphia, PA: Presbyterian and Reformed Publishing Co., 1971.

Vellacott, Philip. *Sophocles and Oedipus: A Study of Oedipus Tyrannus.* Ann Arbor: The University of Michigan Press, 1971.

Von Wahlde, Urban C. "The Johannine Jews: A Critical Survey." *NTS* 28 (1982) 33–60.

Watson, Francis. *Paul, Judaism and the Gentiles.* Cambridge: Cambridge University Press, 1986.

Westphal, Merold. "Nietzsche as a Theological Resource." *Modern Theology* 13 (1997) 213–226.

———. *Suspicion and Faith: The Religious Uses of Modern Atheism.* Grand Rapids: Eerdmans, 1993.

Wiesel, Elie. *Night.* New York: Bantam Books, 1982.

Wilkins, Michael J. and J.P. Moreland, editors. *Jesus Under Fire: Modern Scholarship Reinvents the Historical Jesus.* Grand Rapids: Zondervan, 1995.

Williamson, Clark M. *A Guest in the House of Israel: Post-Holocaust Church Theology.* Louisville: Westminster/John Knox, 1993.

Wykstra, Stephen John. "Rowe's Noseeum Argument from Evil." In *The Evidential Argument from Evil,* edited by Daniel Howard-Snyder. Bloomington: Indiana University, 1996.